THE TIMES
ATLAS OF THE WORLD
MINI EDITION

THE TIMES

ATLAS OF THE WORLD

MINI EDITION

TIMES BOOKS
London

The Times Atlas of the World Mini Edition

Times Books, London
77-85 Fulham Palace Road, London W6 8JB

First published by Bartholomew 1991
First published as The Times Atlas of the World Mini Edition 1994
Revised 1995, 1996, reprinted 1996

The contents of this edition of the Times Atlas of the World Mini Edition are
believed correct at the time of printing. Nevertheless the publisher can accept no
responsibility for errors or omissions, changes in the detail given or for any
expense or loss thereby caused.

Printed in Great Britain by The Edinburgh Press Limited.

ISBN 0 7230 0902 3

KH9139

CONTENTS

Index

WORLD FACTFILE

Abbreviations List

Eng.	English
Ital.	Italian
langs.	languages
Prot.	Protestant
R. Cath.	Roman Catholic
Trad. beliefs	Traditional beliefs
Austr. Dollar	Australian Dollar
CFA Franc	African Financial Community Franc
E. Carib. Dollar	Eastern Caribbean Dollar

The statistics on the following pages are from the latest available sources including UN data.

The Factfile shows capital city names in their English form. In the Atlas, capital city names are in the local form.

Flag	COUNTRY	Status	Area (sq km)	Population ('000)	Capital City
	Afghanistan	Republic	652 225	18 879	Kabul
	Albania	Republic	28 748	3 414	Tirana
	Algeria	Republic	2 381 741	27 325	Algiers
	Andorra	Principality	465	65	Andorra la Vella
	Angola	Republic	1 246 700	10 674	Luanda
	Antigua & Barbuda	Monarchy	442	65	St John's
	Argentina	Republic	2 766 889	34 180	Buenos Aires
	Armenia	Republic	29 800	3 548	Yerevan
	Australia	Federation	7 682 300	17 843	Canberra
	Austria	Republic	83 855	8 031	Vienna
	Azerbaijan	Republic	86 600	7 472	Baku
	The Bahamas	Monarchy	13 939	272	Nassau
	Bahrain	Monarchy	691	549	Manama
	Bangladesh	Republic	143 998	117 787	Dhaka
	Barbados	Monarchy	430	261	Bridgetown
	Belarus	Republic	207 600	10 355	Minsk
	Belgium	Monarchy	30 520	10 080	Brussels
	Belize	Monarchy	22 965	211	Belmopan
	Benin	Republic	112 620	5 246	Porto Novo
	Bhutan	Monarchy	46 620	1 614	Thimphu
	Bolivia	Republic	1 098 581	7 237	La Paz
	Bosnia-Herzegovina	Republic	51 130	3 527	Sarajevo
	Botswana	Republic	581 370	1 443	Gaborone
	Brazil	Republic	8 511 965	153 725	Brasília
	Brunei	Monarchy	5 765	280	Bandar Seri Begawa
	Bulgaria	Republic	110 994	8 443	Sofia
	Burkina	Republic	274 200	9 889	Ouagadougou

Main Languages	Main Religions	Currency
Dari, Pushtu, Uzbek, Turkmen	Muslim	Afghani
Albanian , Greek	Muslim, Orthodox, R. Cath.	Lek
Arabic, French, Berber	Muslim, Roman Catholic	Dinar
Catalan, Spanish, French	Roman Catholic	Franc, Peseta
Portuguese, local langs.	R. Cath., Prot., Trad. beliefs	Kwanza
English, Creole	Protestant, Roman Catholic	E. Carib. Dollar
Spanish, Italian, Amerindian langs.	R. Cath., Prot., Jewish	Peso
Armenian, Azeri, Russian	Orthodox, R. Cath., Muslim	Dram
Eng., Ital., Greek, Aboriginal langs.	Prot., R. Cath., Orthodox	Dollar
German, Serbo-Croat , Turkish	Roman Catholic, Protestant	Schilling
Azeri, Armenian, Russian, Lezgian	Muslim, Orthodox	Manat
English, Creole, French Creole	Protestant, Roman Catholic	Dollar
Arabic, English	Muslim, Christian	Dinar
Bengali, Bihari, Hindi, Eng., local langs.	Muslim, Hindu, Buddhist, Christian	Taka
English, Creole	Protestant, Roman Catholic	Dollar
Belorussian, Russian, Ukrainian	Orthodox, Roman Catholic	Rouble
Dutch , French, German , Italian	Roman Catholic, Protestant	Franc
English, Creole, Spanish, Mayan	R. Cath., Prot., Hindu	Dollar
French, Fon, Yoruba, Adja, local langs.	Trad. beliefs, R. Cath., Muslim	CFA Franc
Dzongkha, Nepali, Assamese, English	Buddhist, Hindu, Muslim	Ngultrum
Spanish, Quechua, Aymara	R. Cath., Prot., Baha'i	Boliviano
Serbo-Croat	Muslim, Orthodox, R. Cath., Prot.	Dinar
English, Setswana, Shona, local langs.	Trad. beliefs, Prot., R. Cath.	Pula
Portuguese, German, Japanese, Ital.	R. Cath., Spiritist, Prot.	Real
Malay, English, Chinese	Muslim, Buddhist, Christian	Dollar (Ringgit)
Bulgarian, Turkish, Romany	Orthodox, Muslim	Lev
French, More, Fulani, local langs.	Trad. beliefs, Muslim, R. Cath.	CFA Franc

Flag	COUNTRY	Status	Area (sq km)	Population ('000)	Capital City
	Burundi	Republic	27 835	6 209	Bujumbura
	Cambodia	Monarchy	181 000	9 968	Phnom Penh
	Cameroon	Republic	475 442	12 871	Yaoundé
	Canada	Federation	9 970 610	29 248	Ottawa
	Cape Verde	Republic	4 033	381	Praia
	Central African Rep.	Republic	622 436	3 235	Bangui
	Chad	Republic	1 284 000	6 183	Ndjamena
	Chile	Republic	756 945	13 994	Santiago
	China	Republic	9 560 900	1 208 841	Beijing
	Colombia	Republic	1 141 748	34 520	Bogotá
	Comoros	Republic	1 862	630	Moroni
	Congo	Republic	342 000	2 516	Brazzaville
	Costa Rica	Republic	51 100	3 011	San José
	Côte d'Ivoire	Republic	322 463	13 695	Yamoussoukro
	Croatia	Republic	56 538	4 504	Zagreb
	Cuba	Republic	110 860	10 960	Havana
	Cyprus	Republic	9 251	734	Nicosia
	Czech Republic	Republic	78 864	10 333	Prague
	Denmark	Monarchy	43 075	5 205	Copenhagen
	Djibouti	Republic	23 200	566	Djibouti
	Dominica	Republic	750	71	Roseau
	Dominican Republic	Republic	48 442	7 769	Santo Domingo
	Ecuador	Republic	272 045	11 221	Quito
	Egypt	Republic	1 000 250	58 326	Cairo
	El Salvador	Republic	21 041	5 641	San Salvador
	Equatorial Guinea	Republic	28 051	389	Malabo
	Eritrea	Republic	117 400	3 437	Asmara

Main Languages	Main Religions	Currency
Kirundi, French	R. Cath., Trad. beliefs, Prot.	Franc
Khmer, Vietnamese	Buddhist, R. Cath., Muslim	Riel
French, Eng., Fang, Bamileke	Trad. beliefs, R. Cath., Muslim	CFA Franc
Eng., French, Amerindian langs.	R. Cath., Prot., Orthodox, Jewish	Dollar
Portuguese, Portuguese Creole	R. Cath., Prot., Trad. beliefs	Escudo
French, Sango, Banda, Baya	Prot., R. Cath., Trad. beliefs	CFA Franc
Arabic, French, local langs.	Muslim, Trad. Beliefs, R. Cath.	CFA Franc
Spanish, Amerindian langs.	Roman Catholic, Protestant	Peso
Chinese, regional langs.	Confucian, Tao., Buddhist, Mus.	Yuan
Spanish, Amerindian langs.	Roman Catholic, Protestant	Peso
Comorian, French, Arabic	Muslim, Roman Catholic	Franc
French, Kongo, Monokutuba	R. Cath., Prot., Trad. beliefs	CFA Franc
Spanish	Roman Catholic, Protestant	Colón
French, Akan, Kru, Gur, local langs.	Trad. beliefs, Muslim, R. Cath.	CFA Franc
Serbo-Croat	R. Cath., Orthodox, Muslim	Kuna
Spanish	Roman Catholic, Protestant	Peso
Greek, Turkish, English	Orthodox, Muslim	Pound
Czech, Moravian, Slovak	Roman Catholic, Protestant	Koruna
Danish	Protestant, Roman Catholic	Krone
Somali, French, Arabic, Issa, Afar	Muslim, Roman Catholic	Franc
English, French Creole	Roman Catholic, Protestant	E. Carib. Dollar
Spanish, French Creole	Roman Catholic, Protestant	Peso
Spanish, Quechua, Amerindian langs.	Roman Catholic, Protestant	Sucre
Arabic, French	Muslim, Coptic	Pound
Spanish	Roman Catholic, Protestant	Colón
Spanish, Fang	R. Cath., Trad. beliefs	CFA Franc
Tigrinya, Arabic, Tigre, English	Muslim, Coptic	Ethiopian Birr

Flag	COUNTRY	Status	Area (sq km)	Population ('000)	Capital City
	Estonia	Republic	45 200	1 541	Tallinn
	Ethiopia	Republic	1 133 880	54 938	Addis Ababa
	Fiji	Republic	18 330	771	Suva
	Finland	Republic	338 145	5 095	Helsinki
	France	Republic	543 965	57 747	Paris
	Gabon	Republic	267 667	1 283	Libreville
	The Gambia	Republic	11 295	1 081	Banjul
	Georgia	Republic	69 700	5 450	Tbilisi
	Germany	Republic	357 868	81 410	Berlin
	Ghana	Republic	238 537	16 944	Accra
	Greece	Republic	131 957	10 426	Athens
	Grenada	Monarchy	378	92	St George's
	Guatemala	Republic	108 890	10 322	Guatemala City
	Guinea	Republic	245 857	6 501	Conakry
	Guinea-Bissau	Republic	36 125	1 050	Bissau
	Guyana	Republic	214 969	825	Georgetown
	Haiti	Republic	27 750	7 041	Port-au-Prince
	Honduras	Republic	112 088	5 770	Tegucigalpa
	Hungary	Republic	93 030	10 261	Budapest
	Iceland	Republic	102 820	266	Reykjavik
	India	Republic	3 287 263	918 570	New Delhi
	Indonesia	Republic	1 919 445	193 017	Jakarta
	Iran	Republic	1 648 000	59 778	Tehran
	Iraq	Republic	438 317	19 925	Baghdad
	Republic of Ireland	Republic	70 282	3 571	Dublin
	Israel	Republic	20 770	5 383	Jerusalem
	Italy	Republic	301 245	57 193	Rome

Main Languages	Main Religions	Currency
Estonian, Russian	Protestant, Orthodox	Kroon
Amharic, Oromo, local langs.	Orthodox, Muslim, Trad. beliefs	Birr
English, Fijian, Hindi	Prot., Hindu, R. Cath., Muslim	Dollar
Finnish, Swedish	Protestant, Orthodox	Markka
French, Fr. dialects, Arabic, German	R. Cath., Prot., Muslim	Franc
French, Fang, local langs.	R. Cath., Prot., Trad. beliefs	CFA Franc
English, Malinke, Fulani, Wolof	Muslim, Protestant	Dalasi
Georgian, Russian, Armenian, Azeri	Orthodox, Muslim	Lari
German, Turkish	Prot., R. Cath., Muslim	Mark
English, Hausa, Akan, local langs.	Prot., R. Cath., Muslim	Cedi
Greek, Macedonian	Orthodox, Muslim	Drachma
English, Creole	Roman Catholic, Protestant	E. Carib. Dollar
Spanish, Mayan langs.	Roman Catholic, Protestant	Quetzal
French, Fulani, Malinke, local langs.	Muslim, Trad. beliefs, R. Cath.	Franc
Portuguese, Port. Creole, local langs.	Trad. beliefs, Muslim, R. Cath.	Peso
Eng., Creole, Hindi, Amerindian langs.	Prot., Hindu, R. Cath., Muslim	Dollar
French, French Creole	R. Cath., Prot., Voodoo	Gourde
Spanish, Amerindian langs.	Roman Catholic, Protestant	Lempira
Hungarian, Romany, German, Slovak	Roman Catholic, Protestant	Forint
Icelandic	Roman Catholic, Protestant	Króna
Hindi, English, regional langs.	Hindu, Muslim, Sikh, Christian	Rupee
Indonesian, local langs.	Muslim, Prot., R. Cath., Hindu	Rupiah
Farsi, Azeri, Kurdish, regional langs.	Muslim, Baha'i, Christian	Rial
Arabic, Kurdish, Turkmen	Muslim, Roman Catholic	Dinar
English, Irish	Roman Catholic, Protestant	Punt
Hebrew, Arabic, Yiddish, English	Jewish, Muslim, Christian, Druze	Shekel
Italian, Italian dialects	Roman Catholic	Lira

Flag	COUNTRY	Status	Area (sq km)	Population ('000)	Capital City
	Jamaica	Monarchy	10 991	2 429	Kingston
	Japan	Monarchy	377 727	124 961	Tokyo
	Jordan	Monarchy	89 206	5 198	Amman
	Kazakhstan	Republic	2 717 300	17 027	Alma-Ata
	Kenya	Republic	582 646	27 343	Nairobi
	Kiribati	Republic	717	77	Bairiki
	Kuwait	Monarchy	17 818	1 620	Kuwait City
	Kyrgyzstan	Republic	198 500	4 596	Bishkek
	Laos	Republic	236 800	4 742	Vientiane
	Latvia	Republic	63 700	2 548	Riga
	Lebanon	Republic	10 452	2 915	Beirut
	Lesotho	Monarchy	30 355	1 996	Maseru
	Liberia	Republic	111 369	2 941	Monrovia
	Libya	Republic	1 759 540	5 225	Tripoli
	Liechtenstein	Monarchy	160	30	Vaduz
	Lithuania	Republic	65 200	3 721	Vilnius
	Luxembourg	Monarchy	2 586	401	Luxembourg
	Macedonia	Republic	25 713	2 142	Skopje
	Madagascar	Republic	587 041	14 303	Antananarivo
	Malawi	Republic	118 484	10 843	Lilongwe
	Malaysia	Federation	332 965	19 489	Kuala Lumpur
	Maldives	Republic	298	246	Male
	Mali	Republic	1 240 140	10 462	Bamako
	Malta	Republic	316	364	Valletta
	Marshall Islands	Republic	181	52	Dalap-Uliga-Darrit
	Mauritania	Republic	1 030 700	2 211	Nouakchott
	Mauritius	Republic	2 040	1 104	Port Louis

Main Languages	Main Religions	Currency
English, Creole	Prot., R. Cath., Rastafarian	Dollar
Japanese	Shintoist, Buddhist, Christian	Yen
Arabic	Muslim, Christian, Muslim	Dinar
Kazakh, Russian, German, Ukrainian	Muslim, Orthodox, Prot.	Tanga
Swahili, English, local langs.	R. Cath., Prot., Trad. beliefs	Shilling
I-Kiribati, English	R. Cath., Prot., Baha'i, Mormon	Austr. Dollar
Arabic	Muslim, Christian, Hindu	Dinar
Kirghiz, Russian, Uzbek	Muslim, Orthodox	Som
Lao, local langs.	Buddhist, Trad. beliefs, R. Cath.	Kip
Latvian, Russian	Prot., R. Cath., Orthodox	Lat
Arabic, French, Armenian	Muslim, Prot., R. Cath.	Pound
Sesotho, English, Zulu	R. Cath., Prot., Trad. beliefs	Loti
English, Creole, local langs.	Trad. beliefs, Muslim, Prot.	Dollar
Arabic, Berber	Muslim, Roman Catholic	Dinar
German	Roman Catholic, Protestant	Swiss Franc
Lithuanian, Russian, Polish	R. Cath., Prot., Orthodox	Litas
Letzeburgish, German, French	Roman Catholic, Protestant	Franc
Macedonian, Albanian, Serbo-Croat	Orthodox, Muslim, R. Cath.	Denar
Malagasy, French	Trad. beliefs, R. Cath., Prot.	Franc
Eng., Chichewa, Lomwe, local langs.	Prot., R. Cath., Trad. beliefs	Kwacha
Malay, English, Chinese, Tamil	Muslim, Buddhist, Hindu	Dollar (Ringgit)
Divehi	Muslim	Rufiyaa
French, Bambara, local langs.	Muslim, Trad. beliefs, R. Cath.	CFA Franc
Maltese, English	Roman Catholic	Lira
Marshallese, English	Protestant, Roman Catholic	US Dollar
Arabic, French, local langs.	Muslim	Ouguiya
English, French Creole, Hindi	Hindu, R. Cath., Muslim, Prot.	Rupee

Flag	COUNTRY	Status	Area (sq km)	Population ('000)	Capital City
	Mexico	Republic	1 972 545	93 008	Mexico City
	Micronesia	Republic	701	121	Palikir
	Moldova	Republic	33 700	4 350	Chişinău
	Monaco	Monarchy	1.95	31	Monaco
	Mongolia	Republic	1 565 000	2 363	Ulan Bator
	Morocco	Monarchy	446 550	26 590	Rabat
	Mozambique	Republic	799 380	15 527	Maputo
	Myanmar	Republic	676 577	45 555	Rangoon
	Namibia	Republic	824 292	1 500	Windhoek
	Nauru	Republic	21	11	Yaren
	Nepal	Monarchy	147 181	21 360	Kathmandu
	Netherlands	Monarchy	41 526	15 380	Amsterdam
	New Zealand	Monarchy	270 534	3 493	Wellington
	Nicaragua	Republic	130 000	4 401	Managua
	Niger	Republic	1 267 000	8 846	Niamey
	Nigeria	Republic	923 768	108 467	Abuja
	North Korea	Republic	120 538	23 483	Pyongyang
	Norway	Monarchy	323 878	4 325	Oslo
	Oman	Monarchy	271 950	2 077	Muscat
	Pakistan	Republic	803 940	126 610	Islamabad
	Panama	Republic	77 082	2 563	Panama City
	Papua New Guinea	Monarchy	462 840	4 205	Port Moresby
	Paraguay	Republic	406 752	4 700	Asunción
	Peru	Republic	1 285 216	23 088	Lima
	Philippines	Republic	300 000	67 038	Manila
	Poland	Republic	312 683	38 544	Warsaw
	Portugal	Republic	88 940	9 830	Lisbon

Main Languages	Main Religions	Currency
Spanish, Amerindian langs.	Roman Catholic, Protestant	Peso
Eng., Trukese, Pohnpeian, local langs.	Protestant, Roman Catholic	US Dollar
Romanian, Russian, Ukrainian, Gagauz	Orthodox	Leu
French, Monegasque, Italian	Roman Catholic	Fr. Franc
Khalka, Kazakh, local langs.	Buddhist, Muslim, Trad. beliefs	Tugrik
Arabic, Berber, French, Spanish	Muslim, Roman Catholic	Dirham
Portuguese, Makua, Tsonga	Trad. beliefs, R. Cath., Muslim	Metical
Burmese, Shan, Karen, local langs.	Buddhist, Muslim, Prot., R. Cath.	Kyat
English, Afrikaans, German, Ovambo	Protestant, Roman Catholic	Dollar
Nauruan, Gilbertese, English	Protestant, Roman Catholic	Austr. Dollar
Nepali, Maithili, Bhojpuri, English	Hindu, Buddhist, Muslim	Rupee
Dutch, Frisian, Turkish	R. Cath., Prot., Muslim	Guilder
English, Maori	Protestant, Roman Catholic	Dollar
Spanish, Amerindian langs.	Roman Catholic, Protestant	Córdoba
French, Hausa, Fulani, local langs.	Muslim, Trad. beliefs	CFA Franc
English, Creole, Hausa, Yoruba, Ibo	Muslim, Prot., Roman Catholic	Naira
Korean	Trad. beliefs, Chondoist, Buddhist	Won
Norwegian	Protestant, Roman Catholic	Krone
Arabic, Baluchi, Farsi, Swahili	Muslim	Rial
Urdu, Punjabi, Sindhi, Pushtu, English	Muslim, Christian, Hindu	Rupee
Spanish, English Creole	R. Cath., Prot., Muslim, Baha'i	Balboa
English, Tok Pisin, local langs.	Prot., R. Cath., Trad. beliefs	Kina
Spanish, Guaraní	Roman Catholic, Protestant	Guaraní
Spanish, Quechua, Aymara	Roman Catholic, Protestant	Sol
English, Filipino, Cebuano, local langs.	R. Cath., Aglipayan, Muslim, Prot.	Peso
Polish, German	Roman Catholic, Orthodox	Złoty
Portuguese	Roman Catholic, Protestant	Escudo

Flag	COUNTRY	Status	Area (sq km)	Population ('000)	Capital City
	Qatar	Monarchy	11 437	540	Doha
	Romania	Republic	237 500	22 736	Bucharest
	Russian Federation	Republic	17 075 400	147 997	Moscow
	Rwanda	Republic	26 338	7 750	Kigali
	St Kitts & Nevis	Monarchy	261	41	Basseterre
	St Lucia	Monarchy	616	141	Castries
	St Vincent	Monarchy	389	111	Kingstown
	São Tomé & Príncipe	Republic	964	130	São Tomé
	Saudi Arabia	Monarchy	2 200 000	17 451	Riyadh
	Senegal	Republic	196 720	8 102	Dakar
	Seychelles	Republic	455	74	Victoria
	Sierra Leone	Republic	71 740	4 402	Freetown
	Singapore	Republic	639	2 930	Singapore
	Slovakia	Republic	49 035	5 347	Bratislava
	Slovenia	Republic	20 251	1 942	Ljubljana
	Solomon Islands	Monarchy	28 370	366	Honiara
	Somalia	Republic	637 657	9 077	Mogadishu
	South Africa	Republic	1 219 080	39 659	Pretoria/Cape Town
	South Korea	Republic	99 274	44 453	Seoul
	Spain	Monarchy	504 782	39 193	Madrid
	Sri Lanka	Republic	65 610	17 865	Colombo
	Sudan	Republic	2 505 813	27 361	Khartoum
	Surinam	Republic	163 820	418	Paramaribo
	Swaziland	Monarchy	17 364	879	Mbabane
	Sweden	Monarchy	449 964	8 794	Stockholm
	Switzerland	Federation	41 293	6 994	Bern
	Syria	Republic	185 180	13 844	Damascus

Main Languages	Main Religions	Currency
Arabic, Indian langs.	Muslim, Christian, Hindu	Riyal
Romanian, Hungarian	Orthodox, R. Cath. protestant	Leu
Russian, Tatar, Ukrainian, local langs.	Orthodox, Muslim, Christian	Rouble
Kinyarwanda, French	R. Cath., Trad. beliefs, Prot.	Franc
English, Creole	Protestant, Roman Catholic	E. Carib. Dollar
English, French Creole	Roman Catholic, Protestant	E. Carib. Dollar
English, Creole	Protestant, Roman Catholic	E. Carib. Dollar
Portuguese, Portuguese Creole	Roman Catholic, Protestant	Dobra
Arabic	Muslim	Riyal
French, Wolof, Fulani, local langs.	Muslim, R. Cath., Trad. beliefs	CFA Franc
Seychellois, English	Roman Catholic, Protestant	Rupee
English, Creole, Mende, Temne	Trad. beliefs, Muslim, Prot.	Leone
Chinese, English, Malay, Tamil	Buddhist, Tao., Muslim, Christian	Dollar
Slovak, Hungarian, Czech	R. Cath., Prot., Orthodox	Koruna
Slovene, Serbo-Croat	Roman Catholic, Protestant	Tólar
Eng., Solomon Is. Pidgin, local langs.	Protestant, Roman Catholic	Dollar
Somali, Arabic	Muslim	Shilling
Afrikaans, English, local langs.	Prot., R. Cath., Muslim, Hindu	Rand
Korean	Buddhist, Prot., R. Cath.	Won
Spanish, Catalan, Galician, Basque	Roman Catholic	Peseta
Sinhalese, Tamil, English	Buddhist, Hindu, Muslim, R. Cath.	Rupee
Arabic, Dinka, Nubian, Beja, Nuer	Muslim, Trad. beliefs, R. Cath.	Dinar
Dutch, Surinamese, English, Hindi	Hindu, R. Cath., Prot., Muslim	Guilder
Swazi, English	Prot., R. Cath., Trad. beliefs	Emalangeni
Swedish	Protestant, Roman Catholic	Krona
German, French, Italian, Romansch	Roman Catholic, Protestant	Franc
Arabic, Kurdish, Armenian	Muslim, Christian	Pound

Flag	COUNTRY	Status	Area (sq km)	Population ('000)	Capital City
	Taiwan	Republic	36 179	21 074	Taipei
	Tajikistan	Republic	143 100	5 751	Dushanbe
	Tanzania	Republic	945 087	28 846	Dodoma
	Thailand	Monarchy	513 115	59 396	Bangkok
	Togo	Republic	56 785	3 928	Lomé
	Tonga	Monarchy	748	98	Nuku'alofa
	Trinidad & Tobago	Republic	5 130	1 257	Port of Spain
	Tunisia	Republic	164 150	8 733	Tunis
	Turkey	Republic	779 452	61 183	Ankara
	Turkmenistan	Republic	488 100	4 010	Ashkhabad
	Tuvalu	Monarchy	25	9	Funafuti
	Uganda	Republic	241 038	20 621	Kampala
	Ukraine	Republic	603 700	51 910	Kiev
	United Arab Emirates	Federation	77 700	1 861	Abu Dhabi
	United Kingdom	Monarchy	244 082	58 091	London
	United States	Republic	9 809 386	260 560	Washington
	Uruguay	Republic	176 215	3 167	Montevideo
	Uzbekistan	Republic	447 400	22 349	Tashkent
	Vanuatu	Republic	12 190	165	Port-Vila
	Venezuela	Republic	912 050	21 177	Caracas
	Vietnam	Republic	329 565	72 509	Hanoi
	Western Samoa	Monarchy	2 831	164	Apia
	Yemen	Republic	527 968	13 873	Sana
	Yugoslavia	Republic	102 173	10 515	Belgrade
	Zaire	Republic	2 345 410	42 552	Kinshasa
	Zambia	Republic	752 614	9 196	Lusaka
	Zimbabwe	Republic	390 759	11 150	Harare

Main Languages	Main Religions	Currency
Chinese, local langs.	Buddhist, Taoist, Confucian	Dollar
Tajik, Uzbek, Russian	Muslim	Rouble
Swahili, Eng., Nyamwezi, local langs.	R. Cath., Muslim, Trad. beliefs	Shilling
Thai, Lao, Chinese, Malay	Buddhist, Muslim	Baht
French, Ewe, Kabre, local langs.	Trad. beliefs, R. Cath., Muslim	CFA Franc
Tongan, English	Prot., R. Cath., Mormon	Pa'anga
English, Creole, Hindi	R. Cath., Hindu, Prot., Muslim	Dollar
Arabic, French	Muslim	Dinar
Turkish, Kurdish	Muslim	Lira
Turkmen, Russian	Muslim	Manat
Tuvaluan, English	Protestant	Dollar
English, Swahili, Luganda, local langs.	R. Cath., Prot., Muslim	Shilling
Ukrainian, Russian, regional langs.	Orthodox, Roman Catholic	Karbovanets
Arabic, English, Hindi, Urdu, Farsi	Muslim, Christian	Dirham
English, S. Indian langs., Chinese	Prot., R. Cath., Muslim, Sikh	Pound
English, Spanish, Amerindian langs.	Prot., R. Cath., Muslim, Jewish	Dollar
Spanish	R. Cath., Prot., Jewish	Peso
Uzbek, Russian, Tajik, Kazakh	Muslim, Orthodox	Som
English, Bislama, French	Prot., R. Cath., Trad. beliefs	Vatu
Spanish, Amerindian langs.	Roman Catholic, Protestant	Bolívar
Vietnamese, Thai, Khmer, Chinese	Buddhist, Taoist, Roman Catholic	Dong
Samoan, English	Prot., R. Cath., Mormon	Tala
Arabic	Muslim	Dinar, Rial
Serbo-Croat, Albanian, Hungarian	Orthodox, Muslim	Dinar
French, Lingala, Swahili, Kongo	R. Cath., Prot., Muslim	Zaïre
English, Bemba, Nyanja, Tonga	Prot., R. Cath., Trad. beliefs, Mus.	Kwacha
English, Shona, Ndebele	Prot., R. Cath., Trad. beliefs	Dollar

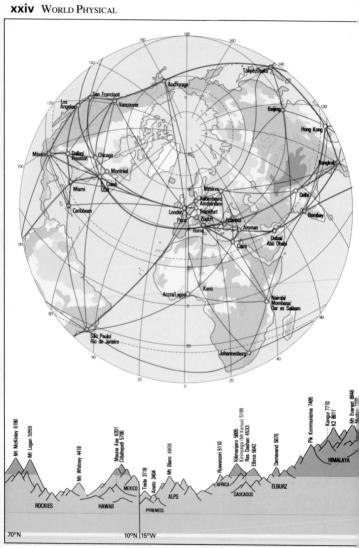

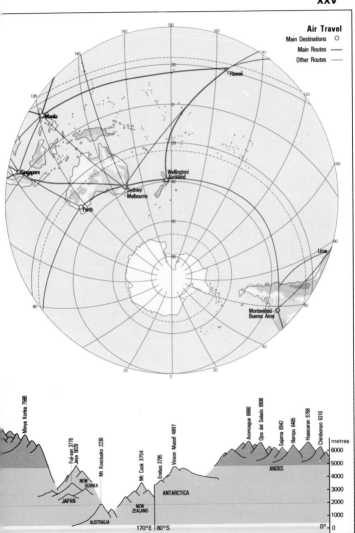

Air Travel

Main Destinations ○
Main Routes ——
Other Routes ——

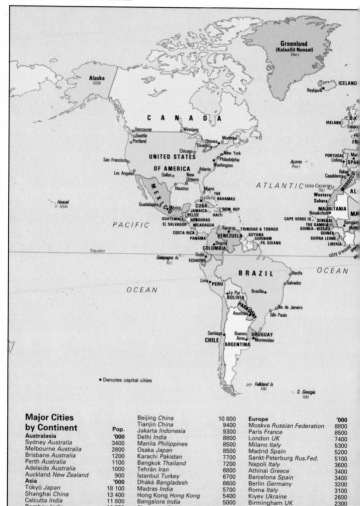

• Denotes capital cities

Major Cities by Continent

	Pop. '000
Australasia	
Sydney *Australia*	3400
Melbourne *Australia*	2800
Brisbane *Australia*	1200
Perth *Australia*	1100
Adelaide *Australia*	1000
Auckland *New Zealand*	900
Asia	'000
Tōkyō *Japan*	18 100
Shanghai *China*	13 400
Calcutta *India*	11 800
Bombay *India*	11 200
Sŏul *South Korea*	11 000

Beijing *China*	10 800
Tianjin *China*	9400
Jakarta *Indonesia*	9300
Delhi *India*	8800
Manila *Philippines*	8500
Osaka *Japan*	8500
Karachi *Pakistan*	7700
Bangkok *Thailand*	7200
Tehrān *Iran*	6800
İstanbul *Turkey*	6700
Dhākā *Bangladesh*	6600
Madras *India*	5700
Hong Kong *Hong Kong*	5400
Bangalore *India*	5000
Shenyang *China*	4800
Lahore *Pakistan*	4100

Europe	'000
Moskva *Russian Federation*	8800
Paris *France*	8500
London *UK*	7400
Milano *Italy*	5300
Madrid *Spain*	5200
Sankt-Peterburg *Rus.Fed.*	5100
Napoli *Italy*	3600
Athinai *Greece*	3400
Barcelona *Spain*	3400
Berlin *Germany*	3200
Roma *Italy*	3100
Kiyev *Ukraine*	2600
Birmingham *UK*	2300
Manchester *UK*	2300
Bucureşti *Romania*	2200

North and Central America	'000	South America	'000	Africa	'000
México *Mexico*	20 200	São Paulo *Brazil*	17 400	Cairo *Egypt*	9000
New York *USA*	16 200	Buenos Aires *Argentina*	11 500	Lagos *Nigeria*	7700
Los Angeles *USA*	11 900	Rio de Janeiro *Brazil*	10 700	Alexandria *Egypt*	3700
Chicago *USA*	7000	Lima *Peru*	6200	Kinshasa *Zaire*	3500
Philadelphia *USA*	4300	Santiago *Chile*	5000	Casablanca *Morocco*	3200
Detroit *USA*	3700	Bogotá *Colombia*	4900	Alger *Algeria*	3000
San Francisco *USA*	3700	Caracas *Venezuela*	4100	Cape Town *South Africa*	2300
Toronto *Canada*	3500	Belo Horizonte *Brazil*	3600	Abidjan *Côte d'Ivoire*	2200
Dallas *USA*	3400	Pôrto Alegre *Brazil*	3100	Tarābulus *Libya*	2100
Guadalajara *Mexico*	3200	Recife *Brazil*	2500	Adis Abeba *Ethiopia*	1900
Houston *USA*	3000	Brasília *Brazil*	2400	Khartoum *Sudan*	1900
Monterrey *Mexico*	3000	Salvador *Brazil*	2400	Dar es Salaam *Tanzania*	1700
Montréal *Canada*	3000	Fortaleza *Brazil*	2100	Johannesburg *South Africa*	1700
Washington *USA*	2900	Curitiba *Brazil*	2000	Luanda *Angola*	1700
Boston *USA*	2800	Guayaquil *Ecuador*	1700	Maputo *Mozambique*	1600

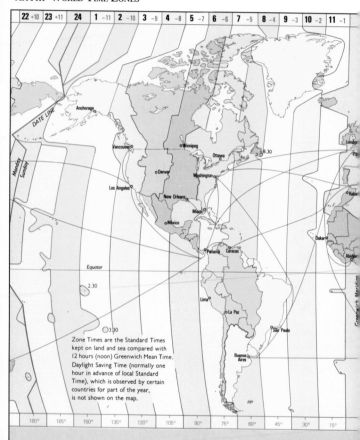

| 22 +10 | 23 +11 | 24 | 1 −11 | 2 −10 | 3 −9 | 4 −8 | 5 −7 | 6 −6 | 7 −5 | 8 −4 | 9 −3 | 10 −2 | 11 −1 |

DATE LINE

Monday / Sunday

Anchorage

Vancouver ○ Winnipeg
Ottawa ○ 8.30
London

Denver ○ Washington
Pa

Los Angeles ○ New Orleans
Rabat ○

Miami ○
Mexico ○

Dakar ○
Panama ○ Caracas

Abidjan

Equator

Greenwich Meridian

2.30

○ 3.30

Lima ○

Zone Times are the Standard Times
kept on land and sea compared with
12 hours (noon) Greenwich Mean Time.
Daylight Saving Time (normally one
hour in advance of local Standard
Time), which is observed by certain
countries for part of the year,
is not shown on the map.

La Paz ○

São Paulo ○

Buenos
Aires ○

| 180° | 165° | 150° | 135° | 120° | 105° | 90° | 75° | 60° | 45° | 30° | 15° |

Journey Times

Sail (via Cape)
164 days

Steam (via Cape)
43 days

Steam (via Suez)
30 days

Supertanker
(via Cape)
28 days

Singapore ◀

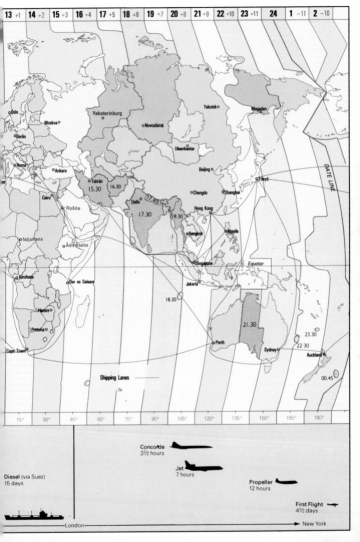

| 13 +1 | 14 +2 | 15 +3 | 16 +4 | 17 +5 | 18 +6 | 19 +7 | 20 +8 | 21 +9 | 22 +10 | 23 +11 | 24 | 1 −11 | 2 −10 |

DATE LINE

Oslo
Moskva
Berlin
Roma
Ankara
Cairo
Al Riyād
Ndjamena
Kinshasa
Dar es Salaam
Harare
Pretoria
Cape Town

Yekaterinburg
Novosibirsk
Ulaanbaatar
Tahrān 15.30
16.30
Delhi 17.30
18.30
Addis Abeba
Singapore
Jakarta
18.30

Yakutsk
Magadan
Beijing
Chengdu
Shanghai
Hong Kong
Bangkok
Manila
Tōkyō

Equator

Perth
21.30
Sydney
22.30
23.30
Auckland
00.45

Shipping Lanes ———

| 15° | 30° | 45° | 60° | 75° | 90° | 105° | 120° | 135° | 150° | 165° | 180° |

Concorde
3½ hours

Jet
7 hours

Propeller
12 hours

First Flight
4½ days

Diesel (via Suez)
15 days

London ———————————————————— → New York

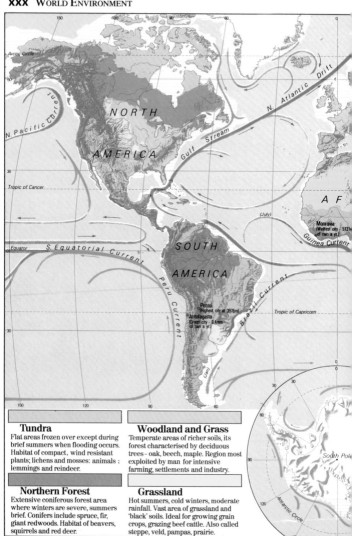

Tundra
Flat areas frozen over except during brief summers when flooding occurs. Habitat of compact, wind resistant plants; lichens and mosses: animals ; lemmings and reindeer.

Northern Forest
Extensive coniferous forest area where winters are severe, summers brief. Conifers include spruce, fir, giant redwoods. Habitat of beavers, squirrels and red deer.

Woodland and Grass
Temperate areas of richer soils, its forest characterised by deciduous trees - oak, beech, maple. Region most exploited by man for intensive farming, settlements and industry.

Grassland
Hot summers, cold winters, moderate rainfall. Vast area of grassland and 'black' soils. Ideal for growing grain crops, grazing beef cattle. Also called steppe, veld, pampas, prairie.

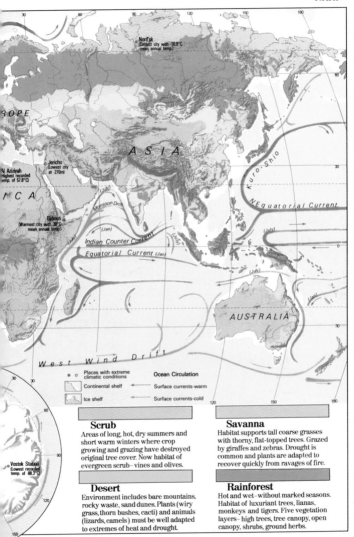

Noril'sk
(Coolest city with -10.9°C
mean annual temp.)

EUROPE

ASIA

Kuro-Shio

N Equatorial Current

AL Aziziyah
Highest recorded
temp. of 57.8°C

Jericho
(Lowest city
at -270m)

AFRICA

Monsoon Drift

(July)

(July)

(July)

Djibouti
(Warmest city with 36°C
mean annual temp.)

Indian Counter Current

(Jan)

Equatorial Current (Jan)

(July)

(July)

AUSTRALIA

(Jan)

West Wind Drift

120

150

180

Places with extreme
climatic conditions

Continental shelf

Ice shelf

Ocean Circulation

Surface currents-warm

Surface currents-cold

Vostok Station
(Lowest recorded
temp. of -88.3°C)

Scrub
Areas of long, hot, dry summers and
short warm winters where crop
growing and grazing have destroyed
original tree cover. Now habitat of
evergreen scrub–vines and olives.

Savanna
Habitat supports tall coarse grasses
with thorny, flat-topped trees. Grazed
by giraffes and zebras. Drought is
common and plants are adapted to
recover quickly from ravages of fire.

Desert
Environment includes bare mountains,
rocky waste, sand dunes. Plants (wiry
grass, thorn bushes, cacti) and animals
(lizards, camels) must be well adapted
to extremes of heat and drought.

Rainforest
Hot and wet–without marked seasons.
Habitat of luxuriant trees, lianas,
monkeys and tigers. Five vegetation
layers–high trees, tree canopy, open
canopy, shrubs, ground herbs.

BOUNDARIES

	International
	International under Dispute
	Cease Fire Line
	Autonomous or State
	Administrative
	Maritime (National)

LETTERING STYLES

CANADA	Independent Nation
FLORIDA	State, Province or Autonomous Region
Gibraltar (U.K.)	Sovereignty of Dependent Territory
Lothian	Administrative Area
LANGUEDOC	Historic Region
Loire **Vosges**	Physical Feature or Physical Region

TOWNS AND CITIES

Square Symbols denote capital cities. Each settlement is given a symbol according to its relative importance, with type size to match.

◼	⬤	**New York**	Major City
◼	●	**Montréal**	City
◻	○	Ottawa	Small City
◼	●	**Québec**	Large Town
◻	○	St John's	Town
◻	○	Yorkton	Small Town
◻	○	Jasper	Village

 Built-up-area

LAKE FEATURES

Permanent

Seasonal

OTHER FEATURES

	River
	Seasonal River
=	Pass, Gorge
	Dam, Barrage
	Waterfall, Rapid
	Aqueduct
	Reef
▲4231	Summit, Peak
.217	Spot Height, Depth
⌣	Well
△	Oil Field
▲	Gas Field
Gas/Oil	Oil/Natural Gas Pipeline
Gemsbok Nat. Pk.	National Park
.UR	Historic Site
	Main Railway
	Other Railway
– – – – –	Under Construction
—+—+—+—	Rail Tunnel
– – – – –	Rail Ferry
	Canal
⊕	International Airport
✦	Other Airport

For pages 102-103, 104-105 only:

0	Sea Level
200m	
2000m	
4000m	
6000m	
	Depth

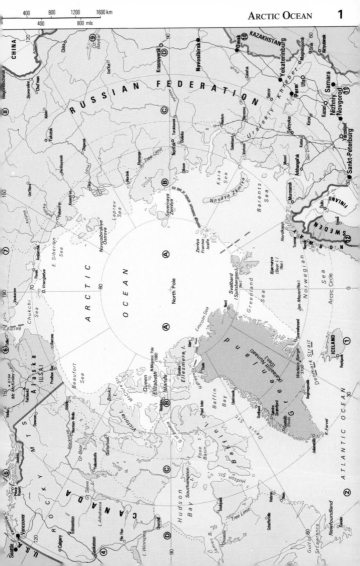

ARCTIC OCEAN

Sverdrup Islands
Prince Gustaf Adolf Sea
Mackenzie King I.
PARRY ISLANDS
B a f f i n
Bathurst Island
Byam Martin I.
Melville Island
Prince Patrick I.
McClure Strait
Eglinton I.
Lougheed I.
Borden I.
Brock I.
Mercy B.
Cornwallis I.
Devon I.
Lowther I.
Bathurst I.
Peel Sound
Prince of Wales Island
Somerset I.
King William Island
Gjoahaven
Boothia Peninsula
McClintock Channel
Viscount Melville Sound
Prince Albert Peninsula
Banks Island
Victoria Island
Stefansson I.
Holman Island
Minto Inlet
Prince Albert Sound
Wollaston Pen.
Dolphin and Union Str.
Coronation Gulf
Cambridge Bay
Bathurst Inlet
Queen Maud Gulf
Perry River
Hadley Bay
Sachs Harbour
Cape Parry
Amundsen Gulf
Dease Strait
Kugluktuk (Coppermine)
Bathurst Inlet
K i t i k m e o t
C. Prince Albert
Nelson Head
Cape Bathurst
Paulatuk
Franklin Bay
Liverpool Bay
Tuktoyaktuk
Inuvik
Aklavik
Fort Good Hope
Norman Wells
Tulita
Colville Lake
Great Bear Lake
Déline
Fort Franklin
Franklin Mts
Mackenzie
N O R T H W E S T   T E R R I T O R I E S
Smith
Fort Smith
Fort Simpson
Nahanni
Liard
Selwyn Mountains
Mackenzie Mountains
Richardson Mts
British Mts
Davidson Mts
Arctic Red
Eagle Plain
Peel
Ogilvie Mts
Eagle
Old Crow
Woodchopper
Porcupine
Y U K O N   T E R R I T O R Y
Dawson
Klondike
Mayo
Pelly
Ross River
Teslin
Whitehorse
Carmacks
Haines Junction
Carcross
Atlin
C a s s i a r
C A R I B O O
Watson Lake
St Elias Mts
Mt Logan
Kluane L.
Wrangell Mts
Mt St Elias
Yakutat
Gulf of Alaska
Alexander Archipelago

BEAUFORT SEA

Pt Barrow
Beechey Pt
Prudhoe Bay
North Slope
Barrow
Pt Lay
Point Lonely
Wainwright
Icy C.
Point Hope
C. Lisburne
Kivalina
Noatak
Kotzebue
Shishmaref
Wales
Seward Peninsula
Nome
Teller
RUS. FED.
Uelen
Lavrentiya
Provideniya
Savoonga
Gambell
St Lawrence I.
Brooks Range
Endicott Mts
Baird Mts
De Long Mts
Umiat
Anaktuvuk Pass
Chandalar
Bettles
Wiseman
Allakaket
Hughes
Shungnak
Kobuk
Selawik
Buckland
Koyuk
Unalakleet
St Michael
A L A S K A   (U.S.A.)
Fairbanks
Eagle
Circle
Fort Yukon
Chicken
Tok
Northway
Delta Junction
Mt McKinley
Mt Foraker
Denali
Talkeetna
Anchorage
Palmer
Copper Center
Valdez
Cordova
Kenai
Kenai Peninsula
Seward
Homer
Kodiak
Kodiak Island
Bethel
Kuskokwim
Aniak
Holy Cross
McGrath
Kaltag
Galena
Ruby
Tanana
Nulato
Poorman
Nenana
Manley
Nikolai
Sleetmute
Kalskag
Russian Mission
Marshall
Mountain Village
St Marys
Alakanuk
Emmonak
Kotlik
Norton Sound
Stebbins
Bering Str.

YUKON
Yukon
Tanana

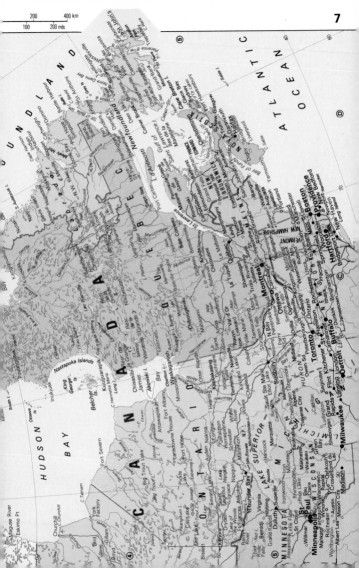

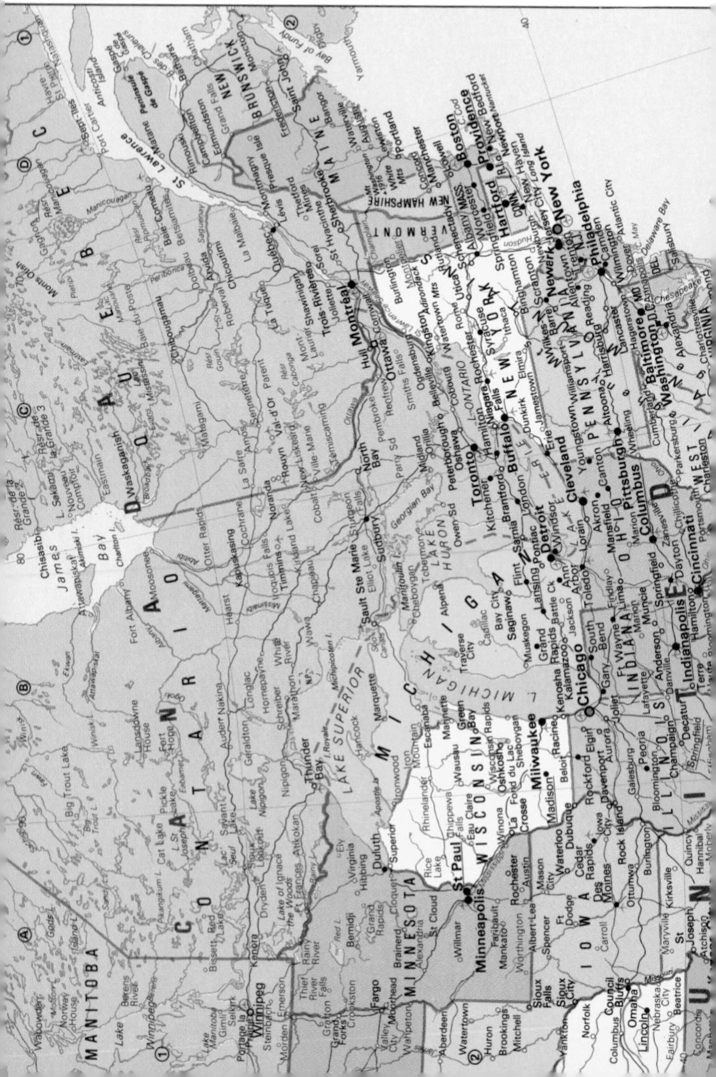

CANADA

MANITOBA

ONTARIO

QUÉBEC

NEW BRUNSWICK

MAINE

NEW HAMPSHIRE

VERMONT

NEW YORK

PENNSYLVANIA

WEST VIRGINIA

OHIO

INDIANA

ILLINOIS

MICHIGAN

WISCONSIN

MINNESOTA

IOWA

Hudson Bay

James Bay

LAKE SUPERIOR

L. MICHIGAN

LAKE HURON

Georgian Bay

Gulf of Maine

Bay of Fundy

Winnipeg

Minneapolis

St. Paul

Madison

Milwaukee

Chicago

Indianapolis

Columbus

Cincinnati

Pittsburgh

Cleveland

Detroit

Toronto

Ottawa

Montréal

Québec

Boston

Providence

Hartford

New York

Newark

Philadelphia

Baltimore

Washington

Albany

Buffalo

Syracuse

Rochester

Sudbury

Saint John

Duluth

Des Moines

Omaha

Lincoln

Sioux Falls

Green Bay

Grand Rapids

Springfield

Peoria

Fort Wayne

Dayton

Columbus

Akron

Canton

Toledo

Flint

Lansing

Saginaw

Kalamazoo

South Bend

Rockford

Dubuque

Cedar Rapids

Waterloo

Rochester

St. Cloud

Eau Claire

La Crosse

Portland

Sault Ste. Marie

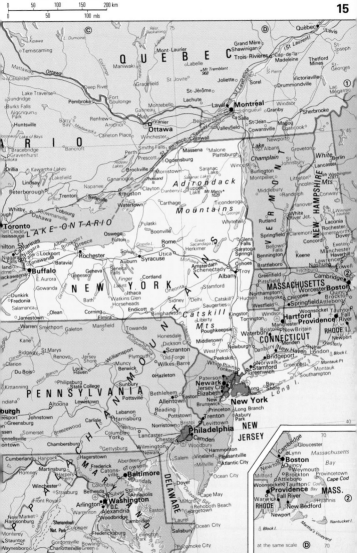

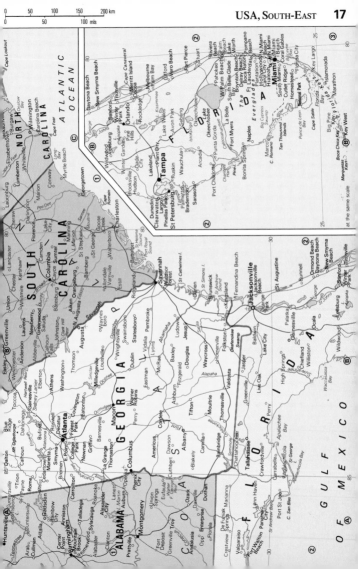

INDIANA

ILLINOIS

KENTUCKY

TENNESSEE

MISSOURI

IOWA

NEBRASKA

KANSAS

OKLAHOMA

Boston Mts

Indianapolis

Nashville

St Louis

Kansas City

Wichita

Tulsa

Springfield

Topeka

Des Moines

Lincoln

Omaha

Columbia

Jefferson City

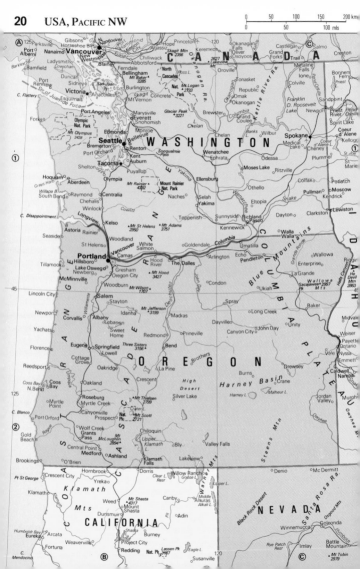

Scale bars:
0 200 400 600 km
0 100 200 300 mls

Ft Smith
Hot Springs
Memphis
Huntsville Chattanooga
SOUTH
C. Fear
Florence Columbia CAROLINA
Orangeburg
Spartanburg
Little Rock
ARKANSAS
Pine Bluff
Tupelo
Gadsden
Athens
Gainesville
Athens
Atlanta
Charleston
Greenwood
Columbus
Birmingham
Tuscaloosa
ALABAMA
Augusta
Macon
Savannah
Greenville
MISSISSIPPI
Shreveport
Jackson
Meridian
Montgomery
Phenix City
GEORGIA
Monroe
Vicksburg
Columbus
Waycross
Brunswick
LOUISIANA
Natchez
Hattiesburg
Laurel
Dothan
Albany
Valdosta
Jacksonville
Alexandria
Baton Rouge
Mobile
Pensacola
Panama City
Tallahassee
St. Augustine
Lake Charles
Lafayette
Biloxi
Apalachee Bay
Gainesville
Daytona Beach
Pt Arthur
Orange
New Orleans
Ocala
Orlando
Galveston
C. Canaveral
Melbourne
Clearwater
St Petersburg
Tampa
Tampa Bay
Ft Pierce
W Palm Beach
Lake Okeechobee
Lake Worth
Little Abaco
Great Abaco
THE
BAHAMAS
Ft Myers
Ft Lauderdale
Hollywood
Berry Is
Eleuthera
Miami
Miami Beach
Nassau
New Providence
Exuma Sound
Cat San Salvador
The Everglades
C. Sable
Andros
Great Exuma
Rum Cay
Long
Key West
Marquesas Keys
Straits of Florida
Great Bahama Bank

GULF OF MEXICO

Habana (Havana)
Matanzas
Cardenas
Arch. de Camagüey
Cayo Romano
Colon
Sta Clara
Pinar del Rio
Guane
G. de Batabano
Cienfuegos
Moron
Ciego de Avila
Camagüey
Holguin
Banes
Yucatan Channel
C. San Antonio
C. Catoche
Sancti Spiritus
CUBA
Victoria de las Tunas
Bayamo
Guantanamo
Jardines de la Reina
Manzanillo
G. de Guacanayabo
Santiago de Cuba
Progreso
Mérida
Tizimin
Pto Juárez
I. de Cozumel
Little Cayman (U.K.)
Cayman Brac
Ciudad del Carmen
Valladolid
Ticul
Peto
B. de la Ascensión
Grand Cayman (U.K.)
Montego Bay
Spanish Town
Port Antonio
Kingston
JAMAICA
Bahia de Campeche
Campeche
Escarcega
Yucatan
Chetumal
Bco Chinchorro
Ambergris Cay
Turneffe I.
Swan (Hond.)
Pedro Cays (Jam.)
CARIBBEAN SEA
Cd del Carmen
Frontera
Términos
Coatzacoalcos
Minatitlán
Istmo de Tehuantepec
Tuxtla Gutiérrez
Villahermosa
Palenque
Flores
Belmopan
BELIZE
Belize
I. de la Bahia
S. Pedro Sula
Sta Rosa
Tela La Ceiba
Trujillo
Pta Gorda
Staan Creek
Pto Barrios
Comitán
S. Cristóbal
Pto Caratasca
Serrana Bank (U.S.A & Col.)
Tonalá
GUATEMALA
Copan
HONDURAS
Juticalpa
Tegucigalpa
Catacamas
Cayos Miskitos
Huixtla
Tapachula
Quezaltenango
Sta Ana
Guatemala
Comayagua
Segovia
Bonanza
Pto Cabezas
I. de Providencia (Col.)
Escuintla
San José
Sonsonate
S. Miguel
La Union
Matagalpa
G. de Fonseca
EL SALVADOR
San Salvador
Chinandega
León
NICARAGUA
Cord. Isabelia
Rio Grande
Prinzapolca
I. del Maiz (Nic & U.S.A.)
Is. de San Andrés (Col.)
Managua
Masaya
Granada
L. de Managua
Bluefields
San Juan del Sur
L. de Nicaragua
San Juan del Norte
G. de Papagayo
Pen. de Nicoya
COSTA RICA
Alajuela
Limón
Pta S. Blas
Colón
G. de los Mosquitos
Puntarenas
San José
Cartago
Chirripó
La Chorrera
Panama
Arch. de las Perlas
G. de Nicoya
David
Santiago
Chitré
Golfo de Panamá
Pto Cortés
Pen. de Osa
G. Dulce
Armuelles
Pen. de Azuero
Pta Solano

① ② ③ ④ (grid references)
Ⓔ Ⓓ Ⓔ

90   80   30   10

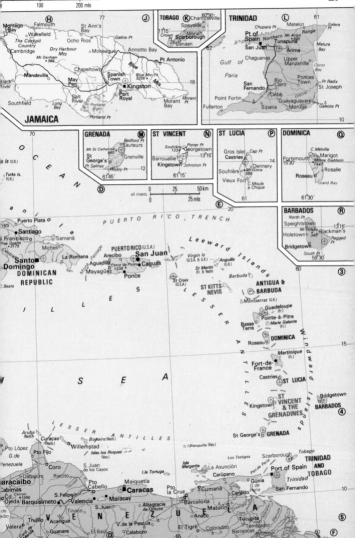

200 400 600 km
100 200 300 mils

BRAZIL

La Serena
Coquimbo
Rivadavia
La Rioja
Sumampa
Reconquista
Vera
Goya
Mercedes
Paso de los Libres
Uruguaiana
Sta Maria
Cruz Alta
Cachoeira do Sul

Punitaqui
Illapel
Jáchal
S. Agustin
Santa Fe
Alegrete
Artigas
Rivera

Los Vilos
San Juan
Olivares
Córdoba
V. Dolores
Rafaela
La Paz
Concordia
Salto
Tacuarembó
Livramento
Bagé

Quillota
S. Felipe
Mendoza
Aconcagua
S. Francisco
Alta Gracia
Villa Maria
Santa Fe
Paraná
Concepción
Paysandú
Melo

Viña del Mar
Valparaíso
S. Antonio
San Luis
Córdoba
Bell Ville
Rosario
San Nicolás
Trinidad
Durazno
Treinta y Tres
URUGUAY

Santiago
S. Bernardo
Rancagua
Mercedes
Río Cuarto
Venado Tuerto
Pergamino
Junin
Buenos Aires
Avellaneda
Colonia
Canelones
Florida
Minas
Rocha

Pichilemu
S. Fernando
S. Rafael
Rufino
Lincoln
Chivilcoy
Mercedes
La Plata
Montevideo
Maldonado
Punta del Este

Curicó
Gral Alvear
ARGENTINA
Buenos Aires
Chascomús
Las Flores
Dolores

Constitución
Talca
Mendoza
San Rafael
Gral Pico
Pehuajó
Olavarría
Azul
Ayacucho
Gral Vedia

Cauquenes
Linares
S. Carlos
Bardas Blancas
Telén
Sta Rosa
Trenque Lauquen
Guaminí
Tandil
Balcarce
Mar del Plata
Miramar
Necochea

Tomé
Talcahuano
Concepción
Coronel
Chillán
Los Angeles
La Pampa
Carhué
Cnl Pringles
Tres Arroyos
Claromecó

Lebu
Angol
Temuco
Neuquén
Gral Roca
Choele Choel
Bahía Blanca
Punta Alta
Bahía Blanca

Carahue
Toltén
Villarrica
Loncoche
Zapala
Río Negro
San Antonio Oeste
Carmen de Patagones
Viedma

Valdivia
Los Lagos
La Unión
Osorno
Paso Limay
Valcheta
Golfo San Matías

Pto Montt
S. Carlos de Bariloche
Maquinchao
Pto Pirámides

Ancud
Castro
El Bolsón
Esquel
Las Plumas
Chubut
Gaimán
Trelew
Rawson
Pto Madryn

Puerto Montt
Chubut
Camarones
C. Dos Bahías

ATLANTIC OCEAN

Pto Aisén
Coihaique
L. Musters
Sarmiento
Golfo San Jorge
Comodoro Rivadavia
Colonia Las Heras
C. Tres Puntas

Caleta Olivia
Deseado
Pta Médanosa

Cochrane
Santa Cruz
Las Heras
Deseado

Esmeralda
S. Martín
S. Julián

Madre de Dios
Lago Argentino
Sta Cruz
FALKLAND ISLANDS (ISLAS MALVINAS) (U.K.)

Calafate
Bahía Grande
Río Turbio
Río Gallegos
West Falkland
East Falkland
Stanley
Weddell
Jason Is.

Arch. de la Reina Adelaida
Punta Arenas
Beauchene Is.

Desolación
Río Grande
Tierra del Fuego
Isla Grande de Tierra del Fuego
Ushuaia
I. de los Estados

at the same scale
Shag Rocks
South Georgia (U.K.)
C. Alexandra
Grytviken
C. Disappointment

Santa Inés
Londonderry
Hoste
C. de Hornos (C. Horn)
Is Wollaston
Is Diego Ramírez

200 400 600 km
100 200 300 mls

(A) (B) 45 (C) 40 (D) 35 (E)

① Equator 0

C. Magiuarinho
f. de Marajó
Salinópolis
Bragança
Capanema
Belém
Abaetetuba
Cametá
Tucurui
Monção
São Luís
Rosário Parnaíba
Pinheiro
Chapadinha
Bacabal
Coroatá
Codó
Caxias
Campo
Maior
Camocim Acaraú
Itapipoca
Sobral Caucaia
Sta Fortaleza (Ceará)
Quiteria
Nova Canindé Aracati
Russas
Morada N Quixadá Areia Branca
Macau Pta do Calcanhar

PARÁ MARANHÃO
Marabá
Imperatriz
Pto Franco
Grajaú
Carolina
Araguaína
Balsas
Teresina
Castelo
Crateús
Mombaça
Taua
Iguatú
Acopiara
Picos J.do Norte Patu
Sousa
Caicó
Mossoró
Natal

CEARÁ
RIO GRANDE DO NORTE
Cabedelo
João Pessoa
Campina Grande

Florano
Oeiras
PIAUÍ
S.Raimundo
Nonato
Paulistana
Ouricuri
Salgueiro
Crato
Sa
Talhada
Limoeiro
Caruaru
PARAÍBA
Olinda
Recife
(Pernambuco)
Jaboatão

TOCANTINS B R A Z I L
Palmas
PERNAMBUCO
Garanhuns
Palmares
Barreiros
Juazeiro
Petrolina
Cach do
S.Francisco
Palmeira dos Ind
ALAGOAS
Maceió

Barra
Jacobina
R.de Jacuípe
Ibotirama
Feira de S.
BAHIA
Propriá Arapiraca
Penedo
SERGIPE
Lagarto
Aracajú
Serrinha
Estância

Barreiras
Iacu
Bom Jesus
da Lapa
Castro
Alves
Cachoeira
Alagoinhas
Salvador (Bahia)
B. de T. os Santos

Aruanã
GOIÁS
Uruaçu
Ceres
Formosa
Jaraguá
Pirenópolis
Anápolis
Goiânia
Goiás
Brasília
São Francisco
Januária
Montes Claros
Porteirinha
Salinas
Caetité
Vitória da
Conquista
Itabuna
Jequié
Ipiaú
Valença
Ilhéus

ATLANTIC OCEAN

15

Rio Verde
Itumbiara
Caldas
Novas
Paracatu
João
Pinheiro
Pirapora
Araçuaí
Teófilo Otôni
Nanuque
Canavieiras
Belmonte
Pôrto Seguro
Itamaraju

São
Francisco
Goiânia
Patos
de Minas
Curvelo
Diamantina
Gov.
Valadares
São Mateus
ESPÍRITO
SANTO

Uberlândia
Araguari
Catalão
MINAS GERAIS
Itabira
Fabriciano
Colatina
Linhares
Vitória
Vila Velha

Ituiutaba
Barragem Água
Vermelha
Araxá
Uberaba
Sete Lagoas
Belo
Horizonte
Caeté
Cng
Caratinga
Manhuacu
Ponte Nova
SANTA
Cachoeiro de Itapemirim

Rubineia
Barretos
São
José
S.J. Rio Prêto
Catanduva
Franca
Passos
Divinópolis
Conselheiro
Carangola
Barbacena
Iúna
Itaperuna

Araçatuba
Ribeirão Prêto
S.João del Rei
Lafaiete
Juiz
de Fora
Nova Friburgo
Campos
S.João da Barra

SÃO PAULO
Pres.
Prudente
Assis
Ourinhos
Londrina
Marília
Bauru
São Carlos
Araraquara
Limeira
Piracicaba
Lavras
Pocos de
Caldas
Volta
Redonda
Barra
Petrópolis
Magé
Niterói

Jacarezinho
Itapeva
Itapetininga
Campinas
Jundiaí
Sorocaba
São Paulo
Santos
São Vicente
Rio de Janeiro

Castro
Ponta
Grossa
Guarapuava
nião
Curitiba
Mafra
Paranaguá
Itararé
Juquiá
São Francisco do Sul
Itanhaém
Iguape

Tropic of Capricorn

45 40 35 25

ARCTIC OCEAN
NORWEGIAN SEA
NORTH SEA
ATLANTIC OCEAN
Greenland (Den.)
Jan Mayen (Nor.)
Arctic Circle
ICELAND
Reykjavik
Foroyar (Den.)
Shetland
Orkney
Aberdeen
Edinburgh
Glasgow
Newcastle
Manchester
Liverpool
Belfast
Dublin
IRELAND
UNITED KINGDOM OF GREAT BRITAIN AND NORTHERN IRELAND
NORWAY
Vesterålen
Lofoten
Narvik
Trondheim
Bergen
Stavanger
Oslo
SWEDEN
Umeå
Sundsvall
Stockholm
Vänern
Jönköping
Göteborg
Malmö
Gotland
Öland
Bornholm
DENMARK
Ålborg
København
Rostock
Gdańsk
Kaliningrad
RUS. FED.
Baltic Sea
Gulf of Bothnia
Åland
FINLAND
Oulu
Vaasa
Tampere
Helsinki
ESTONIA
Tallinn
LATVIA
Riga
LITHUANIA
Vilnius
BELARUS (BELORUSSIA)
Minsk
RUSSIAN FEDERATION
Sankt-Peterburg (Leningrad)
Ladozhskoye Oz.
Onezhskoye Oz.
Murmansk
Arkhangel'sk
O. Kolguyev

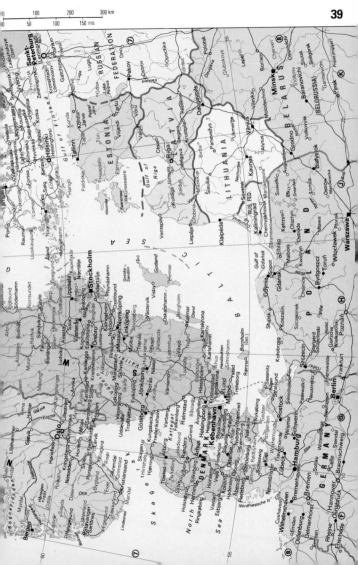

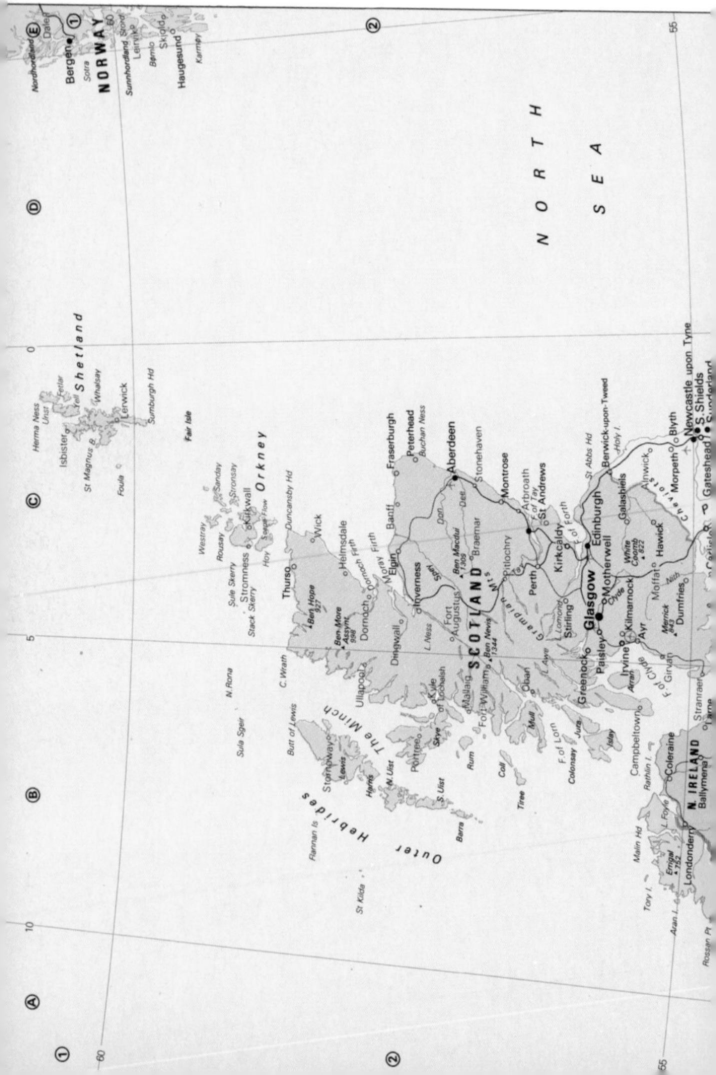

NORWAY

Bergen

Dale

Nordhordland

Stord

Sunnhordland

Leirvik

Bømlo

Haugesund

Karmøy

Skudenes

Herma Ness

Unst

Isbister

St Magnus B.

Shetland

Yell

Whalsay

Lerwick

Foula

Sumburgh Hd

Fair Isle

N O R T H

S E A

Rousay

Westray

Sanday

Stronsay

Kirkwall

Orkney

Stromness

Hoy

South Ronaldsay

Duncansby Hd

C. Wrath

N. Rona

Sula Sgeir

Butt of Lewis

Flannan Is

Stornoway

Lewis

Harris

N. Uist

Benbecula

Outer Hebrides

S. Uist

Barra

St Kilda

Thurso

Wick

Helmsdale

Dunbeath

Stack Skerry

Sule Skerry

Ben More Assynt, 998

Ullapool

Dingwall

Inverness

L. Ness

Ben Nevis, 1344

Fort Augustus

Fort William

Mallaig

Kyle of Lochalsh

Portree

Skye

The Minch

Rum

Eigg

Coll

Tiree

Mull

Jura

Islay

Colonsay

Oban

Fl of Lorn

SCOTLAND

Grampian Mts

Ben Macdui, 1309

Braemar

Pitlochry

Perth

Stirling

Glasgow

Greenock

Paisley

Motherwell

Kilmarnock

Irvine

Ayr

Arran

Kintyre

Campbeltown

Rathlin I.

Grampians

Peterhead

Fraserburgh

Buchan Ness

Aberdeen

Stonehaven

Montrose

Arbroath

St Andrews

Kirkcaldy

Fl of Forth

Edinburgh

Galashiels

Hawick

White Coomb, 822

Moffat

Nith

Dumfries

Merrick, 842

Stranraer

Larne

Ballymena

N. IRELAND

Coleraine

Londonderry

Foyle

Malin Hd

Tory I.

Aran I.

Errigal, 752

Rosan Pt

St Abbs Hd

Berwick-upon-Tweed

Holy I.

Cheviot Hills

The Cheviot, 816

Coldstream

Morpeth

Blyth

Newcastle upon Tyne

Gateshead

S. Shields

Sunderland

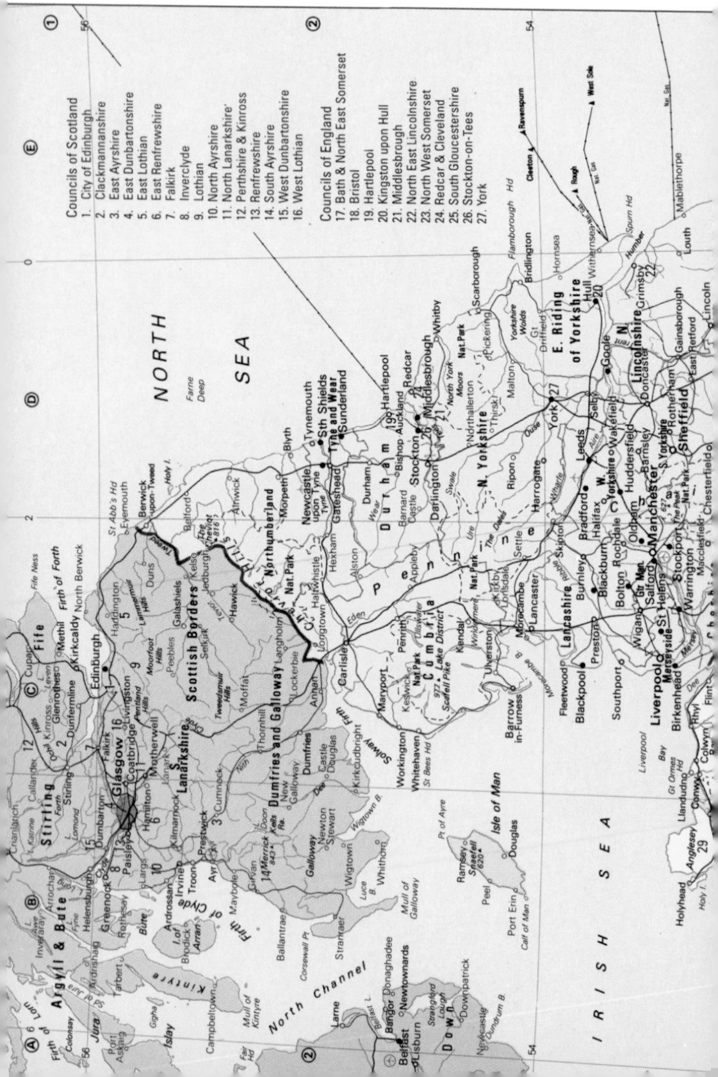

Councils of Scotland
1. City of Edinburgh
2. Clackmannanshire
3. East Ayrshire
4. East Dunbartonshire
5. East Lothian
6. East Renfrewshire
7. Falkirk
8. Inverclyde
9. Lothian
10. North Ayrshire
11. North Lanarkshire
12. Perthshire & Kinross
13. Renfrewshire
14. South Ayrshire
15. West Dunbartonshire
16. West Lothian
Councils of England
17. Bath & North East Somerset
18. Bristol
19. Hartlepool
20. Kingston upon Hull
21. Middlesbrough
22. North East Lincolnshire
23. North West Somerset
24. Redcar & Cleveland
25. South Gloucestershire
26. Stockton-on-Tees
27. York
NORTH SEA
IRISH SEA
North Channel
Argyll & Bute
Stirling
Fife
Glasgow
Lanarkshire
Scottish Borders
Dumfries and Galloway
Northumberland
Tyne and Wear
Durham
Cumbria
N. Yorkshire
E. Riding of Yorkshire
Lancashire
W. Yorkshire
S. Yorkshire
Lincolnshire
Merseyside
Isle of Man
Down
Edinburgh
Newcastle upon Tyne
Carlisle
Leeds
York
Hull
Manchester
Liverpool
Sheffield
Blackpool
Belfast

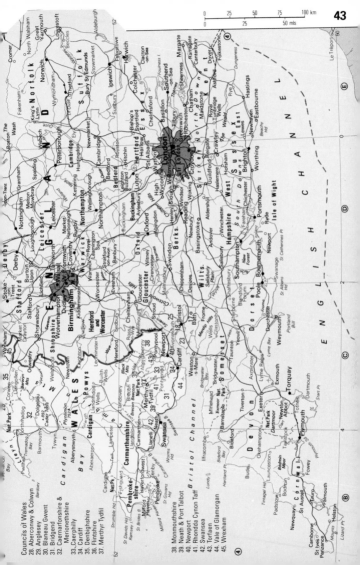

0 25 50 75 100 km
0 25 50 mils

Councils of Wales
28 Aberconwy & Colwyn
29 Anglesey
30 Blaenau Gwent
31 Bridgend
32 Caernarfonshire & Merionethshire
33 Cardiff
34 Caerphilly
35 Denbighshire
36 Flintshire
37 Merthyr Tydfil

38 Monmouthshire
39 Neath & Port Talbot
40 Newport
41 Rhondda Cynon Taff
42 Swansea
43 Torfaen
44 Vale of Glamorgan
45 Wrexham

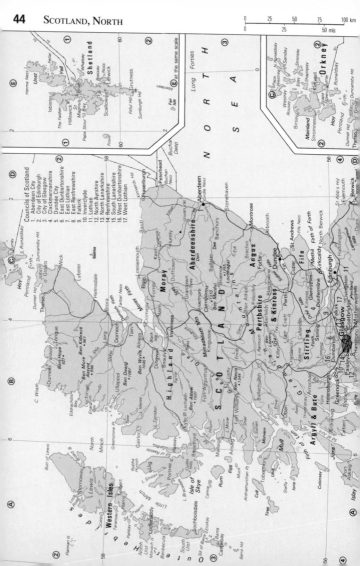

0 25 50 75 100 km
0 25 50 mls

Councils of Scotland
1. Aberdeen City
2. City of Edinburgh
3. City of Glasgow
4. Clackmannanshire
5. Dundee City
6. East Dunbartonshire
7. East Lothian
8. East Renfrewshire
9. Falkirk
10. Inverclyde
11. Lothian
12. Midlothian
13. North Ayrshire
14. North Lanarkshire
15. Renfrewshire
16. South Lanarkshire
17. West Dunbartonshire
18. West Lothian

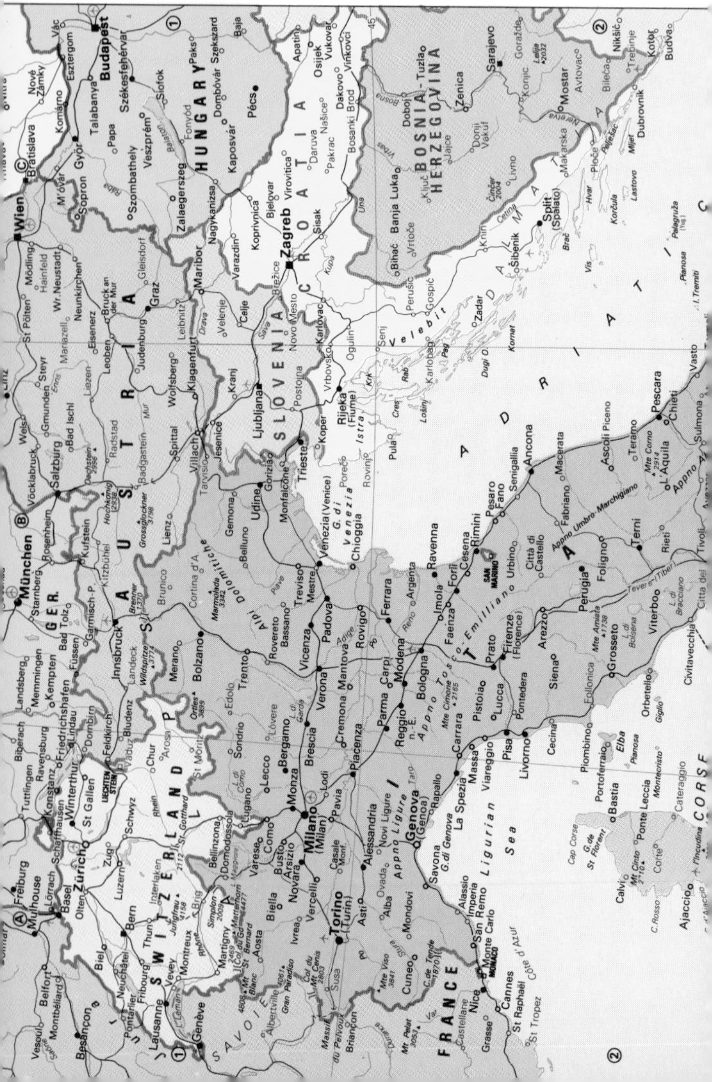
HUNGARY
CROATIA
SLOVENIA
AUSTRIA
SWITZERLAND
BOSNIA-HERZEGOVINA
GER.
FRANCE
ITALIA
ADRIATIC
CORSE
Ligurian Sea
Budapest
Wien
München
Zagreb
Ljubljana
Sarajevo
Bratislava
Salzburg
Innsbruck
Graz
Klagenfurt
Zürich
Bern
Genève
Lausanne
Basel
Milano (Milan)
Torino (Turin)
Genova (Genoa)
Venezia (Venice)
Trieste
Verona
Padova
Bologna
Firenze (Florence)
Pisa
Livorno
Ancona
Pescara
Perugia
Rijeka (Fiume)
Split (Spalato)
Mostar
Nice
Cannes
Monte Carlo
San Remo
Ajaccio
Bastia
Elba
Corse

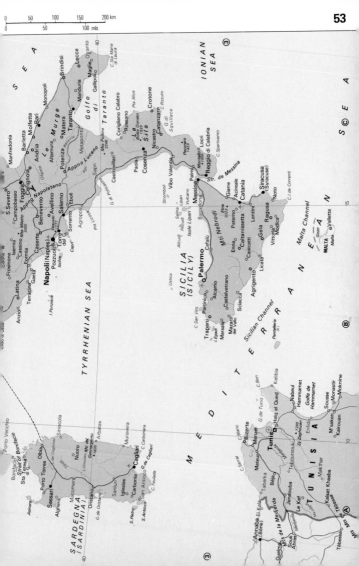

0 50 100 150 200 km
0 50 100 mils

④
③

TURKEY

Bursa
Yalova
Gemlik
Karacabey
Mustafakemalpaşa
Tavşanlı
Akdağ 2089
Simav
Kula
Buldano
Denizli
Nazilli
Aydın
Söke
Milas
Bodrum
İzmir
Menemen
Torbalı
Selçuk
Tire
Ödemiş
Salihli
Turgutlu
Boz Dağları
Manisa
Akhisar
Sındırgı
Balıkesir
Bigadiç
Bandırma
Gönen
Biga
Edremit
Burhaniye
Ayvalık
Soma
Bergama
Çanakkale
Ezine
Ayvacık
Bozcaada
Candarlı

Denizli ③
Muğla
Rhodos
Rhodos
Lindos
Marmaris
Köyceğiz
Fethiye
Kalkan
Göcek K.
Símí
Kós
Nísiros
Tílos
Astipálaia
Kárpathos
Kásos

**SPORÁDHES
(DHODHEKÁNISOS)**

Sámos
Íkaría
Pátmos
Léros
Kálimnos
Kalolimnos
Ikaría
Foúrnoi
Mikonos
Dílos

Khíos
Sakız K.
Psará
Lésvos
Ayvalık K.
Límnos
Áyios Evstrátios
Thásos
Samothráki

Kaválao
Kírton
Dráma
Sérraio
Nígrita
Langadás
K.Strimonikós
Polígiros
K.Toronéos
Skíathos
Skópelos
Alónnisos
Skíros

**AEGEAN
SEA**

Xánthi
Alexandroúpolis
Saros Körfezi
Keşan
Gelibolu
Eceabat
Gökçeada

Sea of
Marmara Adasi

Ténedhos Adi
İzmit
İznik

MACEDONIA

Kavadár
Veles
Prilep
Bítola
Demir
Kavadarci
Gradsko
Negotino
Ohrid
Strumica
Kičevo
Resen

A N I A

Tiranë
Durrës
Elbasan
Lushnjë
Berat
Vlorë
Fier
Gjirokastër
Sarandë
Kükës
Peshkopi
Pogradec
Korçë

**Kórkira
(Corfu)**
Kérkira

**IÓNIOI NÍSOI
(Ionian Islands)**

Levkás
Levkás
Zákinthos
Zákinthos
Kefallinía
Itháki

Ioánnina
Igoumenítsa
Párga
Préveza
Árta
Amfilokhía
Agrínion
Lepanto
Návpaktos
Mesolóngion
Aitolikón

G R E E C E

Grevená
Kalabáka
Tríkala
Kardhítsa
Lárisa
Vólos
Almirós
Fársala
Domokós
Lamía
Amfissa
Livadhiá
Thívai
Khalkís
Kími

Óthris 1728
Óiti 2152
Parnassós 2457

Flórina
Kastoriá
Grámmos 2520
Neápolis
Kozáni
Siátista
Ptolemaís
Édhessa
Véroia
Katerini
Olimbos 2911
Elassón
Larisa

**Thessaloníki
(Salonica)**
Kilkís
Khalkidhikí
Thermaïkós Kólpos

Athína (Athens)
Piraiévs
Mégara
Akharnaí
Eleusís
Elevsís
Koríntos
Korínthos
Sikeón
Argos
Návplion
Trípolis
Megalópolis
Lakonía
Spárti 1935
Parnón 1936
Spárti

Évvoia

Ándros
Kéa
Síros
Tínos
Páros
Náxos
Amorgós
Íos
Síkinos
Folégandros
Thíra
Anáfi
Mílos
Sífnos
Sérifos
Kíthnos
**KIKLÁDHES
(CYCLADES)**

Aíyina
Ídhra
Spétsai
Póros
Méthana

**Gulf of
Argolikós Kólpos**

**Mirtoan
Sea**

Kíthira
Andikíthira

Monemvasía
Yíthion
Neápolis
Ákr. Maléas
Ákr. Tainaron

**Sea of
Crete**

Kríti

Khaniá
Réthimnon
Iráklion
Timbákion
Áyios Nikólaos
Ierápetra
Ídhi Óri 2456
Dhíkti Óri 2148
Léfka Óri 2452
Kastélli
Sitía

Pátrai
Aíyion
Amaliás
Pírgos
Kalámai
Kipárissos
Kiparissía
Filiatrá
Pílos
Méllon
Messíní
Yíthion
Messiniakós Kólpos
Lakonikós Kólpos

Kalávrita
Pýrgos
Trípolis

**IONIAN
SEA**

Strait of Otranto

Brindisi
Lecce
Maglie
Ótranto
C. Sta Maria
di Leuca
Gallipoli

Sea of
Kárpathos

C
25
B
20
A
40

③

④

NORTH SEA

BALTIC SEA

SWEDEN

DENMARK

POLAND

GERMANY

Västervik, Hjältevad, Mönsterås, Nybro, Kalmar, Borgholm, Öland

Exsjö, Huskvarna, Jönköping, Nässjö, Ronneby, Karlskrona

Ulzike, Stegno, Koszalin

Świdwin, Białogard, Szczecinek, Jastrowie, Piła, Poznań

Göteborg, Mölndal, Borås, Kungsbacka, Varberg, Falkenberg, Halmstad, Laholm, Båstad, Ängelholm, Helsingborg, Lund, Malmö, Ystad

Kołobrzeg, Koszalin, Karlino, Białogard, Szczecinek, Gorzów Wielkopolski, Złotów, Skwierzyna, Zielona Góra, Leszno

Skagen, Hirtshals, Frederikshavn, Sæby, Ålborg, Hadsund, Hobro, Randers, Grenå, Århus, Silkeborg, Horsens, Vejle, Fredericia, Kolding, Esbjerg, Varde, Grindsted, Haderslev, Åbenrå

Svendborg, Odense, Nyborg, Korsør, Slagelse, Næstved, Vordingborg, Nykøbing, Gedser

København (Copenhagen), Roskilde, Køge, Hillerød, Helsingør, Helsingborg

Stralsund, Greifswald, Anklam, Pasewalk, Neubrandenburg, Prenzlau, Templin

Wismar, Rostock, Warnemünde, Ribnitz, Güstrow, Schwerin, Ludwigslust, Parchim, Neustrelitz, Neuruppin, Oranienburg, Berlin, Potsdam, Nauen, Brandenburg, Frankfurt (an der Oder), Cottbus

Flensburg, Schleswig, Husum, Heide, Rendsburg, Neumünster, Kiel, Eckernförde

Hamburg, Lübeck, Bad Oldesloe, Itzehoe, Elmshorn, Cuxhaven, Bremerhaven, Stade, Buxtehude, Bremen, Lüneburg, Uelzen, Celle, Wolfsburg, Salzgitter, Braunschweig, Magdeburg, Stendal, Wittenberge, Rathenow, Genthin, Dessau

SCHLESWIG-HOLSTEIN, MECKLENBURG, VORPOMMERN, NIEDERSACHSEN, SACHSEN-ANHALT, BRANDENBURG, NORDRHEIN-WESTFALEN

Wilhelmshaven, Emden, Groningen, Assen, Oldenburg, Leer, Meppen, Lingen, Nordhorn, Rheine, Osnabrück, Minden, Hannover, Hildesheim, Hameln, Bielefeld, Gütersloh, Paderborn, Halberstadt, Aschersleben, Quedlinburg

Den Helder, Alkmaar, Zaandam, Haarlem, Amsterdam, Hilversum, Leiden, 's-Gravenhage (Den Haag), Utrecht, Gouda, Rotterdam, Dordrecht, Amersfoort, Apeldoorn, Zwolle, Deventer, Enschede, Hengelo, Coesfeld, Bocholt, Wesel, Münster, Hamm, Dortmund, Essen, Duisburg

Leeuwarden, Sneek, Heerenveen, Harlingen

Breda, Tilburg, Eindhoven, 's-Hertogenbosch, Nijmegen, Arnhem, Venlo

Antwerpen (Anvers), Mechelen, Brugge, Gent, Oostende, Dunkerque (Duinkerke)

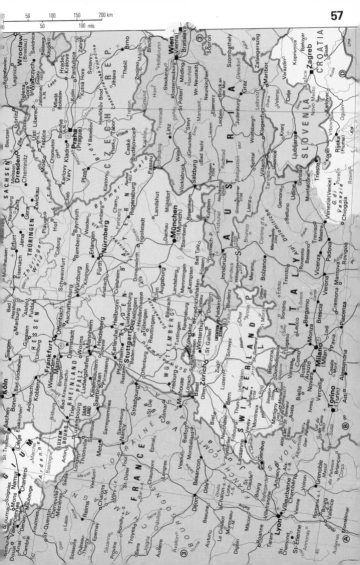

RUSSIAN FEDERATION

LATVIA

Riga

Gulf of Riga

Jūrmala

Daugavpils

LITHUANIA

Šiauliai

Panevėžys

Kaunas (Kovno)

Vilnius

Klaipėda

RUS. FED.

Kaliningrad (Königsberg)

BELARUS (BELORUSSIA)

Minsk

Grodno

Brest

Baranovichi

Pinsk

SWEDEN

Gotland

Öland

Bornholm

BALTIC SEA

Gdynia

Sopot

Gdańsk (Danzig)

Gulf of Gdańsk (Z. Gdański)

Szczecin

POLAND

Poznań

Łódź

Warszawa

Bydgoszcz

Toruń

Białystok

Olsztyn

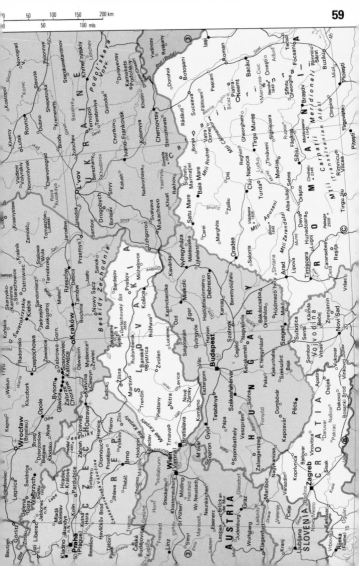

Vel'sk · Krasavino · Gryva · Gayny · Solikamsk · Serov · Sov'va · K
konoshka · Velikiy Ustyug · Luza · Pinyug · Kazhim · Lalsk · Komi- · Permyak · Kudymkar · Kizel · Nov. · Lyalya
Brusenets · Oparino · Vokhma · Kirs · Komi- · Krasnokamsk · Kachkanar · Turinsk
Khar'ovsk · Murashi · Vakhtan · Chusovoy · Nizhniy · Tagil · Irbit · Alapayevsk · Turinsk
Tot'ma · Roslyatino · Murashi · Kotel'nich · Omutninsk · Zuyevka · Vereshchagino · Ocher · Lys'va · Kirovgrad · Rezh · Irbit
Sokol · Buy · Manturovo · **Kirov** · Glazov · Ocher · **Perm** · Kungur · Nizhniye · Nev'yansk · Bogdanovich
ologda · Galich · Kostroma · Vyatka · Zuyevka · Balezino · Bogorodskoye · Ochyor · Krasnoufimsk · Nizhnyaya · Sergi · **Yekaterinburg** (Sverdlovsk)
Kostroma · Makaryev · Sharya · Urdmurtia · Chaykovskiy · Krasnoufimsk · Nizhnyaya · Sergi · Kamensk- · Ural'skiy
Kineshma · Shakhun'ya · Uren · Sovetsk · **Izhevsk** · Sarapul · Chernushka · Nyazepetrovsk · Kasli · Kyshtym
vo · Vichuga · Yoshkar · Urzhum · Mamadysh · Agryz · Kambarka · Pavlovo · **Chelyabinsk**
ovo · Ivanovo · Shuya · Semyonov · Ola · Malmyzh · Mozhga · Birsk · Asha · Bakal · Plast
ovrov · Gorodets · **Nizhniy** · Koz'modemyansk · Cheboksary · **Kazan** · Naberezhnyye · Chelny · Menzelinsk · Pavlovo · Zlatoust · Kopeysk · Chelyabinsk
Vyazniki · Dzerzhinsk · **Novgorod** (Gor'kiy) · Zelenodol'sk · **Tatarstan** · Al'met'yevsk · Ufa · **Bashkortostan** · Tirlyanskiy · Verkhneural'sk
Gus · Khrustalnyy · Nizhniy · Novgorod · Chuvashia · Shumerlya · Chistopol · Leninogorsk · Oktyabr'skiy · Davlekanovo · Tuymazy · Krasnousol' · Magnitogorsk
Murom · Arzamas · Sergach · Alatyr' · Tetyushi · Kuybyshevskoye · Nurlat · Bugul'ma · Belebey · Abdulino · Sterlitamak · Sibay · Kartaly
Pervomaysk · **Mordoviya** · **Simbirsk** · Dimitrovgrad · Sernovodsk · Buguruslan · Salavat · Baymak · Bredy
azan · Sasovo · Kovylkino · **Saransk** · Ul'yanovsk · Tol'yatti · Meleuz · Kumertau
Vsk · Shilovo · Nizhniy · Lomov · **Privolzhskaya** · Nikol'sk · Baryš · **Samara** (Kuybyshev) · Buzuluk · Sorochinsk
Ryazhsk · Morshansk · **Penza** · Kuznetsk · Syzran · **Samara** · Buzuluk · Sorochinsk · Mednogorsk · Disk
haplygin · Tambov · Kamenka · Serdobsk · Khvalynsk · Saratovskoye · Pugachev · **Orenburg** · Saraktash · Kuvandyk · Novotroitsk · Dombarovskiy
ambov · Rasskazovo · Petrovsk · Vol'sk · Balakovo · Pugachev · Orenburg · Sol' · Iletsk · Akbulak · Novotroitsk
ryazi · Rtishchevo · Arkadak · Atkarsk · **Saratov** · Yershov · Ural'sk · Aksay · Novoalekseyevka · Aktyubinsk · Alga
herdevka · Balashov · Povorino · Krasnoarmeysk · Krasnyy · Kut · Novo · Uzensk · Chapayev · Uial · Shubar · Kuduk · Oktyabr'skiy · Emba
nezh · Borisoglebsk · Uryupinsk · Novoanninskiy · Kamyshin · Palasovka · Nikolayevsk · Maksteksay · Inderborskiy · Zharkamys
osh · Kalach · Mikhaylovka · Frolovo · Volzhskiy · Saykhin · **Caspian** · Makat · Kulakshi · Aktumsyq
ostov · **Rostov** · Kalach-na-Donu · **Volgograd** · Volzhskiy · Akhtubinsk · **Lowland** · Gur'yev · Balykshi · Kul'sary
Donu · Shakhty · Morozovsk · **Volgograd** (Stalingrad) · **KAZAKHSTAN** · Ryn · Peski · Sarykamys
Volgodonsk · Kotel'nikovo · **Kalmykia-** · **Astrakhan** · Krasnyy · Yar · Sor · Mertvyy · Ustyurt
Tikhoretsk · Divnoye · **Khalmg** · **Astrakhan** · Mumra · Kultuk · Bevneyev
Kropotkin · **Stavropol'** · Budennovsk · Elista · Yashkul' · Chernyye · Zemli · Lagan' (Kaspiyskiy) · Burynshik · Ustyurt · **UZBEKISTAN**
Labirsk · Armavir · Stavropol' · Kuma · Ova · Tyulen · M. Tyub-Karagan · Polustrov · Say-Utes · **Plateau**
kop · Cherkessk · Kislovodsk · Pyatigorsk · Georgiyevsk · **Dagestan** · Ft Shevchenko · Mangyshlak · Aktau (Shevchenko) · Novyy Uzen · K.-B. · **Kabardino-** · **Balkariya**
Elbrus · Nal'chik · Prokhladnyy · **Chechnya** · Grozny · Fetisovo · K.-C. · **Karachayvo-** · **Cherkesiya**
Abkhazia · Dyuh-Tau · Alagir · **Vladikavkaz** · Buynaksk · **Makhachkala** · S.O. · **Severnaya** · **Osetiya**
khumi · **GEORGIA** · **CASPIAN** · **SEA**

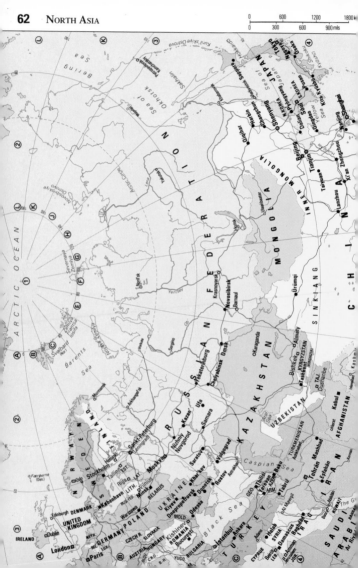

Scale bars

200 400 600 800 km
200 400 mils

Legend

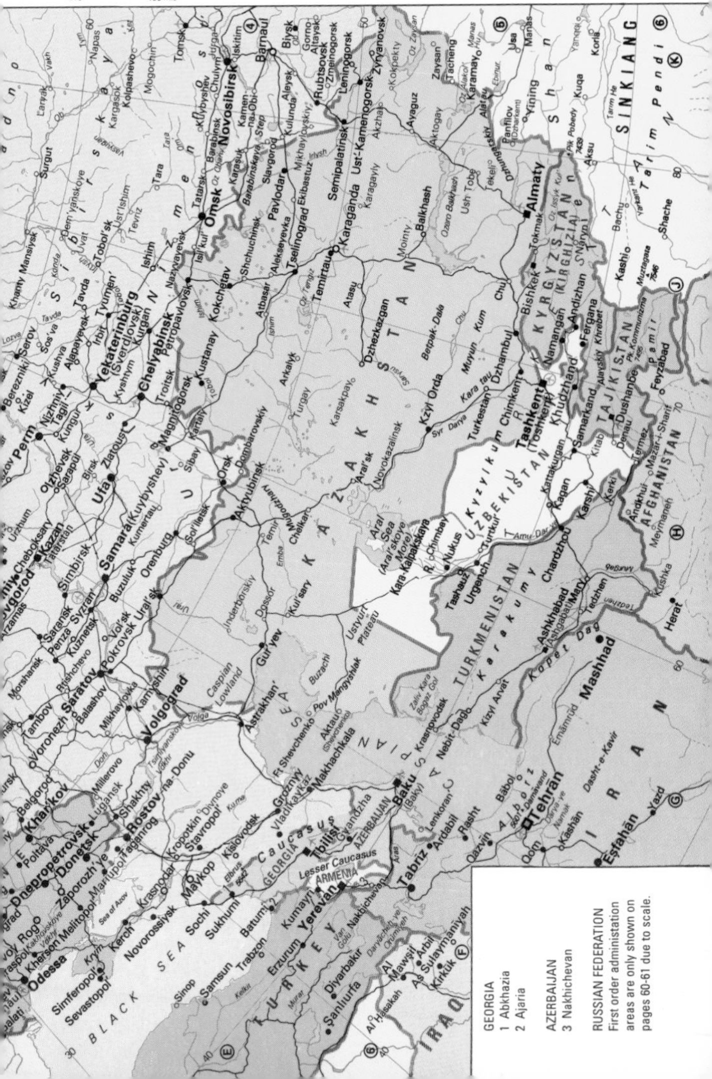

GEORGIA
1 Abkhazia
2 Ajaria

AZERBAIJAN
3 Nakhichevan

RUSSIAN FEDERATION
First order administration
areas are only shown on
pages 60–61 due to scale.

Map labels

Tomsk · Novosibirsk · Barnaul · Biysk · Gorno-Altaysk · Zmeinogorsk · Leninogorsk · Semey · Öskemen · Ust-Kamenogorsk · Tashanta · Ili · Karamay · SINKIANG · Tarim Pendi

Omsk · Pavlodar · Ekibastuz · Semipalatinsk · Karaganda · Balkhash · Ozero Balkhash · Almaty · Shan

Tyumen · Kokchetav · Tselinograd (Akmola) · Astana · Bishkek · KYRGYZSTAN (KIRGHIZIA) · Yining · Kashio

Yekaterinburg (Sverdlovsk) · Chelyabinsk · Kostanay · Atbasar · Taldy-Kurgan · Naryn · Andizhan · Kashgar

Perm · Ufa · Kurgan · Petropavlovsk · Kyzyl Orda · Chimkent · Tashkent · Namangan · Fergana · TAJIKISTAN · Pamir

Magnitogorsk · Aktyubinsk · KAZAKHSTAN · Turkestan · Dzhambul · Khudzhand · Dushanbe

Orenburg · Uralsk · Guryev · Aral · Kzyl Kum · UZBEKISTAN · Samarkand · Kitab · AFGHANISTAN

Samara (Kuybyshev) · Saratov · Kazan · Simbirsk · Ulyanovsk · Syr Darya · Nukus · Bukhara · Karshi · Herat

Volgograd · Astrakhan · Caspian Lowland · TURKMENISTAN · Kara Kum · Ashkhabad · Mary · Mashhad

Rostov-na-Donu · Krasnodar · Stavropol · Caspian Sea · Baku · AZERBAIJAN · Kopet Dag · Tehran · IRAN

Kharkov · Dnepropetrovsk · Donetsk · Mariupol · Sea of Azov · Sochi · GEORGIA · Tbilisi · ARMENIA · Yerevan · Tabriz · Esfahan

Odesa · Simferopol · Sevastopol · BLACK SEA · Novorossiysk · Batumi · Caucasus · Lesser Caucasus · Nakhichevan · TURKEY · Erzurum · Diyarbakir · Sanliurfa · IRAQ

RUSSIA

Black Sea

GREECE
MAC.
ALB.
BULGARIA
Athínai
Sicily

Braşov
Odesa
Dnepropetrovsk
UKRAINE
Donetsk
Kharkov
Saratov
Samara
Ufa
Yekaterinburg
Omsk
Chelyabinsk
Nove

İstanbul
Ankara
TURKEY
Rostov
Volgograd
Astrakhan

KAZAKHSTAN

GEORGIA
Tbilisi
ARM.
Yerevan
AZER.
Baku
Caspian Sea
Aral Sea
Karaganda

CYPRUS
Adana
Alep
Mawgil
Tabriz

LIBYA
Alexandria
Cairo
EGYPT
Aswa

SYRIA
Halab
Damascus
LEB.
Jerusalem
ISRAEL
Amman
JOR.
Baghdad
IRAQ
Tehrān
Mashhad
UZBEKISTAN
Bishkek
Almaty
Tashkent
KYRGYZSTAN
(KIRGHIZIA)
TAJIKISTAN
Dushanbe

TURKMENISTAN
Ashkhabad

SAUDI
ARABIA
Ar Riyād
KUWAIT
Eşfahān
Herat
Kabul
AFGHANISTAN
Islamabad
Kashmir

Buşra
Abādān
IRAN
Kermān

SUDAN
RED SEA
Khartoum

BAHRAIN
QATAR
Abū Dhabī
U.A.E.
The Gulf
Masqat
Lahore
PAKISTAN
Indus
Delhi
NE
Kanpu
Lucknow
Pa

Makkah
Karachi
Hyderābād
Ahmadābād
Jabalpur
INDIA

YEMEN
OMAN
Sana'ã
ARABIAN
SEA
Bombay
Nāgpur
Godavari

ERITREA
Asmara
ETHIOPIA
Addis
Ababa
DJIBOUTI
Aden
G. of Aden
Socotra
(Yemen)
Hyderābād
Krishna

SOMALIA
Bangalore
Madras
Lakshadweep
(Ind.)
Madurai
SRI LANKA
Colombo
Kandy

KENYA
Mombasa
Muqdisho
Equator
MALDIVES

Dar es Salaam
TANZANIA
SEYCHELLES
INDIAN OCEA

Aldabra Is.
(Sey.)
COMOROS

MOZAMBIQUE
Chagos Arch.
(U.K.)

MADAGASCAR
Antananarivo

Don
Krim
Kür

Scale bar
200 400 600 800 km
200 400 mls

Top labels
TAIWAN (FORMOSA)
ai-tung (China Nat. Rep.)
-tung
130 140

PACIFIC

OCEAN

Farallon de Pajaros
Maug Is. 20
Parece Vela
Asuncion
Agrihan
Pagan Alamagan
Guguan
Sarigan
Anatahan
Farallon
de Medinilla
Saipan
Tinian 2
Rota
Guam (U.S.A.)
Nero Deep
9637

Northern Mariana Islands
Northern
Mariana
Islands

MARIANA

Batan Is
C. Engaño
Babuyan Is
Aparri
Tuguegarao
llagan
ulo LUZON
pan Baler
banatuan Polillo Is
uezon City
Manila Catanduanes
Daet
Boac Naga
Bulan Legazpi
Catarman
 blon Masbate Oras
Masbate Samar
nay Catbalogan
Iloilo Roxas Tacloban Guiuan
Bacolod Cebu Leyte
egros Dinagat 10265
Siaton Bohol Siargao
Bohol Surigao
Manukan Butuan
Ozamiz Marawi Cagayan de Oro
Lanao MINDANAO
ambzanga Malaybang Cotabato
ela Davao
olo Digos
Jolo General
u Arch Santos Tinaca Pt

PHILIPPINES

Manila

Mantyu Deep
9818
Challenger Deep
11033 10

Ulithi Fais Gafer Jt

Yap Faraulep

Ngulu Sorol Wolei Lamotrek
Fed.States of Micronesia Ifalik
Palau Eauripik
Islands Koror
Sonsorol Pulo Anna Merir

CAROLINE ISLANDS 3

CELEBES / EBES
SEA

Buol
Manado
Kuandang Belang
Gorontalo Ternate Halmahera
Bacan Weda
Luwuk Obi
Peleng Talaud Mangole
Kep. Banggai
Kendari Wowoni
Kolaka Munia Butung
Baubau Kep.
Tukangbesi

Talaud Karakelong
Tahuna
Sangihe
Kepulauan
Sangihe
Morotai
Tobelo

MOLUCCAS

Waigeo Kwoka Manokwari Supiori
Salawati 800A Cendrawasih Numfoor Biak
Sorong Peg Arfak Yapen
Misool 2835 Teluk
Cendrawasih
Teluk Berau Dom Sarmi
Bula 1340
Faktak Kaimana Mandala
Kokonau Tk Flamingo

Equator 0

Ninigo Group
Wuvulu

IRIAN Aitape Schouten Is 4
Pegunungan Maoke Wewak Karkar
Pk Jaya Sept Long I.
5029 Wewak
JAYA Mt Hagen
Mandala Mendi Goroka
4702 Kubor 4359
Kikori Bulolo
Kerema Wau

PAPUA
NEW GUINEA

CERAM SEA
Namlea Piru 3019
Buru Seram
Ambon
Kep.Banda

Tg d'Urville
Jayapura

BANDA SEA

Kep. Kai Dobo
Kep. Kobroör
Aru
Tranganl

P.Kolepom
Tanahmerah
N E W
G U I N E A
Merauke P A P U A
Komoran Daru

Gulf of
Papua

Port Moresby

Damar
Nila
Teun
Yamdena
Kepulauan
Tanimbar
Selaru

Mulgrave I.
Saibai Torres Strait
Thursday I.
Pr.of Wales C. York
Somerset

Banks I.
CORAL 5

Wetar Romang Babar
Sermata

SIA
SEA

Lomblen
Alor Wetar Kep. Leti
Endeh Dili Atambua
TIMOR
Kupang
Roti

ARAFURA SEA

TIMOR SEA

Savu Sea

C.V. Diemen
Bathurst I. Melville I. Croker I. Coburg Pen
Clarence Str Gunda Str
Darwin Arnhem Land
140

Wessel Is
Goyal C. Arnhem
C. Wilberforce
Gove C. York
Nhulunbuy

AUSTRALIA

Weipa
Iron Range
C. Grenville

Great Barrier Rf

Albatross B.

Grid references: D, E, F (top and bottom)

MONGOLIA

Changchun

Shenyang
Anshan
Benxi
Fushun

Liaoning

KOREA BAY

Dandong

Qinhuangdao
Tangshan
Tianjin (Tientsin)

BO HAI

Dalian
Lüshun

YELLOW SEA (HUANG HAI)

Yantai
Weihai
Wendeng

Qingdao (Tsingtao)

Shandong

Zibo
Jinan (Tsinan)

Weifang
Weihsien

Lianyungang

Jiangsu

Bengbu

Beijing (Peking)
Zhangjiakou
Xuanhua
Baoding
Shijiazhuang
Taiyuan
Yangquan
Hengshui

Hebei

Shanxi

Handan
Anyang
Xinxiang
Zhengzhou
Kaifeng

Henan

Luoyang
Xuchang
Pingdingshan

Datong

Hohhot
Baotou
Dongsheng

Inner Mongolia

Yinshan

Ningxia

Yinchuan
Zhongwei

Qingtongxia

Shaanxi

Yan'an
Xi'an
Xianyang

Qinling

Lanzhou
Linxia

Gansu

Tianshui

Xining

Qinghai

Wuwei

Tengger Shamo

Badain Jaran Shamo

Mu Us Shamo

Erenhot

Erdenet

Ulan Ude

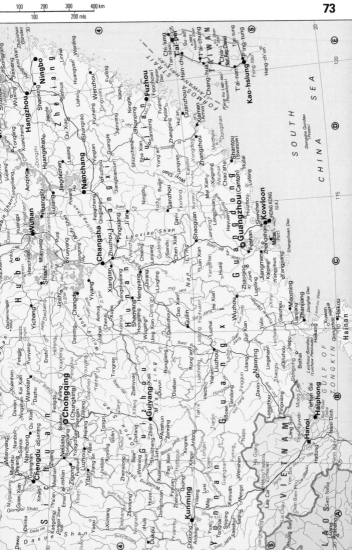

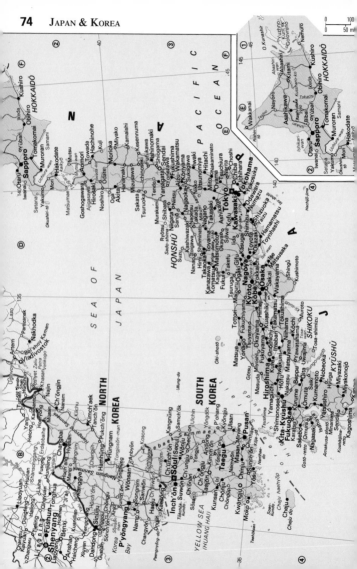

PACIFIC OCEAN

SEA OF JAPAN

HONSHŪ

HOKKAIDŌ

Sapporo

Tōkyō
Yokohama
Kawasaki
Ōsaka
Kyōto
Kōbe
Nagoya

SHIKOKU

KYŪSHŪ

NORTH KOREA

SOUTH KOREA

P'yŏngyang

Sŏul (Seoul)
Inch'ŏn

Taegu
Pusan
Kwangju

YELLOW SEA (HUANG HAI)

Shenyang

Fukuoka
Kita-Kyūshū

Nagasaki

Cheju-do

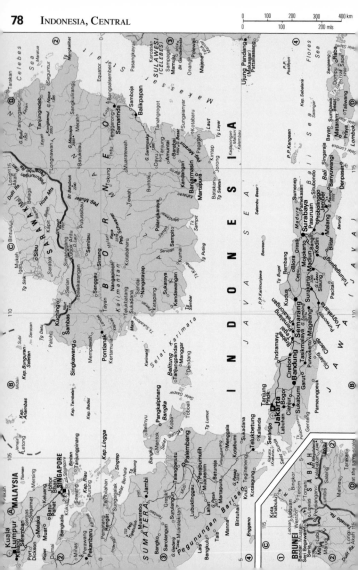

Celebes Sea

SULAWESI (CELEBES)

Makassar Strait

Equator

Ujung Pandang (Makassar)

Flores Sea

SARAWAK

KALIMANTAN

BORNEO

Samarinda
Balikpapan

Banjarmasin
Martapura

Java Sea

Bali
Lombok
Sumbawa

Madura
Surabaya

J A V A

Semarang
Bandung
Jakarta

S U M A T E R A

Palembang

Singapore

MALAYSIA
Kuala Lumpur

BRUNEI
SABAH
Kota Kinabalu

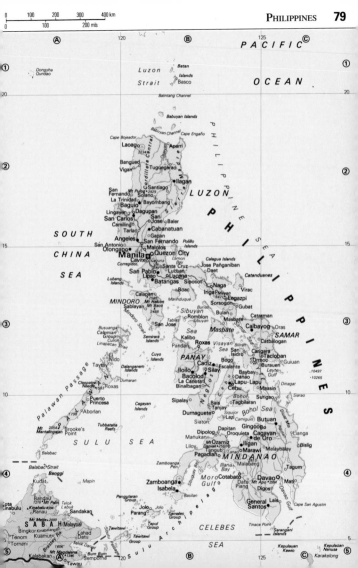

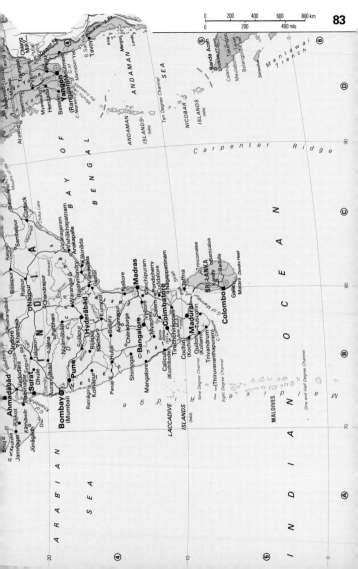

| | 0 | 200 | 400 | 600 | 800 km |
| 0 | | 200 | | 400 mls | |

④

⑤

⑥

Ⓓ

Ⓒ

Ⓑ

Ⓐ

⑤

I N D I A N   O C E A N

A R A B I A N   S E A

B A Y   O F   B E N G A L

A N D A M A N   S E A

Carpenter   Ridge

Mentawai Trench

ANDAMAN
ISLANDS
(India)

NICOBAR
ISLANDS
(India)

LACCADIVE
ISLANDS
(India)

MALDIVES

Ten Degree Channel

Eight Degree Channel

Nine Degree Channel

One and Half Degree Channel

Banda Aceh

Bombay
(Mumbai)

Ahmadābad
Vadodara
Surat
Rajkot
Bhavnagar
Bhuj
Jāmnagar
Junāgadh
G. of Khambhat
Kāthiāwār
Bhachau

Indore
Khandwa
Dhule
Jalgaon
Ujjain

Hoshangābad
Bilāspur
Sambalpur
Raipur
Chandrapur
Cuttack
Bālāsore

Nagpur
I N D I A

Bhubaneswar
Chilka Lake

Pune
Kolhāpur
Solāpur
Hyderābad
Warangal
Vishākhapatnam
Vizianagaram
Rājahmundry
Kākināda
Anakāpalle

Ratnāgiri
Panaji
Hubli
Bijāpur
Rāichur
Kurnool
Guntūr
Vijayawāda
Nellore

Mangalore
Shimoga
Chitradurga
Bangalore
Anantapur
Bellary

Calicut
(Kozhikode)
Mysore
Salem
Vellore
Kānchipuram
Madras
Pondicherry
Cuddalore

Cochin
(Kochi)
Coimbatore
Tiruchchirāppalli
Thanjāvūr
Nāgappattinam

Quilon
(Kollam)
Madurai
Tuticorin
Trivandrum
(Thiruvananthapuram)
C. Comorin

SRI LANKA
Jaffna
Trincomalee
Kandy
Batticaloa
Colombo
Badulla
Galle
Matara   Dondra Head

G. of Mannar

Yangon
(Rangoon)
Bassein
Henzada
Mawlamyine
(Moulmein)
Tavoy
Mergui

Chiang
Mai
Tak

Bhairab Bazar

Mandalay

Aizawl

Silchar

20

10

0

90

80

70

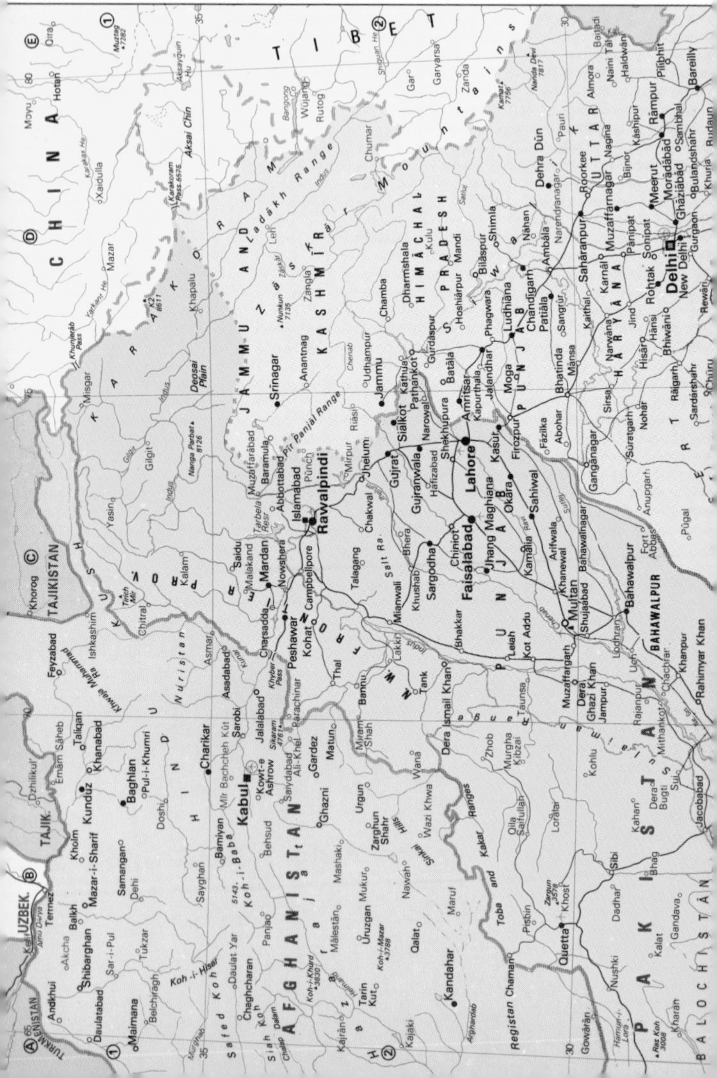

CHINA

TIBET

TAJIKISTAN

UZBEK.

TURKMENISTAN

AFGHANISTAN

PAKISTAN

JAMMU & KASHMIR

HIMACHAL PRADESH

PUNJAB

HARYANA

UTTAR

BALOCHISTAN

KARAKORAM Range

Ladakh Range

Salt Ra.

Aksai Chin

Deosai Plain

Nanga Parbat 8126

Hindu Kush

Koh-i-Baba

Safed Koh

Siah Koh

Registan

Toba

Kirthar Range

Sulaiman Range

New Delhi, Delhi, Rawalpindi, Islamabad, Lahore, Faisalabad, Srinagar, Jammu, Sialkot, Gujranwala, Amritsar, Ludhiana, Jalandhar, Chandigarh, Patiala, Ambala, Saharanpur, Meerut, Moradabad, Rampur, Bareilly, Peshawar, Kabul, Kandahar, Quetta, Bahawalpur, Multan, Sargodha, Jhang, Sahiwal, Okara, Kasur, Dehra Dun, Simla, Shimla, Mandi, Chamba, Dharmshala

0 100 200 300 km
0 50 100 150 mls

Kānpur
Etāwah
Mainpuri
Hamirpur
Rath
Mahoba
Pannā
Auraiya
Kalpi
Orai
Charkhāri
Damoh
Narsimhapur
Seoni
Tirodi
Lakhnadon
Hatrras
Mathura
Āgra
Firozābād
Bhind
Morena
Gwalior
Datia
Jhānsi
Chatarpur
Sāgar
Shora
Tikamgarh
Mahadeo Hills
Chhindwara
Nāgpur
Kāmthi
Umred
Bhāndara
Pauni
Tropic of Cancer
Bharatpur
Dausa
Daulpur
Hindaun
Sawāi Madhopur
Shivpuri
Guna
Sironj
Vidisha
Bhopāl
Hoshangābād
Betūl
Achalpur
Amrāvati
Wardha
Yavatmāl
Pusad
Hinganghāt
Adilābād
Beramapalli
Mancheral
Jagtial
Nizāmābād
Karimnagar
Bodhan
Alwar
Jaipur
Sikar
Didwāna
Kisharigarh
Ajmer
Tonk
Shivpuri
Lalitpur
Rājgarh
Shājapur
Agar
Ujjain
Dewās
Indore
Mhow
Sanawad
Barwāni
Khandwa
Harda
Khargon
Burhānpur
Bhusāwal
Akola
Akot
Khamgaon
Karanja
Washim
Mehkar
Hingoli
Bāsim
Pārbhani
Purna
Nānded
Nirmal
Mānsa
Beāwar
Bhilwāra
Bundi
Kotah
Chittaurgarh
Rawatbhāta
Mandasaur
Nimach
Ratlām
Jāora
Jhābua
Dhār
Sendhwa
Dhule
Amalner
Jalgaon
Malkāpur
Buldāna
Aurangābād
Jālna
Bir
Ladnūn
Nāgaur
Mērta
Bilāra
Kekri
Sojat
Pāli
Sādri
Jālor
Sirohi
Udaipur
Banswāra
Dūngarpur
Dāhod
Godhra
Dabhoi
Rājpipla
Nandurbār
Navāpur
Dhulia
Nāsik
Deolāli
Manmād
Kopārgaon
Malegaon
Sangamner
Dind
Brāhman
Siddhapur
Dānta
Himatnagar
Nadiād
Petlād
Vadodara
Bharuch
Valsād
Silvassa
(D. & D.)
Daman
(D. & D.)
Thāne
Bombay
Jodhpur
Pipar
Bilāra
Bālotra
Pokaran
Shergarh
Devikot
Barmer
Jaisalmer
Rāmgarh
Pāchpadra
Jālor
Palanpur
Pātan
Mahesāna
Radhanpur
Kāndla
Gāndhidhām
Bhuj
Naliya
Mundra
Okha
Dwārka
Porbandar
Mangrol
Verāval
Junāgadh
Gir Hills
Diu
(Goa, Daman & Diu)
Bilimora
Navsāri
Surat
Bhāvnagar
Botad
Jambusar
Dholera
Khambhāt
Gulf of Khambhāt
Dhandhuka
Surendranagar
Limbdi
Morbi
Navlākhi
Wānkāner
Rājkot
Gondal
Jetpur
Dhorāji
Amreli
Kundla
Jāmnagar
Gāndhidhām
Rohri
Khairpur
Nawābshāh
Sartanahu
Sanghar
Mīrpur Khās
Tando Adam
Tando Allāhyār
Hyderabad
Tando
Muhammad
Khān
Badin
Umarkot
Chhachro
Nagar
Parkar
Virāwah
Nawābkot
Kāvda
Lakhpat
Rann of Kachchh
Gulf of Kachchh
S I N D H
Larkāna
Dadu
Sehwan
Kotri
Keti Bandar
Tatta
Sonmiāni
Koraṅgi
Karāchi
Mouths of the Indus
Tropic of Cancer
Nagha
Kalat
Central Makrān Range
Bela
Waṛ
Sonmiāni Bay
Makran Coastal Range
Kīrthar Range
KHAIRPUR
M A D H Y A   P R A D E S H
U T T A R   P R A D E S H
R A J A S T H A N
M A H A R A S H T R A
G U J A R A T
A R A V A L L I   R a n g e
V i n d h y a   R a n g e
S ā t p u r a   R a n g e
T H A R   o r   G R E A T   I N D I A N   D E S E R T
A R A B I A N

S E A

Ganga
Chambal
Betwa
Ken
Son
Narmada R.
Tāpti R.
Tāpi R.
Pune
(Poona)
Kalyān
Karjat
Lonāvale
Pen
Alibāg
Mahād

④
⑤
Ⓒ
Ⓑ
Ⓐ
④
75
70
25
20

0 100 200 300 km
0 50 100 150 mls

MYANMAR (BURMA)

NAGALAND

MANIPUR

MIZORAM

A S S A M

MEGHALAYA

TRIPURA

ARUNĀCHAL Pradesh

BHUTAN

SIKKIM

NEPAL

C H I N A

T I B E T

BANGLADESH

Dhākā (Dacca)

Chittagong

WEST BENGAL

Calcutta

Hāora

Khulna

BAY OF BENGAL

Mouths of the Ganges (Ganga)

BIHAR

Patna

UTTAR PRADESH

Lucknow

Kānpur

Allahābād

Vārānasi

MADHYA PRADESH

Raipur

Bhilai

Durg

ORISSA

Cuttack

Mt Everest

Kathmandu

Gorakhpur

Muzaffarpur

Bhāgalpur

Darbhanga

Gayā

Ranchi

Jamshedpur

Chota Nāgpur

Cherrapunji

Shillong

Gauhāti

Tezpur

Imphāl

Āizawl

Agartala

Comilla

Jessore

Rājshāhi

Rangpur

Mymensingh

Dibrugarh

Siliguri

Kāch Bihār

Gangtok

KAZAKHSTAN

UZBEKISTAN

TURKMENISTAN • Ashkhabad

AFGHANISTAN

IRAN □Tehrān

Mashhad

RUSSIAN FEDERATION

Nizhniy Novgorod

Moskva

Sankt-Peterburg

FINLAND

SWEDEN Stockholm

NORWAY Oslo

Caspian Sea

Volgograd

Rostov

GEORGIA Tbilisi

AZER. Baku

ARM. Yerevan

Tabriz

Baghdad

IRAQ

SYRIA Damascus

KUWAIT

SAUDI ARABIA

Ar Riyāḍ

BAHRAIN QATAR UNITED ARAB EMIRATES

OMAN

YEMEN

ERITREA Asmera

Red Sea

Gulf of Aden

Khar'kov

Kyïv UKRAINE

BELARUS Minsk

LITH. Vilnius

LAT. Riga

EST. Tallinn

Dnipro

Odessa

Black Sea

Kishinev MOLDOVA

Bucureşti ROMANIA

București

Istanbul

Ankara TURKEY

CYPRUS

LEBANON Beirut

ISRAEL Jerusalem

JORDAN Amman

EGYPT

Cairo

Alexandria

Khartoum

SUDAN

POLAND Warszawa

Kraków

SLOVAKIA

Budapest HUNGARY

Beograd

BULGARIA Sofia

GREECE Athína

Mediterranean Sea

LIBYA

Tripoli

Benghazi

CHAD

L. Chad

NIGER

Niamey

Berlin GERMANY

Praha CZECH REPUBLIC

Wien AUSTRIA

München

SWITZ. SLOV. CROATIA

Milano

ITALY

Roma

Napoli

Sicilia

TUNISIA Tunis

MALTA

Hamburg

Bremen

Amsterdam NETH.

BELG. Brussels

LUX.

FRANCE

Paris

Lyon

Marseille

Bordeaux

Corse

Sardegna

ALGERIA

Alger

SAHARA

UNITED KINGDOM

London

Edinburgh

IRELAND Dublin

North Sea

Copenhagen DENMARK

Göteborg

SPAIN

Madrid

Barcelona

Valencia

Zaragoza

Ebro

Bay of Biscay

Bilbao

MOROCCO

Rabat

Casablanca

Marrakech

Western Sahara

MAURITANIA

Nouakchott

MALI

Bamako

BURKINA

Bobo-Dioulasso

SENEGAL Dakar

THE GAMBIA

GUINEA-BISSAU

GUINEA

PORTUGAL Lisboa

Porto

Tropic of Cancer

NORTH ATLANTIC OCEAN

Azores

Islas Canarias (Sp.)

Madeira

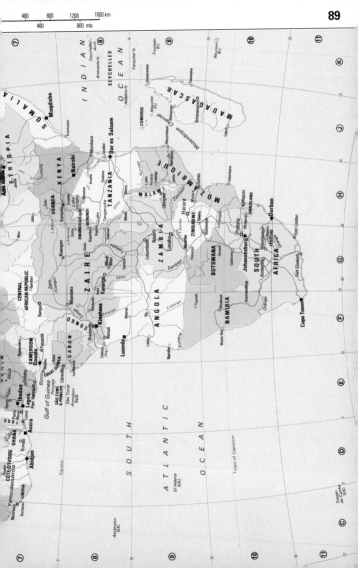

200 400 600 km

100 200 300 mils

ERITREA
DJIBOUTI
ETHIOPIA
SOMALIA
UGANDA
KENYA
RWANDA
BURUNDI
TANZANIA
SEYCHELLES
COMOROS

Gulf of Aden

Asmera
Adan (Aden)
Ta'izz
Al Mukhā (Mocha)
Berbera
Hargeysa
Dire Dawa
Harer
Adis Abeba
Nazret
Gonder
Mek'elē
Kassala
Wad Medani
El Obeid
Kosti
Malakal

Muqdisho (Mugadishu)
Marka
Kismaayo
Baydhabo

Kampala
Jinja
Nairobi
Lake Victoria
Lake Turkana
Kisumu
Nakuru
Mombasa
Kilimanjaro 5895
Arusha
Moshi
Dodoma
Dar es Salaam
Zanzibar
Tabora
Kigoma
Mbeya
Iringa
Mtwara
Lindi

Equator

Moroni
Grande Comore
Anjouan
Mayotte

Caluula
Boosaaso
Hordiyo
Raas Xaafuun
Bandarbeyla
Eyl
Gaalkacyo
Hobyo

at the same scale

ANGOLA
ZAIRE
ZAMBIA
NAMIBIA
BOTSWANA
ZIMBABWE
SOUTH AFRICA
LESOTHO
Luanda
Lobito
Benguela
Huambo (Nova Lisboa)
Namibe (Moçâmedes)
Lubango
Menongue
Cuito Cuanavale
Ondangua
Tsumeb
Grootfontein
Otjiwarongo
Okahandja
Windhoek
Swakopmund
Walvis Bay
Rehoboth
Mariental
Keetmanshoop
Lüderitz
Karasburg
Gobabis
Maun
Ghanzi
Francistown
Serowe
Palapye
Mahalapye
Molepolole
Gaborone
Kanye
Lobatse
Kalahari Desert
Okavango Delta
Makgadikgadi
Lusaka
Kabwe
Kitwe
Ndola
Chingola
Luanshya
Mufulira
Livingstone
Maramba
Lubumbashi (Elisabethville)
Likasi (Jadotville)
Kolwezi
Kamina
Bulawayo
Hwange
Gweru
Kwekwe
Pretoria
Johannesburg
Mmabatho
Rustenburg
Klerksdorp
Potchefstroom
Welkom
Kroonstad
Kimberley
Bloemfontein
Upington
Free State
N. Province
Pietersburg
Northern Cape
W. Cape
E. Cape
Cape Town
Table Mtn 1087
Cape of Good Hope
False Bay
Danger Pt
C. Agulhas
Worcester
Paarl
Beaufort West
Oudtshoorn
George
Mossel Bay
Port Elizabeth
Uitenhage
Grahamstown
East London
King William's Town
Queenstown
Umtata
Great Karoo
Namaqualand
Springbok
Port Nolloth
Alexander Bay
Orange
Port Louis
MAURITIUS
Round I.
St Denis
Réunion (Fr.)
at the same scale
G. Gauteng
M. Mpumalanga
K.-N. Kwazulu-Natal

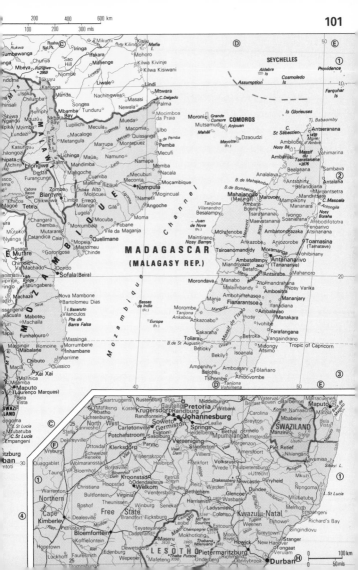

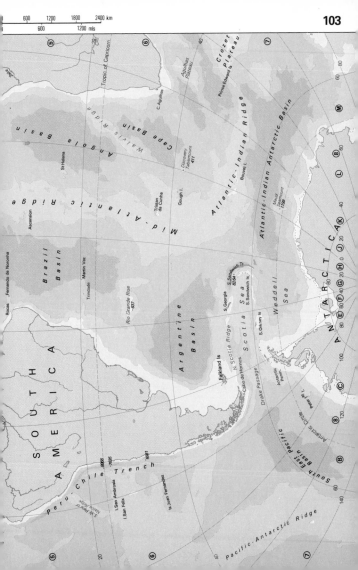

600 1200 1800 2400 km
600 1200 mls

⑤ ⑥ ⑦ Ⓜ ⑧ Ⓛ Ⓚ ⓙ Ⓗ Ⓖ Ⓕ Ⓔ Ⓓ Ⓒ Ⓑ

Tropic of Capricorn

C.Agulhas

Agulhas Plateau

Crozet Plateau

Prince Edward Is.

Atlantic-Indian Ridge

Cape Basin

Walvis Ridge

St.Helena

Angola Basin

Discovery Tablemount 411

Bouvet I.

Atlantic-Indian Antarctic Basin

Gough I.

Tristan da Cunha

Meteor Seamount 1159

M i d - A t l a n t i c   R i d g e

Ascension

Rocas   Fernando de Noronha

Brazil Basin

Martin Vaz

Trindade

Rio Grande Rise 637

Argentine Basin

A N T A R C T I C A

Weddell Sea

S.Sandwich Tr. 8264

S.Georgia

S.Sandwich Is.

Scotia Sea

N.Scotia Ridge

S.Orkney Is.

Falkland Is.

Cabo de Hornos

Antarctic Penin.

Drake Passage

Peter I I.

Antarctic Circle

S O U T H   A M E R I C A

Peru-Chile Trench
6055
2935
7621

I.San Ambrosio
I.San Felix

Nazca Ridge
to Juan F. M.S.

Is.Juan Fernández

South East Pacific Basin

Pacific-Antarctic Ridge

0   600   1200   1800   2400 km
0   600   1200 mls

Emperor Seamount Chain

190

NORTH
AMERICA

2926
Mendocino Seascarp

18

Murray Seascarp

104
Midway Is

Hawaiian
Islands

Tropic of Cancer

C. Falso

Mid-Pacific Mountains

1477

Is Revilla
Gigedo

Clarion Fracture Zone

MARSHALL
ISLANDS

P
O
L
Y
N
E
S
I
A

P   A   C   I   F   I   C

Line Is

O   C   E   A   N

Equator

NAURU

KIRIBATI

Phoenix Is

TUVALU

6150

Tokelau
(N.Z.)

American
Samoa

Is Marquises

SOLOMON
ISLANDS

French Polynesia

Wallis &
(Fr.) Futuna

WRN.
SAMOA

ANUATU

FIJI

TONGA

Cook
Is.
(N.Z.)

Samoa
Is de la
Tahiti Société

Is Tuamotu

Niue

Cook Is

Is Tubuai

Nouvelle
Calédonie
(Fr.)

Horizon Depth
10882

Is Gambier

Pitcairn (U.K.)

S. Fiji
Basin

Norfolk I. Rise

Norfolk I.

10047

N.Cape

Sala y Gómez

i.de Pascua

1344

East Pacific Ridge

NEW
ZEALAND

New Zealand
Plateau

Chatham Is

South West
Pacific
Basin

ckland Is

Campbell I.

G   190

H   160

J   140

K   120   Pacific-Antarctic Ridge

L   100

M

732

Tonga Trench

Kermadec Trench

INTERNATIONAL DATE LINE

① 40

②

③

0

④ 20

20

⑤

40

⑥

PAPUA

NEW GUINEA

Gulf of Papua

Port Moresby

Torres Strait

Cape York

Coen Peninsula

Weipa

Mitchell River

Cooktown

Cairns

Innisfail

Ingham

Palm Is

Townsville

Charters Towers

Ayr

Bowen

Proserpine

Mackay

Sarina

QUEENSLAND

Cloncurry

Hughenden

Richmond

Winton

Longreach

Clermont

Emerald

Rockhampton

Gladstone

Barcaldine

Mount Morgan

Blackall

Theodore

Bundaberg

Windorah

Charleville

Maryborough

Gympie

Quilpie

Roma

Miles

Dalby

Toowoomba

Brisbane

Ipswich

St George

Cunnamulla

Goondiwindi

Warwick

Bourke

Walgett

Moree

Glen Innes

Lismore

Casino

Grafton

Wilcannia

Cobar

Narrabri

Armidale

Broken Hill

Nyngan

Tamworth

Port Macquarie

NEW SOUTH WALES

Dubbo

Taree

Ivanhoe

Bathurst

Maitland

Cessnock

Newcastle

Orange

Lithgow

Griffith

Sydney

Cootamundra

Wollongong

Wagga Wagga

Goulburn

Deniliquin

Albury

Canberra

A.C.T.

Shepparton

VICTORIA

Bendigo

Ballarat

Melbourne

Geelong

Morwell

Colac

Bairnsdale

Bass Strait

King I.

Smithton

Burnie

Devonport

Launceston

Queenstown

St Mary's

TASMANIA

Hobart

Geeveston

PACIFIC OCEAN

Coral Sea Island Territories

Great Barrier Reef

Great Dividing Range

Nouvelle Calédonie

Noumea

Tropic of Capricorn

Norfolk I. (Aust)

Lord Howe I. (Aust)

TASMAN SEA

NEW ZEALAND

South Island

100
200
300 km
50
100
150 mls
Augathella
Mt Hutton
Injune
Taroom
Mundubbera
Biggenden
Maryborough
Gayndah
Double Island Pt
Wandoan
Goomeri
Murgon
Gympie
Tewantin
Wondai
Morven
Mitchell
Roma
Gulugubа
Mungallala
Muckadilla
Wallumbilla
Miles
Chinchilla
Kingaroy
Brooloo
Cooroy
Nambour
Jackson
Jandowae
Nanango
Yarraman
Maroochydore
Caloundra
Condamine
Kilcoy
Surat
Tara
Dalby
Toogoolawah
Caboolture
Moreton I.
Crows Nest
Redcliffe
Glenmorgan
Meandarra
Oakey
Gatton
Brisbane
Darling
Downs
Moonie
Toowoomba
Pittsworth
Ipswich
N. Stradbroke I.
Beenleigh
Millmerran
Clifton
St George
Mt Domville
Allora
Boonah
Beaudesert
Gold Coast
Tweed Heads
Bollon
Warwick
Killarney
Inglewood
Goondiwindi
Murwillumbah
Dirranbandi
Talwood
Thallon
Stanthorpe
Kyogle
Mullumbimby
C. Byron
Hebel
Boggabilla
Texas
Lismore
Mungindi
Goodooga
Yetman
Ballina
Garah
Casino
New Angledool
Croppa Ck
Tenterfield
PACIFIC
Lightning Ridge
Ashley
Moree
Ashford
Woodburn
Collarenebri
Gwydir
Warialda
Deepwater
Yamba
Narran L.
Pokataroo
Gravesend
Maclean
Glen Innes
Rowena
Bellata
Bingara
Inverell
Grafton
Walgett
Burren Jct.
Pian
Wee Waa
Nandewar
Bundarra
Glenreagh
Namoi
Guyra
Dorrigo
Round Mtn
Narrabri
Kaputar
Barraba
Coff's Harbour
OCEAN
Byrock
Gwabegar
Bellingen
Boggabri
Manilla
Uralla
Armidale
Nambucca Heads
Baradine
Gunnedah
Macksville
Coonamble
Smoky C.
Walcha
Coonabarabran
Mullaley
Tamworth
Kempsey
Gulargambone
Werris Creek
Black Sugarloaf
Nyngan
Wauchope
Port Macquarie
Gilgandra
Warren
Quirindi
Liverpool
Murrurundi
Kendall
Nevertire
Coolah
Wingham
Trangie
Dunedoo
Gloucester
Taree
Tottenham
Scone
Merriwa
Narromine
Dubbo
Gulgong
Muswellbrook
Forster
C. Hawke
Yellow Mtn
Wellington
Mudgee
Dungog
Sugarloaf Pt
WALES
Singleton
Maitland
Trundle
Peak Hill
Yeoval
Kandos
Mt Coricudgy
Kurri Kurri
Port Stephens
Condobolin
Cessnock
Raymond Terrace
Molong
Parkes
Newcastle
Morisset
L. Macquarie
Orange
Portland
Cargelligo
Forbes
Bathurst
Lithgow
Wyong
Tuggerah L.
Burcher
L. Cowal
Lachlan
Blayney
Richmond
Windsor
Canowindra
Katoomba
Port Jackson
West Wyalong
Grenfell
Cowra
Parramatta
Sydney
Camden
Campbelltown
L. Burragorang
Young
Picton
Crookwell
Wollongong
Temora
Boorowa
Bowral
Port Kembla
Cootamundra
Murrumburrah
Shellharbour
Goulburn
Burrinjuck Resr
Yass
Coolamon
Junee
Shoalhaven R.
L. George
Nowra
Gundagai
Canberra
Jervis B.
Tumut
A.C.T.
Queanbeyan
Ulladulla
Batlow
Holbrook
Batemans Bay
Tumbarumba
Hume
L. Eucumbene
Moruya
Wodonga
Corryong
Beechworth
Mt Kosciusko
Cooma
Cobargo
Nimmitabel
Bright
Mt Bogong
Snowy Mts
Bega
Australian Alps
Bombala
Merimbula
Delegate
Eden
Genoa
C. Howe
Orbost
Cann River
Bairnsdale
Lakes Entrance
Pt Hicks
Ninety Mile Beach
Wilson's Promontory
Bass Strait
C. Wickham
King I.
Naracoopa
Currie
Grassy
Stokes Pt
C. Frankland
Furneaux Group
Flinders I.
Whitemark
Lady Barron
Cape Barren I.
Hunter Is
C. Grim
Smithton
Stanley
Wynyard
Burnie
Ulverstone
Banks Strait
C. Portland
Marrawah
George Town
Bridport
Gladstone
Eddystone Pt
Devonport
Latrobe
Scottsdale
Launceston
St Helens
Waratah
Deloraine
Longford
Ben Lomond
St Marys
Rosebery
Great L.
Mt Ossa
Queenstown
Strahan
Derwent Br.
Frenchmans Cap
Macquarie Hbr
Oatlands
Freycinet Peninsula
TASMANIA
Tarraleah
Oyster Bay
New Norfolk
Maydena
Sorell
Maria I.
Hobart
Huonville
Tasman Pen
C. Pillar
Geeveston
Storm Bay
Port Davey
S.W. Cape
Bruny I.
S.E. Cape
at the same scale

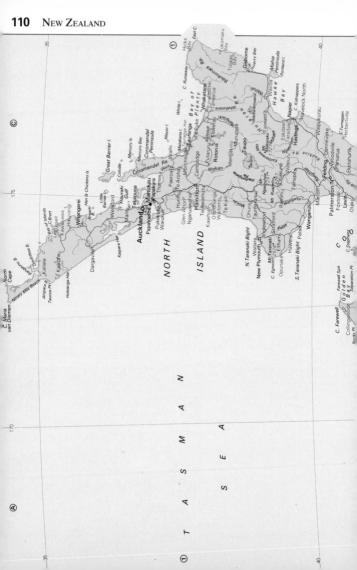

NORTH ISLAND

TASMAN SEA

North Cape
C. Maria van Diemen
Tauroa Pt.
Ahipara B.
Ninety Mile Beach
Reef Pt.
Herekino Har.
Hokianga Har.
Kaitaia
Kaikohe
Bay of Islands
C. Brett
C. Karikari
Doubtless B.
Whangaroa
Waipapakauri

Kaipara Har.
Dargaville
Whangarei
Hen & Chickens Is.
Bream B.
Little Barrier I.
Hauraki Gulf
Great Barrier I.
C. Colville
Mercury Is.
Mercury Bay
Coromandel
Coromandel Peninsula
C. Rodney
Warkworth
Helensville
Taupua
Auckland
Papatoetoe
Manukau
Papakura
Pukekohe
Waiuku
Thames
Paeroa
Waihi
Te Aroha
Huntly
Ngaruawahia
Raglan Har.
Glen Afton
Hamilton
Morrinsville
Matamata
Putaruru
Tokoroa
Cambridge
Te Awamutu
Kawhia
Kawhia Har.
Otorohanga
Te Kuiti
Waitomo

Mokau
Waikato
Taumarunui
N. Taranaki Bight
Waitara
New Plymouth
Inglewood
Mt. Egmont
Stratford
C. Egmont
Eltham
Opunake
Hawera
Ohura
S. Taranaki Bight
Patea
Wanganui

Mercer
Mt. Pirongia
Hauhungaroa Ra.
Mt. Ruapehu
Waiouru
Ohakune
Raetihi
Rangitikei R.
Taihape
Marton
Feilding
Palmerston N.
Foxton
Levin
Otaki

Barrier I.
Waihou
Mayor I.
Tauranga
Tauranga Har.
Te Puke
Maketu
Bay of Plenty
Whakatane I.
White I.
Mt. Edgecumbe
Whakatane
Opotiki
Mokoia I.
Rotorua
Rotorua
Mamaku
Taupo
Lake Taupo
Tongariro

Kawerau
Waioeka
Raukumara Ra.
Te Araroa
Hicks Bay
East C.
C. Runaway

Urewera
Waikaremoana L.
Murupara
Wairoa
Waikari R.
Mohaka R.
Esk R.
Taradale
Napier
Hastings
Havelock North
Waipukurau
Waipawa
Ormondville
Dannevirke
Woodville
Pahiatua
Eketahuna

Mahia Peninsula
Portland I.
Nuhaka
Mangapapa
Gisborne
Poverty Bay
Tokomaru Bay
Tolaga Bay
Okomaru Bay

Hawke Bay
C. Kidnappers
Ruahine Ra.
Tararua Ra.

C. Farewell
Farewell Spit
Golden Bay
Collingwood
Farewell
Separation Pt.
Takaka
Ruby B.
C. Stephens
Collingwood

SOUTH ISLAND

35
175
170
40

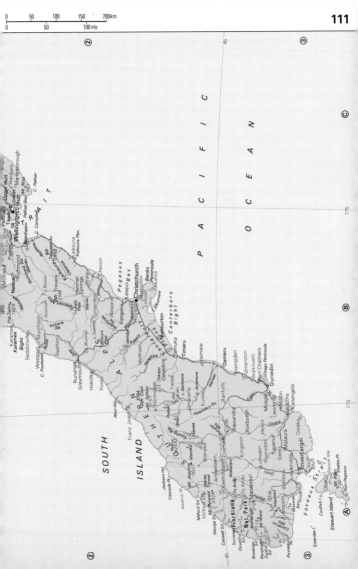

Antarctic Research Stations
1 Artigas (Uruguay)
2 Teniente Rodolfo Marsh Martin (Chile)
3 Bellingshausen (Rus. Fed.)
4 Great Wall (Changcheng) (China)
5 Comandante Ferraz (Brazil)
6 Henryk Arctowski (Poland)
7 Teniente Jubany (Arg.)
8 King Sejong (S. Korea)
9 Capitán Arturo Prat (Chile)
10 General Bernardo O'Higgins (Chile)
11 Esperanza (Arg.)
12 Vicecomodoro Marambio (Arg.)
13 Palmer (USA)
14 Faraday (UK)
15 Rothera (UK)
16 General San Martin (Arg.)

Index

In the index, the first number refers to the page, and the following letter
and letter to the section of the map in which the index entry
can be found. For example, 48C2 **Paris** means that Paris can
be found on page 48 where column C and row 2 meet.

Abbreviations used in the index

Afghan	Afghanistan	Germ	Germany	Par	Paraguay	Arch	Archipelago
Alb	Albania	Hung	Hungary	Phil	Philippines	B	Bay
Alg	Algeria	Ind	Indonesia	Pol	Poland	C	Cape
Ant	Antarctica	Irish Rep	Ireland	Port	Portugal	Chan	Channel
Arg	Argentina	Leb	Lebanon	Rom	Romania	Gl	Glacier
Aust	Australia	Lib	Liberia	Russian Fed	Russian	I(s)	Island(s)
Bang	Bangladesh	Liech	Liechtenstein		Federation	Lg	Lagoon
Belg	Belgium	Lux	Luxembourg	S Arabia	Saudi Arabia	L	Lake
Bol	Bolivia	Madag	Madagascar	Scot	Scotland	Mt(s)	Mountain(s)
Bulg	Bulgaria	Malay	Malaysia	Sen	Senegal	O	Ocean
Burk	Burkina	Maur	Mauritania	S Africa	South Africa	P	Pass
Camb	Cambodia	Mor	Morocco	Switz	Switzerland	Pen	Peninsula
Can	Canada	Mozam	Mozambique	Tanz	Tanzania	Plat	Plateau
CAR	Central African Republic	Myan	Myanmar	Thai	Thailand	Pt	Point
Den	Denmark	Neth	Netherlands	Turk	Turkey	Res	Reservoir
Div	Division	NZ	New Zealand	USA	United States	R	River
Dom Rep	Dominican Republic	Nic	Nicaragua		of America	S	Sea
El Sal	El Salvador	N Ire	Northern Ireland	Urug	Uruguay	Sd	Sound
Eng	England	Nig	Nigeria	Ven	Venezuela	Str	Strait
Eq Guinea	Equatorial Guinea	Nor	Norway	Viet	Vietnam	V	Valley
Eth	Ethiopia	Pak	Pakistan	Yugos	Yugoslavia		
Fin	Finland	PNG	Papua New Guinea	Zim	Zimbabwe		

A

57B2 **Aachen** Germany
46C1 **Aalst** Belg
38K6 **Äänekoski** Fin
47C1 **Aarau** Switz
47B1 **Aare** *R* Switz
72A3 **Aba** China
97C4 **Aba** Nig
99D2 **Aba** Zaire
91A3 **Ābādān** Iran
90B3 **Ābādeh** Iran
96B1 **Abadla** Alg
35B1 **Abaeté** Brazil
35B1 **Abaeté** *R* Brazil
31B2 **Abaetetuba** Brazil
72D1 **Abagnar Qi** China
97C4 **Abakaliki** Nig
63B2 **Abakan** Russian Fed
97C3 **Abala** Niger
96C2 **Abalessa** Alg
32C6 **Abancay** Peru
90B3 **Abarqū** Iran
74E2 **Abashiri** Japan
74E2 **Abashiri-wan** *B* Japan
71F4 **Abau** PNG
99D2 **Abaya** *L* Eth
99D1 **Abbe** *L* Eth
49E1 **Abbe** *L* Eth
48C1 **Abbeville** France
11B4 **Abbeville** Louisiana, USA
17B1 **Abbeville** S Carolina, USA
45B2 **Abbeyfeale** Irish Rep
47C2 **Abbiategrasso** Italy
20B1 **Abbotsford** Can
84C2 **Abbottabad** Pak
61H3 **Abdulino** Russian Fed
98C1 **Abéché** Chad
39F7 **Åbenrå** Den
97C4 **Abeokuta** Nig
99D2 **Abera** Eth
43B3 **Aberaeron** Wales
43C3 **Aberconwy and
Colwyn** County
Wales
15C3 **Aberdeen** Maryland, USA
100B4 **Aberdeen** S Africa
44C3 **Aberdeen** Scot
8D2 **Aberdeen** S Dakota, USA
8A2 **Aberdeen**
Washington, USA
44C3 **Aberdeen City**
Division, Scotland
4J3 **Aberdeen L** Can
44C3 **Aberdeenshire**
Division, Scot
43C4 **Aberdyfi** Wales
43C3 **Abergavenny** Wales
43B3 **Aberystwyth** Wales
81C4 **Abha** S Arabia
90A2 **Abhar** Iran
97B4 **Abidjan** Côte d'Ivoire
18A2 **Abilene** Kansas, USA
9D3 **Abilene** Texas, USA
43D4 **Abingdon** Eng
7B4 **Abitibi** *R* Can
7C5 **Abitibi,L** Can
61F5 **Abkhazia** Division, Georgia
84C2 **Abohar** India
97C4 **Abomey** Benin
98B2 **Abong Mbang** Cam
79A4 **Aborlan** Phil
98B1 **Abou Deïa** Chad
91A4 **Abqaiq** S Arabia
50A2 **Abrantes** Port
95C2 **Abri** Sudan
106A3 **Abrolhos** *Is* Aust
8B2 **Absaroka Range** *Mts* USA
91B5 **Abū al Abyad** / UAE
91A4 **Abū 'Alī** / S Arabia
91B5 **Abu Dhabi** UAE
95C3 **Abu Hamed** Sudan
97C4 **Abuja** Nig
33D5 **Abuná** Brazil
32D6 **Abuná** *R* Bol
93D3 **Abū Sukhayr** Iraq
111B2 **Abut Head** *C* NZ
95C3 **Abu 'Urug** *Well* Sudan
99D1 **Abuye Meda** *Mt* Eth
99C1 **Abu Zabad** Sudan
99D2 **Abwong** Sudan
56B1 **Abv** Den
94B3 **Aby 'Aweigila** *Well* Egypt
99C2 **Abyei** Sudan
24B2 **Acambaro** Mexico
24B2 **Acaponeta** Mexico
24B3 **Acapulco** Mexico
31D2 **Acaraú** Brazil
32D2 **Acarigua** Ven
24C3 **Acatlan** Mexico
23B2 **Acatzingo** Mexico
97B4 **Accra** Ghana
82C4 **Achalpur** India
29B4 **Achao** Chile
47D1 **Achensee** *L* Austria
46E2 **Achern** Germany
41A3 **Achill** / Irish Rep
63B2 **Achinsk** Russian Fed
53C3 **Acireale** Italy
26C2 **Acklins** / Caribbean S
32C6 **Acobamba** Peru
29B2 **Aconcagua** *Mt* Chile
31D3 **Acopiara** Brazil
26A5 **Açores** *Is* Atlantic O
A Coruña = La Coruña
47C2 **Acqui** Italy
108A2 **Acraman,L** Aust
4C3 **Acre** = 'Akko
32C5 **Acre** State, Brazil
32C5 **Acre** *R* Brazil
22C3 **Acton** USA
23B1 **Actopan** Mexico
19A3 **Ada** USA
50B1 **Adaja** *R* Spain
91C5 **Adam** Oman
35A2 **Adamantina** Brazil
98B2 **Adamaoua** Region, Nig/Cam
47D1 **Adamello** *Mt* Italy
16C1 **Adams** USA
87B3 **Adam's Bridge** India/ Sri Lanka
13D2 **Adams L** Can
8A2 **Adams,Mt** USA
87C3 **Adam's Peak** *Mt* Sri Lanka
81C4 **'Adan** Yemen
92C2 **Adana** Turk
60D5 **Adapazari** Turk
112B7 **Adare,C** Ant
108B1 **Adavale** Aust
74E2 **Adda** *R* Italy
91A4 **Ad Dahna'** Region, S Arabia
96A2 **Ad Dakhla** Mor
81C4 **Ad Dālī'** Yemen
91B4 **Ad Dammam** S Arabia
91A4 **Ad Dibdibah** Region, S Arabia
91A5 **Ad Dilam** S Arabia
91A5 **Ad Dir'īyah** S Arabia
93D3 **Ad Diwaniyah** Iraq
93D3 **Ad Duwayd** S Arabia
106C4 **Adelaide** Aust
4J3 **Adelaide Pen** Can
22D3 **Adelanto** USA
Aden = 'Adan
81C4 **Aden,G of** Yemen/ Somalia
97C3 **Aderbissinat** Niger
94C2 **Adhra** Syria
71E4 **Adi** / Indon
52B1 **Adige** *R* Italy
99D1 **Adigrat** Eth
85D5 **Adilābād** India
20B1 **Adin** USA
15D2 **Adirondack Mts** USA
99D2 **Adis Abeba** Eth
95C3 **Adi Ugai** Eritrea
93C2 **Adiyaman** Turk
54C1 **Adjud** Rom
4E4 **Admiralty I** USA
6B2 **Admiralty Inlet** *B* Can
12B1 **Adoni** India
48B3 **Adour** *R* France

Adrar

96A2 Adrar Region, Maur
96C2 Adrar Mts Alg
96A2 Adrar Soufouf Region, Maur
98C1 Adré Chad
95A2 Adri Libya
47E2 Adria Italy
14B2 Adrian Michigan, USA
52B2 Adriatic S S Europe
99D1 Adwa Eth
61F5 Adygeya Division, Russian Fed
97B4 Adzopé Côte d'Ivoire
55B3 Aegean S Greece
80E2 Afghanistan Republic, Asia
99E2 Afgooye Somalia
97C4 Afikpo Nig
38G6 Afjord Nor
96C1 Aflou Alg
99E2 Afmadu Somalia
97A3 Afollé Region, Maur
94B2 Afula Israel
92C2 Afyon Turk
95A3 Agadem Niger
97C3 Agadez Niger
96B1 Agadir Mor
85D4 Agar India
86C2 Agartala India
2081 Agassiz Can
97B4 Agboville Côte d'Ivoire
93E1 Agdam Azerbaijan
75B1 Agematsu Japan
48C3 Agen France
90A3 Agha Jāri Iran
96A2 Aghwinit Well Mor
47D2 Agno R Italy
47E1 Agordo Italy
48C3 Agout R France
85D3 Agra India
93D2 Ağri Turk
53C2 Agri R Italy
53B3 Agrigento Italy
55B3 Agrinion Greece
34A3 Agrio R Chile
53B2 Agropoli Italy
61H2 Agryz Russian Fed
6E3 Agto Greenland
27D3 Aguadilla Puerto Rico
24B1 Agua Prieta Mexico
24B2 Aguascalientes Mexico
23A1 Aguascalientes State, Mexico
35C1 Aguas Formosas Brazil
50A1 Agueda Port
96C3 Aguelhok Mali
50B2 Águilas Spain
23A2 Aguililla Mexico
100B4 Agulhas,C S Africa
79C4 Agusan R Phil
93E2 Ahar Iran
110B1 Ahipara B NZ
85C4 Ahmadābād India
87A1 Ahmadnagar India
99E2 Ahmar Mts Eth
46D1 Ahr R Germany
46D1 Ahrgebirge Region, Germany
23A1 Ahuacatlan Mexico
23A1 Ahualulco Mexico
39G7 Åhus Sweden
90A3 Ahvān Iran
90A3 Ahvāz Iran
26A4 Aiajuela Costa Rica
47B1 Aigle Switz
47B2 Aiguille d'Arves Mt France
47B2 Aiguille de la Grand Sassière Mt France
75B1 Aikawa Japan
17B1 Aiken USA
73A5 Ailao Shan Upland China
35C1 Aimorés Brazil
96B1 Ain Beni Mathar Mor
95B2 Ain Dalla Well Egypt
51C2 Ain el Hadjel Alg
95A3 Ain Galakka Chad

96B1 Ain Sefra Alg
92B4 'Ain Sukhna Egypt
75A2 Aioi Japan
96B2 Aioun Abd el Malek Well Maur
96A3 Aïoun El Atrouss Maur
30C2 Aiquile Bol
97C3 Air Desert Region Niger
21C3 Airdrie Can
46B1 Aire France
42D3 Aire R Eng
46C2 Aire R France
6C3 Airforce I Can
47C1 Airolo Switz
43E3 Aishihik Can
12C2 Aishihik L Can
46B2 Aisne Department, France
46B2 Aisne R France
49C2 Aix-en-Provence France
49D3 Aix-en-Provence France
47C2 Aix-les-Bains France
86B2 Aiyar Res India
55B3 Aiyion Greece
55B3 Aíyna I Greece
86C2 Aizawl India
100A3 Aizeb R Namibia
74E3 Aizu-Wakamatsu Japan
52A2 Ajaccio Corse
23B2 Ajalpan Mexico
65F5 Ajaria Division, Georgia
95B1 Ajdabiyā Libya
74E2 Ajigasawa Japan
94B2 Ajlun Jordan
91C4 Ajman UAE
85C3 Ajmer India
9B3 Ajo USA
23A2 Ajuchitan Mexico
55C3 Ak R Turk
87B1 Akalkot India
111B2 Akaroa NZ
75A2 Akashi Japan
61J3 Akbulak Russian Fed
93C2 Akçakale Turk
96A2 Akchar Watercourse Maur
55C3 Akdağ Mt Turk
98C2 Aketi Zaire
93D1 Akhalkalaki Georgia
93D1 Akhalsikhe Georgia
55B3 Akharnái Greece
12D3 Akhiok USA
92A2 Akhisar Turk
58D1 Akhiste Latvia
95C2 Akhmim Egypt
61G4 Akhtubinsk Russian Fed
60D4 Akhtyrka Ukraine
75A2 Aki Japan
78A1 Akimiski I Can
74E3 Akita Japan
96A3 Akjoujt Maur
94B2 'Akko Israel
4E3 Aklavik Can
94B2 Aklé Aouana Desert Region Maur
99D2 Akobo Sudan
99D2 Akobo R Sudan
84B2 Aköba Afghan
85D4 Akola India
85D4 Akot India
6D3 Akpatok I Can
55B3 Ákra Kafírévs C Greece
55B4 Ákra Maléa C Greece
38A2 Akranes Iceland
55C3 Ákra Sídheros C Greece
55B3 Ákra Spátha C Greece
55B3 Ákra Taínaron C Greece
10B2 Akron USA
94A1 Akrotíri B Cyprus

84D1 Aksai Chin Mts China
92B2 Aksaray Turk
61H3 Aksay Kazakhstan
84D1 Aksayquin Hu L China
92B2 Akşehir Turk
92B2 Akseki Turk
63D1 Aksenovo Zilovskoye Russian Fed
68D1 Aksha Russian Fed
82C1 Aksu China
61H5 Aktau Kazakhstan
65J5 Aktogay Kazakhstan
61J4 Aktumsyk Kazakhstan
65G4 Aktyubinsk Kazakhstan
38B1 Akureyri Iceland
Akyab = Sittwe
65J4 Akzhal Kazakhstan
11B3 Alabama State, USA
11B3 Alabama R USA
17A1 Alabaster USA
92C2 Ala Dağlari Mts Turk
61F5 Alagir Russian Fed
47B2 Alagna Italy
31D3 Alagoas State, Brazil
31D4 Alagoinhas Brazil
51B1 Alagón Spain
93E4 Al Ahmadi Kuwait
25D3 Alajuela Costa Rica
12B2 Alakanuk USA
38B1 Alakurtti Russian Fed
93E3 Al Amārah Iraq
21A2 Alameda USA
23B1 Alamo Mexico
9C3 Alamogordo USA
9C3 Alamosa USA
39H6 Åland I Fin
92B2 Alanya Turk
17B1 Alapaha R USA
65H4 Alapayevsk Russian Fed
92A2 Alaşehir Turk
68C3 Ala Shan Mts China
4C3 Alaska State, USA
4C3 Alaska,G of USA
12C3 Alaska Pen USA
4C3 Alaska Range Mts USA
52A2 Alassio Italy
12D1 Alatna R USA
61G3 Alatyr' Russian Fed
108B2 Alawoona Aust
91C5 Al'Ayn UAE
82B2 Alaysky Khrebet Mts Tajikistan
49D3 Alba Italy
92C1 Al Bāb Syria
51B2 Albacete Spain
50A1 Alba de Tormes Spain
93D2 Al Badi Iraq
93B2 Alba Iulia Rom
54A2 Albania Republic, Europe
106A4 Albany Aust
17B1 Albany Georgia, USA
15D2 Albany New York, USA
8A2 Albany Oregon, USA
7B4 Albany R Can
34B2 Albardón Arg
91C5 Al Batinah Region, Oman
71F5 Albatross B Aust
95B1 Al Baydā Libya
13C2 Albemarle Sd USA
50B1 Alberche R Spain
108A1 Alberga Aust
46B1 Albert France
5G4 Alberta Province, Can
99D2 Albert,L Uganda/Zaire
12B2 Albert Lea USA
99D2 Albert Nile R Uganda
49D2 Albertville France
48C3 Albi France
18B1 Albia USA
33G2 Albina Suriname
14B2 Albion Michigan, USA

15C2 Albion New York, USA
91A5 Al Bi'r S Arabia
91A5 Al Biyadh Region, S Arabia
50B2 Alborán I Spain
39G7 Alborg Den
93D3 Al Bū Kamāl Syria
47C1 Albula R Switz
9C3 Albuquerque USA
91C5 Al Buraymi Oman
95A1 Al Burayqah Libya
95A1 Al Burdi Libya
107D4 Albury Aust
93E3 Al Buşayyah Iraq
50B1 Alcalá de Henares Spain
53B3 Alcamo Italy
51B1 Alcaniz Spain
31C2 Alcântara Brazil
50B2 Alcaraz Spain
50B2 Alcázar de San Juan Spain
51B2 Alcira Spain
35D1 Alcobaça Brazil
50B1 Alcolea de Pinar Spain
51B2 Alcoy Spain
51C2 Alcudia Spain
89J8 Aldabra Is Indian O
63E2 Aldan Russian Fed
63E2 Aldan R Russian Fed
Aldanskoye Nagor'ye Upland Russian Fed
43E3 Aldeburgh Eng
43B4 Alderney I UK
43D4 Aldershot Eng
97A3 Aleg Maur
30E4 Alegrete Brazil
34C2 Alejandro Roca Arg
30H6 Alejandro Selkirk I Chile
65J4 Aleksandrovsk Sakhalinskiy Russian Fed
65J4 Alekseyevka Kazakhstan
60E3 Aleksin Russian Fed
58B1 Alem Sweden
35C2 Além Paraiba Brazil
49C2 Alençon France
21C4 Alenuihaha Chan Hawaiian Is
Aleppo = Halab
6D1 Alert Can
49C3 Alès France
52A2 Alessandria Italy
64B3 Ålesund Nor
12C3 Aleutian Range Mts USA
4E4 Alexander Arch USA
100A3 Alexander Bay S Africa
17A1 Alexander City USA
112C3 Alexander I Ant
111A3 Alexandra NZ
29G8 Alexandra,C South Georgia
6C2 Alexandra Fjord Can
95B1 Alexandria Egypt
11A3 Alexandria Louisiana, USA
10A2 Alexandria Minnesota, USA
10C3 Alexandria Virginia, USA
55C2 Alexandroúpolis Greece
13C2 Alexis Creek Can
94B2 Aley Leb
65K4 Aleysk Russian Fed
93D3 Al Fallūjah Iraq
51B1 Alfaro Spain
35B2 Alfatar Bulg
93E3 Al Fāw Iraq
35B2 Alfenas Brazil
47D2 Alfiós R Greece
47D2 Alfonsine Italy
35C2 Alfonzo Cláudio Brazil
35C2 Alfredo Chaves Brazil
61J4 Alga Kazakhstan
34B3 Algarrobo del Aguila Arg
50A2 Algeciras Spain

96C1 Alger Alg
96B2 Algeria Republic, Africa
53A2 Alghero Sardegna
Algiers = Alger
15C1 Algonquin Park Can
91C5 Al Hadd Oman
93D3 Al Hadithah Iraq
92C3 Al Hadithah S Arabia
93D2 Al Hadr Iraq
91C5 Al Hajar al Gharbi Mts Oman
91C5 Al Hajar ash Sharqi Mts Oman
93C3 Al Hamad Desert Region Jordan/S Arabia
93E4 Al Haniyah Desert Region Iraq
91A5 Al Harq S Arabia
93C3 Al Harrah Desert Region S Arabia
95A2 Al Haruj al Aswad Upland Libya
91A4 Al Hasa Region, S Arabia
93D2 Al Hasakah Syria
93C4 Al Hawja' S Arabia
93E3 Al Hayy Iraq
94C2 Al Hijanah Syria
93D3 Al Hillah Iraq
91A5 Al Hillah S Arabia
96B1 Al Hoceima Mor
91A4 Al Hufuf S Arabia
91B5 Al Humrah Region, UAE
91C5 Al Huwatsah Oman
90A2 Aliabad Iran
91C4 Aliabad Iran
55B2 Aliákmon R Greece
93E3 Ali al Gharbi Iraq
87A1 Alibag India
51B2 Alicante Spain
9D4 Alice USA
106C3 Alice Springs Aust
53B3 Alicudi I Italy
84D3 Aligarh India
90A3 Aligúdarz Iran
84B2 Ali-Khel Afghan
55C3 Alimniá I Greece
86B1 Alipur Duár India
14B2 Aliquippa USA
22B2 Alisal USA
93C3 Al' Isawiyah S Arabia
100B4 Aliwal North S Africa
95B2 Al Jaghbub Libya
93D3 Al Jalamid S Arabia
95B2 Al Jawf Libya
93C4 Al Jawf S Arabia
94A2 Al Jazirah Desert Region Syria/Iraq
50A2 Aljezur Port
91A4 Al Jubayl S Arabia
91C5 Al Kamil Oman
93D2 Al Khábúr R Syria
91C5 Al Khabúrah Oman
93D3 Al Khális Iraq
91C4 Al Khasab Oman
91B4 Al Khawr Qatar
95A1 Al Khums Libya
91B5 Al Kidan Region, S Arabia
94C2 Al Kiswah Syria
56B2 Alkmaar Neth
95B2 Al Kufrah Oasis Libya
93E3 Al Kut Iraq
92C2 Al Ládhiqiyah Syria
86A1 Allahabad India
94C2 Al Lajáh Mt Syria
12D1 Allakaket USA
76B2 Allanmyo Myan
95C2 'Allaqi Watercourse Egypt
17B1 Allatoona L USA
15C2 Allegheny R USA
10C3 Allegheny Mts USA
17B1 Allendale USA
111A3 Allen,Mt NZ
15C2 Allentown USA
87B3 Alleppey India
56C2 Aller R Germany
47D1 Allgáu Mts Germany
8C2 Alliance USA
81C3 Al Lith S Arabia

91B5 Al Liwá Region, UAE
109D1 Allora Aust
14B2 Alma Michigan, USA
Alma Ata = Almaty
50A2 Almada Port
Al Madinah = Medina
71F2 Almagan I Pacific O
91B4 Al Manámah Bahrain
93D3 Al Ma'niyah Iraq
21A1 Almanor,L USA
51B2 Almansa Spain
13B1 Alma Peak Mt Can
91B5 Al Máriyyah UAE
95B1 Al Marj Libya
82B1 Almaty Kazakhstan
93D2 Al Mawsil Iraq
50B1 Almazán Spain
35C1 Almenara Brazil
50B1 Almería Spain
61H3 Al'met'yevsk Russian Fed
56C1 Almhult Sweden
93E3 Al Miqdádiyah Iraq
112C3 Almirante Brown Base Ant
34A1 Almirante Latorre Chile
55B3 Almirós Greece
91A4 Al Mish'ab S Arabia
50A2 Almodóvar Port
84D3 Almora India
91A4 Al Mubarraz S Arabia
92C4 Al Mudawwara Jordan
91C5 Al Mudaybi Oman
91B4 Al Muharraq Bahrain
91A5 Al Mukalla Yemen
81C4 Al Mukha Yemen
93D3 Al Musayyib Iraq
44B3 Alness Scot
93D3 Al Nu'maniyah Iraq
42D2 Alnwick Eng
71D4 Alor I Indon
77C4 Alor Setar Malay
Alost = Aalst
107E2 Alotau PNG
106B3 Aloysius,Mt Aust
34C3 Alpachiri Arg
14B1 Alpena USA
47B2 Alpes du Valais Mts Switz
52B1 Alpi Dolomitiche Mts Italy
47B2 Alpi Graie Mts Italy
9C3 Alpine Texas, USA
47C1 Alpi Orobie Mts Italy
47B2 Alpi Pennine Mts Italy
47C1 Alpi Retiche Mts Switz
47D1 Alpi Venoste Mts Italy
52A1 Alps Mts Europe
95A1 Al Qaddáhíyah Libya
94C1 Al Qadmús Syria
93D3 Al Qá'im Iraq
93C4 Al Qálibah S Arabia
92C2 Al Qámishlí Syria
95A1 Al Qaryah ash Sharqiyah Libya
92C3 Al Qaryatayn Syria
91A4 Al Qátif S Arabia
95A2 Al Qatrún Libya
91A4 Al Qaysámah S Arabia
94C2 Al Quatayfah Syria
50A2 Alqueva R Port
92C3 Al Qunaytirah Syria
81C4 Al Qunfidhah S Arabia
93E3 Al Qurnah Iraq
94C1 Al Qusayr Syria
92C3 Al Qutayfah Syria
56B1 Als I Den
49D2 Alsace Region France
57B2 Alsfeld Germany
42C2 Alston Eng
38J5 Alta Nor
29D2 Alta Gracia Arg
27D5 Altagracia de Orituco Ven
68A2 Altai Mts Mongolia
17B1 Altamaha R USA

33G4 Altamira Brazil
23B1 Altamira Mexico
53C2 Altamura Italy
68C1 Altanbulag Mongolia
71F4 Altape PNG
24B2 Altata Mexico
63A3 Altay China
63B3 Altay Mongolia
63A2 Altay Mts Russian Fed
47C1 Altdorf Switz
46D1 Altenkirchen Germany
34B3 Altiplanicie del Payún Plat Arg
47B1 Altkirch France
101C2 Alto Molócue Mozam
10A3 Alton USA
15C2 Altoona USA
34B2 Alto Pencoso Mts Arg
35A1 Alto Sucuriú Brazil
23B2 Altotonga Mexico
23A2 Altoyac de Alvarez Mexico
82C2 Altun Shan Mts China
21B2 Alturas USA
19A4 Altus USA
9D3 Alva USA
91B5 Al'Ubaylah S Arabia
93C4 Al Uruyq Desert Region, S Arabia
91B5 Al'Uruq ad Mu'taridah Region, S Arabia
9D2 Alva USA
23B2 Alvarado Mexico
19A3 Alvarado USA
39G6 Álvdalen Sweden
19A4 Alvin USA
38J5 Alvsbyn Sweden
80B3 Al Wajh S Arabia
85D3 Alwar India
91B5 Al Widyan Desert Region Iraq/S Arabia
72A2 Alxa Yogi China
93E2 Alyat Azerbaijan
39J8 Alytus Lithuania
46E2 Alzey Germany
23B2 Amacuzac R Mexico
99D1 Amadi Sudan
93D3 Amadiyah Iraq
6C3 Amadjuak L Can
74B4 Amakusa-shotó I Japan
39G7 Amål Sweden
63D2 Amalat R Russian Fed
55B3 Amaliás Greece
85D4 Amalner India
69E4 Amami I Japan
69E4 Amami guntó Arch Japan
100C4 Amanzimtoti S Africa
33G3 Amapá Brazil
33G3 Amapá State, Brazil
9C3 Amarillo USA
60E5 Amasya Turk
23A1 Amatitan Mexico
Amazonas = Solimões
32D4 Amazonas State, Brazil
28 Amazonas R Brazil
85D3 Ambála India
87C3 Ambalangoda Sri Lanka
101D3 Ambalavao Madag
98B2 Ambam Cam
101D2 Ambanja Madag
1C7 Ambarchik Russian Fed
32B4 Ambato Ecuador
101D2 Ambato-Boeny Madag
101D2 Ambatolampy Madag
101D2 Ambatondrazaka Madag
57C3 Amberg Germany
25D3 Ambergris Cay Belize
86A2 Ambikápur India
101D2 Ambilobe Madag

101D3 Ambosary Madag
101D2 Ambodifototra Madag
101D3 Ambohimahasoa Madag
71D4 Ambon Indon
101D3 Ambositra Madag
101D3 Ambovombe Madag
98B3 Ambriz Angola
98C1 Am Dam Chad
64H3 Amderma Russian Fed
16C1 Amherst Massachusetts, USA
Amherst = Kyaikkami
87B2 Amhúr India
48C2 Amiens France
75B1 Amino Japan
94B1 Amioune Leb
89K8 Amirante Is Indian O
86A1 Amlekhgan Nepal
32B5 Amotape Peru
38K6 Ammarnäs Sweden
56B2 Ammersfoort Neth
90B2 Amol Iran
55C3 Amorgós I Greece
7C5 Amos Can
Amoy = Xiamen
101D3 Ampanihy Madag
35B2 Amparo Brazil
51C1 Amposta Spain
85D4 Amravati India
85C4 Amreli India
84C2 Amritsar India
56A2 Amsterdam Neth
101H1 Amsterdam S Africa
15D2 Amsterdam USA
98C1 Am Timan Chad
88L3 Amu Darya R Uzbekistan
6A2 Amund Ringes I Can
4F2 Amundsen G Can
112B4 Amundsen S Ant
80E Amundsen-Scott Base Ant
78D3 Amuntai Indon
63E2 Amur R Russian Fed
33E2 Anaco Ven
8B2 Anaconda USA
20B1 Anacortes USA
55C3 Anáfi I Greece
93D3 'Anah Iraq
21B3 Anaheim USA
87B2 Anaimalai Hills India
12E1 Anaktuvuk P USA
101D2 Analalava Madag
92B2 Anamur Turk
75A2 Anan Japan
87B2 Anantapur India
84D2 Anantnag India
31B5 Anápolis Brazil
90C3 Anár Iran
90B3 Anarak Iran
71F2 Anatahan I Pacific O
30D4 Añatuya Arg
74B3 Anbyon N Korea
22C4 Anacapa Is USA
4D3 Anchorage USA
30C2 Ancohuma Mt Bol
32B6 Ancón Peru

Auxerre

49C2 Auxerre France
46B1 Auxi-le-Châteaux France
49C2 Auxonne France
22C4 Avalon USA
7E5 Avalon Pen Can
35B2 Avaré Brazil
90D3 Avaz Iran
94B3 Avedat Hist Site Israel
33F4 Aveiro Brazil
50A1 Aveiro Port
29E2 Avellaneda Arg
53B2 Avellino Italy
46B1 Avesnes-sur-Helpe France
39H6 Avesta Sweden
52B2 Avezzano Italy
44C3 Aviemore Scot
111B2 Aviemore,L NZ
47B2 Avigliana Italy
49C3 Avignon France
50B1 Avila Spain
50A1 Aviles Spain
47D1 Avisio R Italy
43D3 Avoca R Aust
43D4 Avon R Dorset, Eng
43D3 Avon R Warwick, Eng
43C4 Avonmouth Wales
17B2 Avon Park USA
48B2 Avre R France
54A2 Avtovac Bosnia-Herzegovina
94C2 A'waj R Syria
74D4 Awaji-shima R Japan
99E2 Awara R NZ
99E2 Awarua Pt NZ
99E2 Awash Eth
99E2 Awash R Eth
75B1 Awa-shima I Japan
111B2 Awatere R NZ
98A3 Awbari Libya
95A2 Aweil Sudan
95B2 Awjilah Libya
96A2 Awserd Well Mor
43C4 Axminster Eng
75B1 Ayabe Japan
29E3 Ayacucho Arg
32C6 Ayacucho Peru
65K5 Ayaguz Kazakhstan
82C2 Ayakkum Hu L China
50A2 Ayamonte Spain
63F2 Ayan Russian Fed
32C6 Ayaviri Peru
92A2 Aydin Turk
55C3 Áyios Evstrátios I Greece
43D4 Aylesbury Eng
13D2 Aylmer,Mt Can
94C2 'Ayn al Fijah Syria
93D2 Ayn Zálah Iraq
95B2 Ayn Zuwayyah Well Libya
99D2 Ayod Sudan
107D2 Ayr Aust
42B2 Ayr Scot
42B2 Ayr R Scot
42B2 Ayre,Pt of Eng
54C2 Aytos Bulg
76C3 Aythaya Thai
23A1 Ayutla Mexico
55C3 Ayvacik Turk
55C3 Ayvalik Turk
86A1 Azamgarh India
97B3 Azaouad Desert Region Mali
97D3 Azare Nig
92C2 A'Záz Syria
Azbine = Aïr
65F5 Azerbaijan Republic Asia
32B4 Azogues Ecuador
Azores = Açores
98C1 Azoum R Chad
60E4 Azov,Sea of Russian Fed/Ukraine
Azovskoye More = Azov, Sea of
96B1 Azrou Mor
34D3 Azucena Arg

32A2 Azuero,Pen de Panama
29E3 Azul Arg
94C2 Az-Zabdani Syria
91C5 Az Záhirah Mts Oman
95A2 Az Zafra Iraq
96A2 Azzeffal R Maur
93E3 Az Zubayr Iraq

B

94B2 Ba'abda Leb
92C3 Ba'albek Leb
94B3 Ba'al Hazor Mt Israel
99E2 Baardheere Somalia
54C2 Babadag Rom
92A1 Babaeski Turk
32A4 Babahoyo Ecuador
81C4 Bab al Mandab Str Djibouti/Yemen
71D4 Babar I Indon
99D3 Babati Tanz
60E2 Babayevo Russian Fed
14B2 Baberton USA
13B1 Babine R Can
5F4 Babine L Can
90B2 Babol Iran
79B2 Babuyan Chan Phil
79B2 Babuyan Is Phil
31C2 Bacabal Brazil
71D4 Bacan I Indon
60C4 Bacău Rom
76D1 Bac Can Viet
108B3 Bacchus Marsh Aust
82B2 Bachu China
4J3 Back R Can
12J2 Backbone Ranges Mts Can
76D1 Bac Ninh Viet
79B3 Bacolod Phil
79B3 Baco,Mt Phil
87B2 Badagara India
72A1 Badain Jaran Shamo Desert China
50A2 Badajoz Spain
51C1 Badalona Spain
93D3 Badanah S Arabia
46D2 Bad Bergzabern Germany
46D1 Bad Ems Germany
47C1 Baden Switz
57B3 Baden-Baden Germany
57C3 Badgastein Austria
22C2 Badger USA
46D2 Bad-Godesberg Germany
57B2 Bad Hersfeld Germany
46D1 Bad Honnef Germany
85B4 Badin Pak
52B1 Bad Ischl Austria
93C3 Badiyat ash Sham Desert Region Jordan/Iraq
57B3 Bad-Kreuznach Germany
46D1 Bad Nevenahr-Ahrweiler Germany
47C1 Bad Ragaz Switz
57C3 Bad Tölz Germany
87C3 Badulla Sri Lanka
50B2 Baena Spain
97A3 Bafatá Guinea-Bissau
4H2 Baffin Region Can
6C2 Baffin B Greenland/Can
6C2 Baffin I Can
98B2 Bafia Cam
97B3 Bafing R Mali
97A3 Bafoulabé Mali
98B2 Bafoussam Cam
90C3 Bafq Iran
60E5 Bafra Burun Pt Turk
90C3 Báft Iran
98C2 Bafwasende Zaïre
86A1 Bagaha India
87B1 Bágalkot India
99D3 Bagamoyo Tanz
29F2 Bagé Brazil

93D3 Baghdād Iraq
86B2 Bagherhat Bang
91C3 Bághin Iran
84B1 Baghlan Afghan
49C3 Bagnols-sur-Cèze France
97B3 Bagoé R Mali
79B2 Baguio Phil
86B1 Bāhādurābād India
11C4 Bahamas,The Is Caribbean S
86B2 Baharampur India
92A4 Bahariya Oasis Egypt
84C3 Bahawalpur Pak
84C3 Bahawalpur Province, Pak
85C3 Bahawalnagar Pak
Bahia = Salvador
31C4 Bahia State, Brazil
29D3 Bahía Blanca Arg
29D3 Bahía Blanca B Arg
34A3 Bahía Concepción B Chile
35C2 Bahia da Ilha Grande B Brazil
24B2 Bahía de Banderas B Mexico
24C2 Bahía de Campeche B Mexico
25D3 Bahía de la Ascensión B Mexico
24B3 Bahía de Petacalco B Mexico
96A2 Bahía de Rio de Oro B Mor
35C2 Bahia de Sepetiba B Brazil
29C6 Bahía Grande B Arg
9B4 Bahía Kino Mexico
24A2 Bahía Magdalena B Mexico
24A2 Bahía Sebastia Vizcaino B Mexico
99D1 Bahar Dar Eth
86A1 Bahraich India
80D3 Bahrain Sheikdom, Arabian Pen
93D3 Bahr al Milh L Iraq
98C2 Bahr Aouk R Chad/CAR
Bahret Lut = Dead S
98C2 Bahr al Arab Watercourse Sudan
99D2 Bahr el Ghazal R Sudan
98B1 Bahr el Ghazal Watercourse Chad
101H1 Baía de Maputo B Mozam
31B2 Baia de Marajó B Brazil
101D2 Baía de Pemba B Mozam
31C2 Baía de São Marcos B Brazil
50A2 Baia de Setúbal B Port
31D4 Baia de Todos os Santos B Brazil
100A2 Baia dos Tigres Angola
60B4 Baia Mare Rom
98B2 Baibokoum Chad
69E2 Baicheng China
101E2 Baie Antongila B Madag
7D5 Baie-Comeau Can
101D2 Baie de Bombetoka B Madag
101D2 Baie de Mahajamba B Madag
101D3 Baie de St Augustin B Madag
94B2 Baie de St Georges B Leb
10D2 Baie des Chaleurs B Can
7C4 Baie-du-Poste Can
72B3 Baihe China
72C3 Bai He R China
93D3 Ba'iji Iraq
86A2 Baikunthpur India

Baile Atha Cliath = Dublin
54B2 Băilesti Rom
46B1 Bailleul France
72A3 Baima China
17B1 Bainbridge USA
12B2 Baird Inlet USA
4B3 Baird Mts USA
72D1 Bairin Youqi China
72D1 Bairin Zuoqi China
107D4 Bairnsdale Aust
79B4 Bais Phil
54A1 Baja Hung
9B3 Baja California State, Mexico
24A1 Baja California Pen Mexico
61J2 Bakal Russian Fed
98C2 Bakala CAR
97A3 Bakel Sen
8C2 Baker Montana, USA
8B2 Baker Oregon, USA
6A3 Baker Foreland Pt Can
4J3 Baker L Can
4J3 Baker Lake Can
8A2 Baker,Mt USA
9B3 Bakersfield USA
90C2 Bakharden Turkmenistan
90C2 Bakharok Turkmenistan
60D3 Bakhmach Ukraine
38C1 Bakkafloi R Iceland
99D2 Bako Eth
98C2 Bakouma CAR
65F5 Baku Azerbaijan
Baky = Baku
92B2 Balâ Turk
79A4 Balabac I Phil
70C3 Balabac Str Malay
78C2 Balaikarangan Indon
108A2 Balaklava Aust
61G3 Balakovo Russian Fed
86A2 Balāngir India
61F3 Balashov Russian Fed
86B2 Balasore India
80A3 Balât Egypt
52C1 Balaton L Hung
45C2 Balbriggan Irish Rep
29E3 Balcarce Arg
54C2 Balchik Bulg
111B3 Balclutha NZ
18B2 Bald Knob USA
17B1 Baldwin USA
9C3 Baldy Peak Mt USA
Balearic Is = Islas Baleares
78C2 Baleh R Malay
79B2 Baler Phil
61H2 Balezino Russian Fed
106A1 Bali I Indon
92A2 Balikesir Turk
87B3 Balikh R Syria
78D3 Balikpapan Indon
79B2 Balintang Chan Phil
78C4 Bali S Indon
35A1 Baliza Brazil
84B1 Balkh Afghan
65J5 Balkhash Kazakhstan
44B3 Ballachulish Scot
45B2 Ballaghaderreen Irish Rep
42B2 Ballantrae Scot
4G2 Ballantyne Str Can
87B2 Ballapur India
108B3 Ballarat Aust
44C3 Ballater Scot
112C7 Balleny Is Ant
86A1 Ballia India
109D1 Ballina Aust
41B3 Ballina Irish Rep
45B2 Ballinasloe Irish Rep
45B2 Ballinrobe Irish Rep
55A2 Ballsh Alb
45C1 Ballycastle Irish Rep
45C1 Ballycastle N Ire
45C1 Ballymena N Ire
45C1 Ballymoney N Ire
45B1 Ballyshannon Irish Rep

45B2 Ballyvaghan Irish Rep
108B3 Balmoral Aust
34C2 Balnearia Arg
84B3 Balochistān Region, Pak
100A2 Balombo Angola
109C1 Balonn R Aust
85C3 Balotra India
86A1 Balrāmpur India
107D4 Balranald Aust
31B3 Balsas Brazil
23B2 Balsas Mexico
24B3 Balsas R Mexico
60C4 Balta Ukraine
39H7 Baltic S N Europe
92B3 Baltim Egypt
45B3 Baltimore Irish Rep
10C3 Baltimore USA
86B1 Bālurghāt India
61H4 Balykshi Kazakhstan
91C4 Bam Iran
98B1 Bama Nig
97B3 Bamako Mali
98C2 Bambari CAR
17B1 Bamberg USA
57C3 Bamberg Germany
98C2 Bambili Zaire
35B2 Bamboi Brazil
98B2 Bamenda Cam
13C3 Bamfield Can
98B2 Bamingui R CAR
98B2 Bamingui Bangoran National Park CAR
84B2 Bamiyan Afghan
91D4 Bampur Iran
91D4 Bampur R Iran
98C2 Banalia Zaire
97B3 Banamba Mali
76C3 Ban Aranyaprathet Thai
76C2 Ban Ban Laos
77C4 Ban Betong Thai
45C1 Banbridge N Ire
43D3 Banbury Eng
44C3 Banchory Scot
25D3 Banco Chinchorro Is Mexico
15C1 Bancroft Can
84B3 Bānda India
70A3 Banda Aceh Indon
84B3 Bandama R Côte d'Ivoire
91C4 Bandar Abbās Iran
90A2 Bandar Anzali Iran
99F2 Bandarbeyla Somalia
91B4 Bandar-e Daylam Iran
91B4 Bandar-e Lengeh Iran
91B4 Bandar-e Māqām Iran
91B4 Bandar-e Rig Iran
91B4 Bandar-e Torkoman Iran
91A3 Bandar Khomeyní Iran
78C2 Bandar Seri Begawan Brunei
71D4 Banda S Indon
91C4 Band Boni Iran
35C2 Bandeira Mt Brazil
91B3 Bandiagara Mali
60C5 Bandirma Turk
45B3 Bandon Irish Rep
98B3 Bandundu Zaire
25E2 Banes Cuba
13D2 Banff Can
44C3 Banff Scot
5G4 Banff R Can
13D2 Banff Nat Pk Can
87B2 Bangalore India
82C3 Bangassou CAR
70C3 Banggi I Malay
98B2 Banghāzi Libya
76D2 Bang Hieng R Laos
78B3 Bangka I Indon
78A3 Bangko Thai
76C3 Bangkok Thai
82C3 Bangladesh Republic, Asia
84D2 Bangong Co L China
10D2 Bangor Maine, USA

45D1 Bangor N Ire
16B2 Bangor Pennsylvania, USA
42B3 Bangor Wales
78D3 Bangsalsembera Indon
76B3 Bang Saphan Yai Thai
79B2 Bangued Phil
98B2 Bangui CAR
100C2 Bangweulu L Zambia
77C4 Ban Hat Yai Thai
76C2 Ban Hin Heup Laos
76C1 Ban Houei Sai Laos
76B3 Ban Hua Hin Thai
97B3 Bani R Mali
97C3 Bani Bangou Niger
95A1 Bani Walid Libya
92C3 Bāniyās Syria
94B2 Baniyas Syria
52C2 Banja Luka Bosnia-Herzegovina
78C3 Banjarmasin Indon
97A3 Banjul The Gambia
77B4 Ban Kantang Thai
76D2 Ban Khemmarat Thai
77B4 Ban Khok Kloi Thai
71F5 Banks I Aust
5E4 Banks I British Columbia, Can
4F2 Banks I Northwest Territories, Can
20C1 Banks L USA
111B2 Banks Pen NZ
109C4 Banks Str Aust
86B2 Bankura India
76C2 Ban Mae Sariang Thai
76B2 Ban Mae Sot Thai
76C2 Ban Me Thuot Viet
45C1 Bann R N Ire
77B4 Ban Na San Thai
84C2 Bannu Pak
34A3 Baños Maule Chile
76C2 Ban Pak Neun Laos
77C4 Ban Pak Phanang Thai
76B2 Ban Ru Kroy Camb
76B2 Ban Sai Yok Thai
76C3 Ban Sattahip Thai
59B3 Banská Bystrica Slovakia
85C4 Bānswāra India
77B4 Ban Tha Kham Thai
76D2 Ban Thateng Laos
76C2 Ban Tha Tum Thai
45B3 Bantry Irish Rep
41A3 Bantry B Irish Rep
76D3 Ban Ya Soup Viet
78C4 Banyuwangi Indon
72C3 Baofeng China
76C1 Bao Ha Viet
72B3 Baoji China
76D3 Bao Loc Viet
68B4 Baoshan China
72C1 Baotou China
46B1 Bapaume France
93D3 Ba'Qūbah Iraq
32J7 Baquerizo Morena Ecuador
54A2 Bar Montenegro, Yugos
99D1 Bara Sudan
99E2 Baraawe Somalia
78D3 Barabai Indon
86A1 Bāra Banki India
65J4 Barabinsk Russian Fed
65J4 Barabinskaya Step Steppe Kazakhstan, Russian Fed
50B1 Baracaldo Spain
26C2 Baracoa Cuba
94C3 Baradá R Syria
109C2 Baradine Aust
87A1 Bārāmati India
84C2 Baramula Pak
85D3 Bārān India
4E4 Baranof I USA
60C3 Baranovichi Belarus

108A2 Baratta Aust
86B1 Barauni India
31C6 Barbacena Brazil
27F4 Barbados / Caribbean S
101H1 Barberton S Africa
48B2 Barbezieux France
27E3 Barbosa Colombia
27E3 Barbuda / Caribbean S
107D3 Barcaldine Aust
Barce = Al Marj
53C3 Barcellona Italy
53C2 Barcelona Spain
33E1 Barcelona Ven
107D3 Barcoo R Aust
34B3 Barda del Medio Arg
95A2 Bardaï Chad
29C3 Bardas Blancas Arg
86B2 Barddhaman India
59C3 Bardejov Slovakia
47C2 Bardi Italy
47B2 Bardonecchia Italy
43B3 Bardsey / Wales
84D3 Bareilly India
64D2 Barentsøya / Barents S
64E2 Barents S Russian Fed
95C3 Barentu Eritrea
86A2 Bargarh India
47B2 Barge Italy
63D2 Barguzin Russian Fed
63D2 Barguzin R Russian Fed
86B2 Barharwa India
53C2 Bari Italy
51D2 Barika Alg
32C2 Barinas Ven
86B1 Baripāda India
84B1 Barī Sādri India
86C2 Barisal Bang
78C3 Barito R Indon
95A2 Barjuj Watercourse Libya
73A3 Barkam China
18C2 Barkley,L USA
100B4 Barkly East S Africa
106C2 Barkly Tableland Mts Aust
46C2 Bar-le-Duc France
106A3 Barlee,L Aust
106A3 Barlee Range Mts Aust
53C2 Barletta Italy
85C3 Barmer India
108B2 Barmera Aust
43B3 Barmouth Wales
42D2 Barnard Castle Eng
65K4 Barnaul Russian Fed
16B3 Barnegat B USA
6C2 Barnes Icecap Can
17B1 Barnesville Georgia, USA
18C3 Barnesville Ohio, USA
43D3 Barnsley Eng
43B4 Barnstaple Eng
97C4 Baro Nig
86C1 Barpeta India
32D1 Barquisimeto Ven
31C4 Barra Brazil
44A3 Barra / Scot
109D2 Barraba Aust
23A2 Barra de Navidad Mexico
31C6 Barra de Pirai Brazil
35A1 Barra de São Simão Brazil
35A1 Barra do Garças Brazil
35B1 Barragem Agua Vermelha Res Brazil
50A2 Barragem da Castelo do Bode Res Port
50A2 Barragem do Maranhão Res Port
35A2 Barragem Trés Irmãos Res Brazil
44A3 Barra Head Pt Scot

31C6 Barra Mansa Brazil
32B6 Barranca Peru
32C2 Barrancabermeja Colombia
33E2 Barrancas Ven
30E4 Barranqueras Arg
32C1 Barranquilla Colombia
44A3 Barra,Sound of Chan Scot
16C1 Barre USA
34B2 Barreal Arg
31C4 Barreiras Brazil
50A2 Barreiro Port
31D3 Barreiros Brazil
107D5 Barren,C Aust
12D3 Barren Is USA
31B6 Barretos Brazil
13E2 Barrhead Can
14C2 Barrie Can
13C2 Barrière Can
108B2 Barrier Range Mts Aust
107E4 Barrington,Mt Aust
27N2 Barrouaillie St Vincent and the Grenadines
4C2 Barrow USA
45C2 Barrow R Irish Rep
106C3 Barrow Creek Aust
106A3 Barrow I Aust
42C2 Barrow-in-Furness Eng
4C2 Barrow,Pt USA
6A2 Barrow Str Can
15C1 Barry's Bay Can
87B1 Barsi India
9B3 Barstow USA
49C2 Bar-sur-Aube France
33F2 Bartica Guyana
92B1 Bartin Turk
107D2 Bartle Frere,Mt Aust
9D3 Bartlesville USA
101C3 Bartolomeu Dias Mozam
58C2 Bartoszyce Pol
78C4 Barung I Indon
85C4 Barwāh India
85C4 Barwāni India
109C1 Barwon R Aust
61G3 Barysh Russian Fed
98B3 Basankusu Zaire
34D2 Basavilbaso Arg
79B1 Basco Phil
52A1 Basel Switz
53C2 Basento R Italy
13E2 Bashaw Can
79B1 Bashi Chan Phil
61K3 Bashkortostan Division, Russian Fed
79B4 Basilan I Phil
43E4 Basildon Eng
43C4 Basingstoke Eng
8B2 Basin Region USA
93E3 Basra Iraq
46D2 Bas-Rhin Department, France
76C2 Bassac R Camb
52B1 Bassano Italy
47D2 Bassano del Grappa Italy
97C4 Bassari Togo
101C3 Bassas da India I Mozam Chan
76A2 Bassein Myan
27E3 Basse Terre Guadeloupe
97C4 Bassila Benin
22C2 Bass Lake USA
10C2 Bass Str Aust
39G7 Båstad Sweden
91B4 Bastak Iran
86A1 Basti India
52A2 Bastia Corse
57B3 Bastogne Belg
19B3 Bastrop Louisiana, USA
19A3 Bastrop Texas, USA
98A2 Bata Eq Guinea
78C3 Batakan Indon
84D2 Batala India
68B3 Batang China
98B2 Batangafo CAR

79B1 Batan Is Phil
35B2 Batatais Brazil
15C2 Batavia USA
90D3 Batemans Bay Aust
17B1 Batesburg USA
18B2 Batesville Arkansas, USA
19C3 Batesville Mississippi, USA
43C4 Bath Eng
15C2 Bath New York, USA
98B1 Batha R Chad
43C4 Bath and North East Somerset County Eng
107D4 Bathurst Aust
7D6 Bathurst Can
4F2 Bathurst,C Can
106C2 Bathurst I Aust
4H2 Bathurst I Can
4H3 Bathurst Inlet B Can
97B3 Batié Burkina
90B3 Bātlāq-e-Gavkhūni Salt Flat Iran
109C3 Batlow Aust
93D2 Batman Turk
96C1 Batna Alg
11A3 Baton Rouge USA
94B1 Batroun Leb
76C3 Battambang Camb
87C3 Batticaloa Sri Lanka
13F2 Battle R Can
10B2 Battle Creek USA
7E4 Battle Harbour Can
20C2 Battle Mountain USA
78D2 Batukelau Indon
65F5 Batumi Georgia
77C5 Batu Pahat Malay
78A3 Baturaja Indon
94B2 Bat Yam Israel
71D4 Baubau Indon
97C3 Bauchi Nig
47B2 Bauges Mts France
7E4 Bauld,C Can
47B1 Baumes-les-Dames France
63D2 Baunt Russian Fed
31B6 Bauru Brazil
35A1 Baus Brazil
57C2 Bautzen Germany
78C4 Baween I Indon
95B2 Bawiti Egypt
97B3 Bawku Ghana
76B2 Bawlake Myan
108A2 Bawlen Aust
17B1 Baxley USA
25E2 Bayamo Cuba
78C2 Bayan Indon
68C2 Bayandzürh Mongolia
68B3 Bayan Har Shan Mts China
72A1 Bayan Mod China
72B1 Bayan Obo China
47A2 Bayard P France
12J3 Bayard,Mt Can
63D3 Bayasgalant Mongolia
79B1 Baybay Phil
93D1 Bayburt Turk
10B2 Bay City Michigan, USA
19A4 Bay City Texas, USA
92B2 Bay Dağlari Turk
64H3 Bayaratskaya Guba B Russian Fed
99E2 Baydhabo Somalia
48B2 Bayeux France
47B1 Bayerische Alpen Mts Germany
57C3 Bayern State, Germany
92C3 Bāyir Jordan
63C2 Baykalskiy Khrebet Mts Russian Fed
63B1 Baykit Russian Fed
63B3 Baylik Shan Mts China/Mongolia
61J3 Baymak Russian Fed
79B2 Bayombong Phil
48B3 Bayonne France
57C3 Bayreuth Germany
19C3 Bay St Louis USA

15D2 Bay Shore USA
15C1 Bays,L of Can
68A2 Baytik Shan Mts China
Bayt Lahm = Bethlehem
19B4 Baytown USA
50B2 Baza Spain
59D3 Bazaliya Ukraine
48B3 Bazas France
73B3 Bazhong China
91D4 Bazmān Iran
94C1 Bcharre Leb
16B3 Beach Haven USA
43E4 Beachy Head Eng
16C2 Beacon USA
101D2 Bealanana Madag
18B1 Beardstown USA
22B1 Bear Valley USA
8D2 Beatrice USA
44C2 Beatrice Oilfield N Sea
13C1 Beatton R Can
5F4 Beatton River Can
29E6 Beauchene Is Falkland Is
109D1 Beaudesert Aust
1B5 Beaufort S Can
100B4 Beaufort West S Africa
15D1 Beauharnois Can
44B3 Beauly Scot
21B3 Beaumont California, USA
11A3 Beaumont Texas, USA
49C2 Beaune France
48C2 Beauvais France
12E1 Beauval Can
12E1 Beaver Alaska, USA
13F2 Beaver R Saskatchewan, Can
4D3 Beaver Creek Can
12E1 Beaver Creek Can
13E2 Beaver Dam Kentucky, USA
14B3 Beaverhill L Can
14A1 Beaver I USA
18B2 Beaver L USA
13D1 Beaverlodge Can
85C3 Beawar India
35B2 Beazley Arg
35B2 Bebedouro Brazil
43E3 Beccles Eng
54B1 Bečej Serbia, Yugos
96B1 Béchar Alg
12C3 Becharof L USA
11B3 Beckley USA
43D3 Bedford County, Eng
43D3 Bedford Eng
14A3 Bedford Indiana, USA
27M2 Bedford Pt Grenada
4D2 Beechey Pt USA
109D1 Beechworth Aust
109C3 Beenleigh Aust
92B3 Beersheba Israel
Beer Sheva = Beersheba
94B3 Beér Sheva R Israel
9D4 Beeville USA
98C2 Befale Zaire
101D2 Befandriana Madag
109C3 Bega Aust
91B3 Behbehan Iran
12H3 Behm Canal Sd USA
90B2 Behshahr Iran
84B2 Behsūd Afghan
69E2 Bei'an China
73B5 Beihai China
72D2 Beijing China
76E1 Beiliu China
73B4 Beipan Jiang R China
72E1 Beipiao China
Beira = Sofala
94C2 Beirut Leb
72A2 Bei Shan Mts China
94B2 Beit ed Dine Leb
94B3 Beit Jala Israel
50A2 Beja Port
96C1 Beja Tunisia
96C1 Bejaïa Alg

50A1 Béjar Spain
90C3 Bejestān Iran
59C3 Békéscsaba Hung
101D3 Bekily Madag
86A1 Bela India
85B3 Bela Pak
78C2 Belaga Malay
16A3 Bel Air USA
87B1 Belamnalli India
71D3 Belang Indon
70A3 Belangpidie Indon
58C2 Belarus Republic, Europe
Belau = Palau Is.
101C3 Bela Vista Mozam
70A3 Belawan Indon
61J2 Belaya R Ukraine
6C2 Belcher Chan Can
7C4 Belcher Is Can
84B1 Belchiragh Afghan
61H3 Belebey Russian Fed
99E2 Beled Weyne Somalia
31B2 Belém Brazil
32B3 Belén Colombia
34D2 Belén Urug
9C3 Belen USA
45D1 Belfast N Ire
101H1 Belfast S Africa
45D1 Belfast Lough Estuary N Ire
99D1 Bēlfodiyo Eth
42D2 Belford Eng
49D2 Belfort France
87A1 Belgaum India
56A2 Belgium Kingdom, N W Europe
60E3 Belgorod Russian Fed
60E3 Belgorod Division, Russian Fed
60D4 Belgorod Dnestrovskiy Ukraine
Belgrade = Beograd
95A2 Bel Hedan Libya
78B3 Belinyu Indon
78B3 Belitung I Indon
25D3 Belize Belize
25D3 Belize Republic, Cent America
47D2 Bellac France
5F4 Bella Coola Can
47C2 Bellagio Italy
19A4 Bellaire USA
47C1 Bellano Italy
87B1 Bellary India
109C1 Bellata Aust
47B2 Belledonne Mts France
8C2 Belle Fourche USA
49D2 Bellegarde France
17B2 Belle Glade USA
7E4 Belle I Can
48B2 Belle-Île I France
7E4 Belle Isle,Str of Can
7C5 Belleville Can
18A2 Belleville Kansas, USA
20B1 Bellevue Washington, USA
109D2 Bellingen Aust
8A2 Bellingham USA
112C2 Bellingshausen Base Ant
112C3 Bellingshausen S Ant
52A1 Bellinzona Switz
32B2 Bello Colombia
107E3 Bellona Reefs Nouvelle Calédonie
22B1 Bellota USA
15D2 Bellows Falls USA
6B3 Bell Pen Can
52B1 Belluno Italy
29D2 Bell Ville Arg
31C6 Belmonte Brazil
25D3 Belmopan Belize
45B1 Belmullet Irish Rep
69E1 Belogorsk Russian Fed
101D3 Beloha Madag
31C5 Belo Horizonte Brazil
10B2 Beloit Wisconsin, USA

64E3 Belomorsk Russian Fed
61J3 Beloretsk Russian Fed
Belorussia = Belarus
101D2 Belo-Tsiribihina Madag
64E3 Beloye More S Russian Fed
60E1 Beloye Ozero L Russian Fed
60E1 Belozersk Russian Fed
14B3 Belpre USA
108A2 Beltana Aust
19A3 Belton USA
59D3 Bel'tsy Moldova
16B2 Belvidere New Jersey, USA
98B3 Bembe Angola
97C3 Bembéréke Benin
10A2 Bemidji USA
39G6 Bena Nor
98C3 Bena Dibele Zaire
108C3 Benalla Aust
44B3 Ben Attow Mt Scot
50B2 Benavente Spain
44A3 Benbecula I Scot
106A4 Bencubbin Aust
8A2 Bend USA
44B3 Ben Dearg Mt Scot
60C4 Bendery Ukraine
107D4 Bendigo Aust
57C3 Benešov Czech Republic
52B2 Benevento Italy
83C4 Bengal,B of Asia
96D1 Ben Gardane Tunisia
72D3 Bengbu China
78A3 Bengkalis Indon
78A3 Bengkulu Indon
100A2 Benguela Angola
92B3 Benha Egypt
44B2 Ben Hope Mt Scot
98C2 Beni Zaire
32D6 Béni R Bol
96B1 Beni Abbes Alg
51C1 Benicarló Spain
51B2 Benidorm Spain
51C2 Beni Mansour Alg
95C2 Beni Mazar Egypt
96B1 Beni Mellal Mor
97C4 Benin Republic, Africa
97C4 Benin City Nig
95C2 Beni Suef Egypt
44B2 Ben Kilbreck Mt Scot
44B3 Ben Lawers Mt UK
109C4 Ben Lomond Mt Aust
44C3 Ben Macdui Mt Scot
44B2 Ben More Assynt Mt Scot
111B2 Benmore,L NZ
44B3 Ben Nevis Mt Scot
15D2 Bennington USA
94B2 Bent Jbail Leb
98B2 Benoué R Cam
9B3 Benson Arizona, USA
99C2 Bentiu Sudan
19B3 Benton Arkansas, USA
18C2 Benton Kentucky, USA
14A2 Benton Harbor USA
97C4 Benue R Nig
45B1 Benwee Hd C Irish Rep
44B3 Ben Wyvis Mt Scot
72E1 Benxi China
54B2 Beograd Serbia, Yugos
86A2 Beohari India
74C4 Beppu Japan
55A2 Berat Alb
95C3 Berber Sudan
99E1 Berbera Somalia
98B2 Berbérati CAR
46A1 Berck France
60C4 Berdichev Ukraine
60E4 Berdyansk Ukraine
97B4 Berekum Ghana
22B2 Berenda USA

Blanco

34A2 Blanco R Arg
34B1 Blanco R Arg
8A2 Blanco,C USA
7E4 Blanc Sablon Can
43C4 Blandford Forum Eng
43C4 Blaneau Gwent County Wales
46A2 Blangy-sur-Bresle France
46B1 Blankenberge Belg
101C2 Blantyre Malawi
48B2 Blaye France
109C2 Blayney Aust
111B2 Blenheim NZ
96C1 Blida Alg
14B1 Blind River Can
108A2 Blinman Aust
78C4 Blitar Indon
15D2 Block I USA
16D2 Block Island Sd USA
101G1 Bloemfontein S Africa
101G1 Bloemhof S Africa
101G1 Bloemhof Dam Res S Africa
33F3 Blommesteinmeer L Surinam
38A1 Blonduós Iceland
45B1 Bloody Foreland C Irish Rep
14A3 Bloomfield Indiana, USA
18B1 Bloomfield Iowa, USA
10B2 Bloomington Illinois, USA
14A3 Bloomington Indiana, USA
16A2 Bloomsburg USA
78C4 Blora Indon
6H3 Blosseville Kyst Mts Greenland
57B3 Bludenz Austria
11B3 Bluefield USA
32A1 Bluefields Nic
26B3 Blue Mountain Peak Mt Jamaica
16A2 Blue Mts USA
109D2 Blue Mts Aust
27J1 Blue Mts Jamaica
8A2 Blue Mts USA
Blue Nile = Bahr el Azraq
99D1 Blue Nile R Sudan
4G3 Bluenose L Can
11B3 Blue Ridge Mts USA
13D2 Blue River Can
45B1 Blue Stack Mt Irish Rep
111A3 Bluff NZ
106A4 Bluff Knoll Mt Aust
30C4 Blumenau Brazil
49D2 Blundez Austria
20B2 Bly USA
12E3 Blying Sd USA
42D2 Blyth Eng
98J3 Blythe USA
11B3 Blytheville USA
97A4 Bo Sierra Leone
79B3 Boac Phil
72D2 Boading China
14B2 Boardman USA
63C3 Boatou China
33E3 Boa Vista Brazil
97A4 Boa Vista I Cape Verde
76E1 Bobai China
47C2 Bóbbio Italy
97B3 Bobo Dioulasso Burkina
60C3 Bobruysk Belarus
17B2 Boca Chica Key I USA
32D5 Bôca do Acre Brazil
35C1 Bocaiúva Brazil
98B2 Bocaranga CAR
17B2 Boca Raton USA
55C3 Bochnia Pol
56B2 Bocholt Germany
46D1 Bochum Germany
100A2 Bocoio Angola
98B2 Boda CAR
63D2 Bodaybo Russian Fed

21A2 Bodega Head Pt USA
95A3 Bodélé Region Chad
38J5 Boden Sweden
47C1 Bodensee L Switz/Germany
87B1 Bodhan India
87B2 Bodinayakkanür India
43B4 Bodmin Eng
43B4 Bodmin Moor Upland Eng
38G5 Bodø Nor
55C3 Bodrum Turk
98C3 Boende Zaïre
97A3 Boffa Guinea
76B2 Bogale Myan
19C3 Bogalusa USA
109C2 Bogan R Aust
97B3 Bogandé Burkina
6H3 Bogarnes Iceland
92C2 Boğazlıyan Turk
61K2 Bogdanovich Russian Fed
68A2 Bogda Shan Mt China
100A3 Bogenfels Namibia
109D1 Boggabilla Aust
109C2 Boggabri Aust
45B2 Boggeragh Mts Irish Rep
79B3 Bogo Phil
109C3 Bogong,Mt Aust
78B4 Bogor Indon
61H2 Bogorodskoye Russian Fed
32C3 Bogotá Colombia
63A2 Bogotol Russian Fed
86B2 Bogra Bang
72D2 Bo Hai B China
46B2 Bohain-en-Vermandois France
72D2 Bohai Wan B China
57C3 Böhmer-Wald Upland Germany
79B4 Bohol I Phil
79B4 Bohol S Phil
35A1 Bois R Brazil
14B1 Bois Blanc I USA
8B2 Boise USA
96A2 Bojador,C Mor
79B2 Bojeador,C Phil
90C2 Bojnûrd Iran
97A3 Boké Guinea
109C1 Bokhara R Aust
39F7 Boknafjord Inlet Nor
98B3 Boko Congo
76C3 Bokor Camb
98C3 Bokungu Zaïre
98B1 Bol Chad
23A1 Bolaános Mexico
97A3 Bolama Guinea-Bissau
23A1 Bolanos R Mexico
48C2 Bolbec France
97B4 Bole Ghana
59B2 Boleslawiec Pol
97B3 Bolgatanga Ghana
60C4 Bolgrad Ukraine
34C3 Bolivar Arg
18B2 Bolivar Missouri, USA
18C2 Bolivar Tennessee, USA
30C2 Bolivia Republic, S America
32C2 Bolivar Mt Ven
30C2 Bollnäs Sweden
109C1 Bollon Aust
52B2 Bologna Italy
60D2 Bologoye Russian Fed
69F2 Bolon' Russian Fed
61G3 Bol'shoy Irgiz R Russian Fed
74C2 Bol'shoy Kamen Russian Fed
Bol'shoy Kavkaz = Caucasus
61G4 Bol'shoy Uzen R Kazakhstan
9C4 Bolson de Mapimi Desert Mexico
43C3 Bolton Eng

92B1 Bolu Turk
38A1 Bolungarvik Iceland
92B2 Bolu Türk
52B1 Bolzano Italy
98B3 Boma Zaïre
107D4 Bombala Aust
87A1 Bombay India
99D2 Bombo Uganda
35B1 Bom Despacho Brazil
86C1 Bomdila India
97A4 Bomi Hills Lib
31C4 Bom Jesus da Lapa Brazil
63C2 Bomnak Russian Fed
99C2 Bomokandi R Zaïre
98C2 Bomu R CAR/Zaïre
27F2 Bonaire I Caribbean S
12F2 Bona,Mt USA
25D3 Bonanza Nic
7E5 Bonavista Can
108A2 Bon Bon Aust
98C2 Bondo Zaïre
97B4 Bondoukou Côte d'Ivoire
Bône = 'Annaba
33E3 Bonfim Guyana
98C2 Bongandanga Zaïre
98B1 Bongor Chad
19A3 Bonham USA
53A2 Bonifacio France
52A2 Bonifacio,Str of Chan Medit S
Bonin Is = Ogasawara Gunto
17B2 Bonita Springs USA
52B2 Bonn Germany
20C1 Bonners Ferry USA
12H1 Bonnet Plume R Can
13E2 Bonnyville Can
97A4 Bonthe Sierra Leone
79B2 Bontoc Phil
98E3 Booaal Somalia
99E1 Boonaal Aust
15C2 Boonville USA
109C2 Boorowa Aust
6A2 Boothia,G of Can
6A2 Boothia Pen Can
98B3 Booué Gabon
108A1 Bopeechee Aust
99D2 Bor Sudan
92B2 Bor Turk
54B2 Bor Serbia, Yugos
8B2 Borah Peak Mt USA
39G7 Borås Sweden
108A3 Borda,C Aust
48B3 Bordeaux France
4B3 Borden I Can
16B2 Borden Pen Can
108B3 Bordertown Aust
96C2 Bordj Omar Dris Alg
8D1 Borens River Can
38B2 Borgarnes Iceland
9C3 Borger USA
38H7 Borgholm Sweden
47C2 Borgosia Italy
47D1 Borgo Valsugana Italy
59C3 Borislav Ukraine
61F3 Borisoglebsk Russian Fed
60C3 Borisov Belarus
60E3 Borisovka Russian Fed
95A3 Borkou Region Chad
38H6 Borlänge Sweden
47C2 Bormida Italy
47D1 Bormio Italy
67F5 Borneo I Malay/Indon
39H7 Bornholm I Den
55C3 Bornova Turk
98C2 Boro R Sudan
97B3 Boromo Burkina
60D2 Borovichi Russian Fed
106C2 Borroloola Aust
54B1 Borsa Rom
90A3 Borüjed Iran
90B3 Borüjen Iran
58B2 Bory Tucholskie Region, Pol

63D2 Borzya Russian Fed
73B5 Bose China
101G1 Boshof S Africa
54A2 Bosna R Bosnia-Herzegovina
37E4 Bosnia-Herzegovina Republic, Europe
75C1 Bösö-hantö B Japan
Bosporus = Karadeniz Boğazi
51C2 Bosquet Alg
98B2 Bossangoa CAR
98B2 Bossèmbélé CAR
19B3 Bossier City USA
65K5 Bosten Hu L China
43D3 Boston Eng
10C2 Boston USA
11A3 Boston Mts USA
85C4 Botäd India
54B2 Botevgrad Bulg
101G1 Bothaville S Africa
64C3 Bothnia,G of Sweden/Fin
100B3 Botletli R Botswana
60C4 Botosani Rom
100B3 Botswana Republic, Africa
53C3 Botte Donato Mt Italy
46D1 Bottrop Germany
35B2 Botucatu Brazil
7E5 Botwood Can
89D7 Bouaké Côte d'Ivoire
98B2 Bouar CAR
96B1 Bouârfa Mor
98B2 Bouca CAR
51C2 Boufarik Alg
Bougie = Bejaia
97B3 Bougouni Mali
46C2 Bouillon France
96B2 Bou Izakarn Mor
46D2 Boulay-Moselle France
8C2 Boulder Colorado, USA
9B3 Boulder City USA
22A2 Boulder Creek USA
48C1 Boulogne France
98B2 Boumba R CAR
97B4 Bouna Côte d'Ivoire
8B3 Boundary Peak Mt USA
97B4 Boundiali Côte d'Ivoire
107F3 Bourail Nouvelle Calédonie
97B3 Bourem Mali
49D2 Bourg France
49D2 Bourg de Péage France
48C2 Bourges France
48C3 Bourg-Madame France
49C2 Bourgogne Region, France
47B2 Bourg-St-Maurice France
108C2 Bourke Aust
43D4 Bournemouth Eng
96C1 Bou Säada Alg
98B1 Bousso Chad
97A3 Boutilmit Maur
103J7 Bouvet I Atlantic O
34D2 Bowen Arg
13E2 Bow R Can
107D2 Bowen Aust
19A3 Bowie Texas, USA
13E2 Bow Island Can
11B3 Bowling Green Kentucky, USA
18B2 Bowling Green Missouri, USA
14B2 Bowling Green Ohio, USA
15C3 Bowling Green Virginia, USA
15C2 Bowmanville Can
109D2 Bowral Aust
13C2 Bowron R Can
72D3 Bo Xian China
72D2 Boxing China
92B1 Boyabat Turk
98B2 Boyali CAR
5J4 Boyd Can

16B2 Boyertown USA
13E2 Boyle Can
41B3 Boyle Irish Rep
45C2 Boyne R Irish Rep
17B2 Boynton Beach USA
98C2 Boyoma Falls Zaïre
55C3 Bozca Ada I Turk
55C3 Boz Dağlari Mts Turk
8B2 Bozeman USA
Bozen = Bolzano
98B2 Bozene Zaïre
80A2 Bozoum CAR
47B2 Bra Italy
52C2 Brač I Croatia
15C1 Bracebridge Can
95A2 Brach Libya
38H6 Bräcke Sweden
17B2 Bradenton USA
42D3 Bradford Eng
44E1 Brae Scot
44E3 Braemar Scot
50A1 Braga Port
34C3 Bragado Arg
50A1 Bragança Port
31B2 Bragança Brazil
35B2 Bragança Paulista Brazil
86C2 Brahman-Baria Bang
86B2 Brahmani R India
86C2 Brahmaputra R India
7E5 Braie Verte Can
60C4 Brăila Rom
10A2 Brainerd USA
97A3 Brakna Region, Maur
5F4 Bralorne Can
14C2 Brampton Can
33E3 Branco R Brazil
100A3 Brandberg Mt Namibia
56C2 Brandenburg Germany
56C2 Brandenburg State, Germany
101G1 Brandfort S Africa
8D2 Brandon Can
100B4 Brandvlei S Africa
57C2 Brandys nad Lebem Czech Republic
58B2 Braniewo Pol
10B2 Brantford Can
108B3 Branxholme Aust
7D5 Bras D'Or L Can
35C1 Brasília de Minas Brazil
32D6 Brasiléia Brazil
31B5 Brasília Brazil
54C1 Brasov Rom
78D1 Brassey Range Mts Malay
59B3 Bratislava Slovakia
63C2 Bratsk Russian Fed
15C2 Brattleboro USA
56C2 Braunschweig Germany
97A4 Brava I Cape Verde
9B3 Brawley USA
45C2 Bray Irish Rep
6C3 Bray I Can
13D2 Brazeau R Can
13D2 Brazeau,Mt Can
28D4 Brazil Republic, S America
103G5 Brazil Basin Atlantic O
9D3 Brazos R USA
98B3 Brazzaville Congo
57C3 Brdy Upland Czech Republic
111A3 Breaksea Sd NZ
110B1 Bream B NZ
78A4 Brebes Indon
44C3 Brechin Scot
46C1 Brecht Belg
59B3 Břeclav Czech Republic
43C4 Brecon Wales
43C4 Brecon Beacons Mts Wales
43B3 Brecon Beacons Nat Pk Wales
56A2 Breda Neth
100B4 Bredasdorp S Africa
38H6 Bredbyn Sweden

61J3 Bredy Russian Fed
15C2 Breezewood USA
47C1 Bregenz Austria
47C1 Bregenzer Ache R Austria
38A1 Breiðafjörður B Iceland
47C2 Brembo R Italy
17A1 Bremen USA
56B2 Bremen Germany
56B2 Bremerhaven Germany
20B1 Bremerton USA
19A3 Brenham USA
57C3 Brenner P Austria/Italy
47D2 Breno Italy
47D2 Brenta R Italy
22B2 Brentwood USA
52B1 Brescia Italy
Breslau = Wrocław
52B1 Bressanone Italy
44E1 Bressay I Scot
48B2 Bressuire France
58C2 Brest Belarus
48B2 Brest France
48B2 Bretagne Region, France
46B2 Breteuil France
46B2 Breton Woods USA
110B1 Brett,C NZ
109C1 Brewarrina Aust
16C2 Brewster New York, USA
20C1 Brewster Washington, USA
101G1 Breyten S Africa
52C1 Brežice Slovenia
98C2 Bria CAR
49C2 Briare France
43C4 Bridgend County Wales
21B2 Bridgeport California, USA
15D2 Bridgeport Connecticut, USA
16B3 Bridgeport Texas, USA
27F4 Bridgetown Barbados
10D2 Bridgewater Can
43C4 Bridgwater Eng
43C4 Bridgwater B Eng
42D2 Bridlington Eng
109C4 Bridport Aust
47B1 Brienzer See L Switz
46C2 Briey France
52A1 Brig Switz
8B2 Brigham City USA
109C3 Bright Aust
43D4 Brighton Eng
46E1 Brilon Germany
55A2 Brindisi Italy
19B3 Brinkley USA
107E3 Brisbane Aust
15D2 Bristol Connecticut, USA
43C4 Bristol County Eng
43C4 Bristol Eng
15D2 Bristol Pennsylvania, USA
16D2 Bristol Rhode Island, USA
11B3 Bristol Tennessee, USA
12B3 Bristol B USA
43B4 Bristol Chan Eng/Wales
4D3 British Mts USA
5F4 British Columbia Province, Can
6B1 British Empire Range Mts Can
101G1 Brits S Africa
100B4 Britstown S Africa
48C2 Brive France
59B3 Brno Czech Republic
17B1 Broad R USA
7C4 Broadback R Can
44A2 Broad Bay Inlet Scot

44B3 Broadford Scot
5H4 Brochet Can
4G2 Brock I Can
15C2 Brockport USA
16D1 Brockton USA
15C2 Brockville Can
6B2 Brodeur Pen Can
42B2 Brodick Scot
58B2 Brodnica Pol
60C3 Brody Ukraine
19B3 Broken Bow Oklahoma, USA
23B1 Broken Bow L USA
107D4 Broken Hill Aust
47C2 Broni Italy
38G5 Brønnøysund Nor
26C2 Bronx Borough, New York, USA
79A4 Brooke's Point Phil
17B2 Brookfield Missouri, USA
11A3 Brookhaven USA
20B2 Brookings Oregon, USA
8D2 Brookings South Dakota, USA
16D1 Brookline USA
16C2 Brooklyn Borough, New York, USA
5G4 Brooks, Can
12C3 Brooks,L USA
12A1 Brooks Mt USA
4C3 Brooks Range Mts USA
17B2 Brooksville USA
109D1 Brooloo Aust
106B2 Broome Aust
44C2 Brora Scot
20B2 Brothers USA
95A3 Broulkou Chad
13C3 Browning USA
9D4 Brownsville USA
9D3 Brownwood USA
46B1 Bruay-en-Artois France
106A3 Bruce,Mt Aust
14B1 Bruce Pen Can
59B3 Brück an der Mur Austria
Bruges = Brugge
46B1 Brugge Belg
46D1 Brühl Germany
78C2 Brunei Sultanate, S E Asia
52B1 Brunico Italy
111B2 Brunner,L NZ
11B3 Brunswick Georgia, USA
18B2 Brunswick Mississippi, USA
29B6 Brunswick,Pen de Chile
109C4 Bruny I Aust
61F1 Brusenets Russian Fed
26A3 Brus Laguna Honduras
Brüssel = Bruxelles
56A2 Bruxelles Belg
9D3 Bryan USA
108A2 Bryan,Mt Aust
60D3 Bryansk Russian Fed
60D3 Bryansk Division, Russian Fed
19B3 Bryant USA
59B2 Brzeg Pol
84C2 Bübiyan I Kuwait/Iraq
99D3 Bubu R Tanz
32C2 Bucaramanga Colombia
44D3 Buchan Oilfield N Sea
44A3 Buchanan Lib
44D3 Buchan Deep N Sea
6C2 Buchan G Can
40C2 Buchan Ness Pen Scot
7E5 Buchans Can
34C2 Buchardo Arg
Bucharest = Bucureşti
44C3 Buchs Switz
43D3 Buckingham Eng
12B1 Buckland USA

12B1 Buckland R USA
108A2 Buckleboo Aust
98B3 Buco Zau Congo
54C2 Bucureşti Rom
59B3 Budapest Hung
84D3 Budaun India
43B4 Bude Eng
19B3 Bude USA
61F5 Budennovsk Russian Fed
54A2 Budva Montenegro, Yugos
98A2 Buea Cam
22B3 Buellton USA
34B2 Buena Esperanza Arg
32B3 Buenaventura Colombia
23A2 Buenavista Mexico
29E2 Buenos Aires Arg
29D3 Buenos Aires State, Arg
18B2 Buffalo Mississippi, USA
10C2 Buffalo New York, USA
8C2 Buffalo South Dakota, USA
19A3 Buffalo Texas, USA
8C2 Buffalo Wyoming, USA
101H1 Buffalo R S Africa
13E2 Buffalo L Alberta, Can
5G3 Buffalo L Northwest Territories, Can
5H4 Buffalo Narrows Can
17B1 Buford USA
59C2 Bug R Pol/Ukraine
32B3 Buga Colombia
90B2 Bugdayli Turkmenistan
61H3 Bugulma Russian Fed
61H3 Buguruslan Russian Fed
93C2 Buhayrat al Asad Res Syria
41C3 Builth Wells Wales
34A2 Buin Chile
99C3 Bujumbura Burundi
99C3 Bukama Zaïre
99C3 Bukavu Zaïre
80E2 Bukhara Uzbekistan
78C2 Bukit Batubrok Mt Indon
70B4 Bukittinggi Indon
99D3 Bukoba Tanz
78D3 Buku Gandadiwata Mt Indon
71E4 Bula Indon
79B3 Bulan Phil
84D3 Bulandshahr India
100B3 Bulawayo Zim
58D4 Buldan Turk
68C2 Bulgan Mongolia
54B2 Bulgaria Republic, Europe
47B1 Bulle Switz
111B2 Buller R NZ
109C3 Buller,Mt Aust
106A4 Bullfinch Aust
108B1 Bulloo R Aust
108B1 Bulloo Downs Aust
108B1 Bulloo L Aust
18B2 Bull Shoals Res USA
34A3 Bulnes Chile
71F4 Bulolo PNG
101G1 Bultfontein S Africa
98C2 Bumba Zaïre
76B2 Bumphal Dam Thai
99D2 Buna Kenya
106A4 Bunbury Aust
45C1 Buncrana Irish Rep
107E3 Bundaberg Aust
109D2 Bundarra Aust
85D3 Bündi India
45B1 Bundoran Irish Rep
109C1 Bungil R Aust
98B3 Bungo Angola
75A2 Bungo-suidō Str Japan
70B3 Bunguran I Ind

14B2	**Charlotte** Michigan, USA	
11B3	**Charlotte** N Carolina, USA	
17B2	**Charlotte Harbor** B USA	
10C3	**Charlottesville** USA	
7D5	**Charlottetown** Can	
27K1	**Charlotteville** Tobago	
108B3	**Charlton** Aust	
10C1	**Charlton I** Can	
84C2	**Charsadda** Pak	
107D3	**Charters Towers** Aust	
48C2	**Chartres** France	
29E3	**Chascomús** Arg	
13D2	**Chase** Can	
44B2	**Châteaubriant** France	
48C2	**Châteaudun** France	
48B2	**Châteaulin** France	
48C2	**Châteauroux** France	
46D2	**Château-Salins** France	
49C2	**Chateau-Thierry** France	
46C1	**Châtelet** Belg	
48C2	**Châtellerault** France	
43E4	**Chatham** Eng	
7D5	**Chatham** New Brunswick, Can	
16C1	**Chatham** New York, USA	
14B2	**Chatham** Ontario, Can	
13A2	**Chatham Sd** Can	
12H3	**Chatham Str** USA	
49C2	**Châtillon** France	
47B2	**Châtillon** Italy	
16B3	**Chatsworth** USA	
17B1	**Chattahoochee** USA	
17A1	**Chattahoochee** R USA	
11B3	**Chattanooga** USA	
76A1	**Chauk** Myan	
49D2	**Chaumont** France	
66A2	**Chauny** France	
77D3	**Chau Phu** Viet	
50A1	**Chaves** Port	
61H2	**Chaykovskiy** Russian Fed	
50B2	**Chazaouet** Alg	
34C2	**Chazón** Arg	
32C2	**Chcontá** Colombia	
57C2	**Cheb** Czech Republic	
65F4	**Cheboksary** Russian Fed	
10B2	**Cheboygan** USA	
61G5	**Chechnya** Division, Russian Fed	
74B3	**Chech'on** S Korea	
85C3	**Chechro** Pak	
18A2	**Checotah** USA	
76A2	**Cheduba** I Myan	
108B1	**Cheepie** Aust	
86A3	**Chegga** Maur	
100C2	**Chegutu** Zim	
20B1	**Chehalis** USA	
74B4	**Cheju** S Korea	
74B4	**Cheju do** / S Korea	
74B4	**Cheju-haehyŏp** Str S Korea	
63F2	**Chekunda** Russian Fed	
20B1	**Chelan,L** USA	
90B2	**Cheleken** Turkmenistan	
34B3	**Chelforo** Arg	
80B1	**Chelkar** Kazakhstan	
59C2	**Chelm** Pol	
58B2	**Chelmno** Pol	
43E4	**Chelmsford** Eng	
43C4	**Cheltenham** Eng	
61K2	**Chelyabinsk** Russian Fed	
61K3	**Chelyabinsk** Division, Russian Fed	
101C2	**Chemba** Mozam	
57C2	**Chemnitz** Germany	
84D2	**Chenab** R India/Pak	
96B2	**Chenachane** Alg	
20C1	**Cheney** USA	
18A2	**Cheney Res** USA	
72D1	**Chengda** China	
73A3	**Chengdu** China	
72E2	**Chengshan Jiao** Pt China	
73C4	**Chenxi** China	
73C4	**Chen Xian** China	
73D3	**Cheo Xian** China	
32B5	**Chepén** Peru	
34B2	**Chepes** Arg	
48C2	**Cher** R France	
23A2	**Cheran** Mexico	
17C1	**Cheraw** USA	
48B2	**Cherbourg** France	
96C1	**Cherchell** Alg	
63C2	**Cheremkhovo** Russian Fed	
60E2	**Cherepovets** Russian Fed	
60D4	**Cherkassy** Ukraine	
61F5	**Cherkessk** Russian Fed	
60D3	**Chernigov** Ukraine	
60D3	**Chernobyl** Ukraine	
60C4	**Chernovtsy** Ukraine	
61J2	**Chernushka** Russian Fed	
60B3	**Chernyakhovsk** Russian Fed	
61G4	**Chernyye Zemli** Region, Russian Fed	
18A2	**Cherokees,L o'the** USA	
34A3	**Cherquenco** Chile	
86C1	**Cherrapunji** India	
60C3	**Cherven'** Belarus	
59C2	**Chervonograd** Ukraine	
10C3	**Chesapeake** B USA	
42C3	**Cheshire** County, Eng	
16C1	**Cheshire** USA	
64F3	**Chéshskaya Guba** B Russian Fed	
21A1	**Chester** California, USA	
42C3	**Chester** Eng	
18C2	**Chester** Illinois, USA	
16C1	**Chester** Massachusets, USA	
15C3	**Chester** Pennsylvania, USA	
17B1	**Chester** S Carolina, USA	
16A3	**Chester** R USA	
42D3	**Chesterfield** Eng	
6A3	**Chesterfield Inlet** Can	
16A3	**Chestertown** USA	
25D3	**Chetumal** Mexico	
13C1	**Chetwynd** Can	
12A2	**Chevak** USA	
111B2	**Cheviot** NZ	
40C2	**Cheviots** Hills Eng/Scot	
13D3	**Chewelah** USA	
8C2	**Cheyenne** USA	
86A1	**Chhapra** India	
86C1	**Chhātak** Bang	
85D4	**Chhatarpur** India	
85D4	**Chhindwāra** India	
86C1	**Chhuka** Bhutan	
73E5	**Chia'l** Taiwan	
100A2	**Chiange** Angola	
76C2	**Chiang Kham** Thai	
76B2	**Chiang Mai** Thai	
47C1	**Chiavenna** Italy	
74E3	**Chiba** Japan	
86B2	**Chibāsa** India	
100A2	**Chibia** Angola	
7C4	**Chibougamau** Can	
75A1	**Chiburi-jima** / Japan	
101C3	**Chibuto** Mozam	
10B2	**Chicago** USA	
14A2	**Chicago Heights** USA	
12G3	**Chichagof I** USA	
43D4	**Chichester** Eng	
75B1	**Chichibu** Japan	
69G4	**Chichi-jima** / Japan	
11B3	**Chickamauga L** USA	
19C3	**Chickasawhay** R USA	
9D3	**Chickasha** USA	
12F2	**Chicken** USA	
32A5	**Chiclayo** Peru	
8A3	**Chico** USA	
29C4	**Chico** R Arg	
101C2	**Chicoa** Mozam	
15D2	**Chicoutimi** Can	
7C5	**Chicoutimi** Can	
101C3	**Chicualacuala** Mozam	
87B2	**Chidambaram** India	
6D3	**Chidley,C** Can	
17B2	**Chiefland** USA	
99C3	**Chiengi** Zambia	
47B2	**Chieri** Italy	
47D2	**Chiese** R Italy	
52B2	**Chieti** Italy	
72D1	**Chifeng** China	
12C3	**Chiginagak,Mt** USA	
4C3	**Chigmit Mts** USA	
23B2	**Chignahuapán** Mexico	
12C3	**Chignik** USA	
24B2	**Chihuahua** Mexico	
87B2	**Chik Ballāpur** India	
87B2	**Chikmagalūr** India	
12C	**Chikuminuk L** USA	
101C2	**Chikwawa** Malawi	
76A1	**Chi-kyaw** Myan	
87C1	**Chilakalūrupet** India	
23B2	**Chilapa** Mexico	
87B3	**Chilaw** Sri Lanka	
28B6	**Chile** Republic	
34B2	**Chilecito** Mendoza, Arg	
100B2	**Chililabombwe** Zambia	
86B2	**Chilka** L India	
13C2	**Chilko** R Can	
13C2	**Chilkotin** R Can	
34A3	**Chillán** Chile	
34D3	**Chillar** Arg	
18B2	**Chillicothe** Missouri, USA	
14B3	**Chillicothe** Ohio, USA	
13C3	**Chilliwack** Can	
13C3	**Chilo** R India	
101C2	**Chilongozi** Zambia	
20B2	**Chiloquin** USA	
24C3	**Chilpancingo** Mexico	
43D4	**Chiltern Hills** Upland Eng	
14A2	**Chilton** USA	
101C2	**Chilumba** Malawi	
69E4	**Chi-lung** Taiwan	
101C2	**Chilwa** L Malawi	
100C2	**Chimanimani** Zim	
46C1	**Chimay** Belg	
65G5	**Chimbay** Uzbekistan	
32B4	**Chimborazo** Mt Ecuador	
32B5	**Chimbote** Peru	
65H5	**Chimkent** Kazakhstan	
101C2	**Chinoio** Mozam	
67E3	**China** Republic, Asia	
	China National Republic = Taiwan	
25D3	**Chinandega** Nic	
32B6	**Chincha Alta** Peru	
10D1	**Chinchilla** Aust	
101C2	**Chinde** Mozam	
86C2	**Chindwin** R Myan	
100B2	**Chingola** Zambia	
100A2	**Chinguar** Angola	
96A2	**Chinguetti** Maur	
74B3	**Chinhae** S Korea	
100C2	**Chinhoyi** Zim	
12D3	**Chiniak,C** USA	
84C2	**Chiniot** Pak	
74B3	**Chinju** S Korea	
98C2	**Chinko** R CAR	
101C2	**Chinsali** Zambia	
52B1	**Chioggia** Italy	
101C2	**Chipata** Zambia	
101C3	**Chipinge** Zim	
32A4	**Chira** R Peru	
87C1	**Chirāla** India	
101C3	**Chiredzi** Zim	
95A2	**Chirfa** Niger	
32A2	**Chiriquí** Mt Panama	
54C2	**Chirpan** Bulg	
32A2	**Chirripo Grande** Mt Costa Rica	
100B2	**Chirundu** Zim	
100B2	**Chisamba** Zambia	
7C4	**Chisasibi** Can	
73B4	**Chishui He** R China	
	Chişinău = Kishinev	
47B2	**Chisone** R Italy	
61H2	**Chistopol** Russian Fed	
68D1	**Chita** Russian Fed	
100A2	**Chitado** Angola	
100A2	**Chitembo** Angola	
12F2	**Chitina** USA	
12F2	**Chitina** USA	
87B2	**Chitradurga** India	
84C1	**Chitral** Pak	
32A2	**Chitré** Panama	
86C2	**Chittagong** Bang	
85C4	**Chittaurgarh** India	
87B2	**Chittoor** India	
100B2	**Chiume** Angola	
47B2	**Chivasso** Italy	
100C2	**Chivhu** Zim	
29D2	**Chivilcoy** Arg	
100C2	**Chivu** Zim	
73A4	**Chizu** Japan	
29C3	**Choele Choel** Arg	
34C3	**Choique** Arg	
24B2	**Choix** Mexico	
58B2	**Chojnice** Pol	
99D1	**Choke** Eth	
48B2	**Cholet** France	
23B2	**Cholula** Mexico	
100B2	**Choma** Zambia	
86B1	**Chomo Yummo** Mt China/India	
57C2	**Chomutov** Czech Republic	
63C1	**Chona** R Russian Fed	
74B3	**Ch'ŏnan** S Korea	
76C3	**Chon Buri** Thai	
32A4	**Chone** Ecuador	
74B2	**Ch'ŏngjin** N Korea	
74B3	**Chŏngju** S Korea	
74B3	**Ch'ŏngju** S Korea	
100A2	**Chongoroi** Angola	
73B4	**Chongqing** China	
74B3	**Chŏnju** S Korea	
86B1	**Chooyu** Mt China/Nepal	
59D3	**Chortkov** Ukraine	
74B3	**Ch'ŏrwŏn** N Korea	
59B2	**Chorzow** Pol	
74E3	**Choshi** Japan	
24B3	**Chos-Malal** Arg	
58B2	**Choszczno** Pol	
86A2	**Chotanagpur** Region, India	
96C1	**Chott Melrhir** Alg	
22B2	**Chowchilla** USA	
63D3	**Choybalsan** Mongolia	
6A3	**Chrantrey Inlet** B Can	
111B2	**Christchurch** NZ	
101G1	**Christiana** S Africa	
6D2	**Christian,C** Can	
12H3	**Christian Sd** USA	
6E3	**Christianshaab** Greenland	
104D4	**Christmas I** Indian O	
65J5	**Chu** Kazakhstan	
65J5	**Chu** R Kazakhstan	
29C4	**Chubut** State, Arg	
29C4	**Chubut** R Arg	
60D2	**Chudovo** Russian Fed	
	Chudskoye Ozero = Peipus, Lake	
4D3	**Chugach Mts** USA	
12E2	**Chugiak** USA	
75A1	**Chūgoku-sanchi** Mts Japan	
29F2	**Chuí** Brazil	
29B3	**Chuillán** Chile	
77C5	**Chukai** Malay	
76D2	**Chu Lai** Viet	

34D2 Colonia del Sacramento Urug
34B2 Colonia 25 de Mayo Arg
29C5 Colonia Las Heras Arg
44A3 Colonsay I Scot
23A1 Colontlán Mexico
27E5 Coloradito Ven
8C3 Colorado State, USA
9B3 Colorado R Arizona, USA
29D3 Colorado R Buenos Aires, Arg
9D3 Colorado R Texas, USA
9B3 Colorado Plat USA
8C3 Colorado Springs USA
22D3 Colton USA
16A3 Columbia Maryland, USA
19C3 Columbia Mississippi, USA
10A3 Columbia Missouri, USA
15C2 Columbia Pennsylvania, USA
11B3 Columbia S Carolina, USA
11B3 Columbia Tennessee, USA
13D2 Columbia R Can
8A2 Columbia R USA
20C1 Columbia Plat USA
11B3 Columbus Georgia, USA
14A3 Columbus Indiana, USA
11B3 Columbus Mississippi, USA
8D2 Columbus Nebraska, USA
10B2 Columbus Ohio, USA
19A4 Columbus Texas, USA
20C1 Colville USA
4C3 Colville R USA
110C1 Colville,C NZ
4F3 Colville L Can
42C3 Colwyn Bay Wales
47E2 Comacchio Italy
72B1 Comanche Res USA
112C2 Comandante Ferraz Base Ant
25D3 Comayagua Honduras
34A2 Combarbalá Chile
45C2 Comeragh Mts Irish Rep
86C2 Comilla Bang
25C3 Comitán Mexico
46C2 Commercy France
6B3 Committees B Can
52A1 Como Italy
29C5 Comodoro Rivadavia Arg
23A1 Comonfort Mexico
87B3 Comorin,C India
70C4 Comoros Is Indian O
49C2 Compiègne France
23A1 Compostela Mexico
34B2 Comte Salas Arg
86C1 Cona China
74A4 Conakry Guinea
34B2 Concarán Arg
48B2 Concarneau France
35D1 Conceição da Barra Brazil
31B3 Conceição do Araguaia Brazil
35C1 Conceiçao do Mato Dentro Brazil
29B3 Concepción Chile
30E3 Concepción Par
29E2 Concepción R Arg
24B2 Concepcion del Oro Mexico
34D2 Concepción del Uruguay Arg
9A3 Conception,Pt USA
35B2 Conchas Brazil
9C4 Conchos R Mexico

21A2 Concord California, USA
10C2 Concord New Hampshire, USA
29E2 Concordia Arg
8D3 Concordia USA
20B1 Concrete USA
109D1 Condamine Aust
107D4 Condobolin Aust
20B1 Condon USA
46C1 Condroz Mts Belg
17A1 Conecuh R USA
47E2 Conegliano Italy
89F8 Congo R Congo
Congo,R = Zaire
14B1 Coniston Can
45B2 Connaught Region, Irish Rep
14B2 Conneaut USA
10C2 Connecticut State, USA
15D2 Connecticut R USA
15C2 Connellsville USA
45B2 Connemara,Mts of Irish Rep
14A3 Connersville USA
108B2 Conoble Aust
19A3 Conroe USA
35C2 Conselheiro Lafaiete Brazil
77D4 Con Son Is Viet
Constance,L = Bodensee
60C5 Constanta Rom
96C1 Constantine Alg
12C3 Constantine,C USA
29B3 Constitución Chile
13F3 Consul Can
47E2 Contarina Italy
31C4 Contas R Brazil
23B2 Contreras Mexico
4H3 Contuoyto L Can
11A3 Conway Arkansas, USA
15D2 Conway New Hampshire, USA
17C1 Conway South Carolina, USA
108A1 Conway,L Aust
42C3 Conwy Wales
106C3 Coober Pedy Aust
110B2 Cook Str NZ
13B2 Cook,C Can
4C5 Cook Inlet B USA
105H4 Cook Is Pacific O
11B2 Cook,Mt NZ
107D2 Cooktown Aust
109C2 Coolabah Aust
108C1 Cooladdi Aust
109C2 Coolamon Aust
106B4 Coolgardie Aust
109C3 Cooma Aust
109C2 Coonabarabran Aust
109C2 Coonamble Aust
108B2 Coonbah Aust
108A2 Coondambo Aust
108C1 Coongoola Aust
106C3 Coorong,The Aust
109D1 Cooroy Aust
20B2 Coos B USA
20B2 Coos Bay USA
107D4 Cootamundra Aust
45C1 Cootehill Irish Rep
23B2 Copala Mexico
23B2 Copalillo Mexico
Copenhagen = Kobenhavn
30B4 Copiapó Chile
47D2 Copparo Italy
12F2 Copper R USA
4D3 Copper Centre USA
14B1 Copper Cliff Can
23A2 Copper Canyon = Qurlurtuuk
Coppermine = Qurlurtuuk
4G3 Coppermine R Can
Coquilhatville = Mbandaka

30B4 Coquimbo Chile
54B2 Corabia Rom
17B2 Coral Gables USA
6B3 Coral Harbour Can
107D2 Coral S Aust/PNG
104F4 Coral Sea Basin Pacific O
107E2 Coral Sea Island Territories Aust
108B3 Corangamite,L Aust
33F3 Corantijn Surinam/Guyana
46B2 Corbeil-Essonnes France
50A1 Corcubion Spain
11B3 Cordele USA
50A1 Cordillera Cantabrica Spain
26C3 Cordillera Central Mts Dom Rep
79B2 Cordillera Central Mts Phil
34B2 Cordillera de Ansita Arg
32B5 Cordillera de los Andes Mts Peru
30C4 Cordillera del Toro Mt Arg
32C2 Cordillera de Mérida Ven
34A3 Cordillera de Viento Arg
25D3 Cordillera Isabella Mts Nic
32B3 Cordillera Occidental Mts Colombia
32B3 Cordillera Oriental Mts Colombia
108B1 Cordillo Downs Aust
29D2 Córdoba Arg
24C3 Córdoba Mexico
50B2 Córdoba Spain
29D2 Córdoba State, Arg
4D3 Cordova USA
Corfu = Kérkira
109D2 Coricudgy,Mt Aust
53C3 Corigliano Calabro Italy
11B3 Corinth Mississippi, USA
31C5 Corinto Brazil
45B2 Cork County, Irish Rep
41B3 Cork Irish Rep
92A1 Çorlu Turk
31C5 Cornel Fabriciano Brazil
35A2 Cornélio Procópio Brazil
7E5 Corner Brook Can
109C3 Corner Inlet B Aust
15C2 Corning USA
7C5 Cornwall Can
43B4 Cornwall County, Eng
43B4 Cornwall,C Eng
6A2 Cornwallis I Can
32D1 Coro Ven
31C2 Coroatá Brazil
30D2 Coroico Bol
35B1 Coromandel Brazil
87C2 Coromandel Coast India
110C1 Coromandel Pen NZ
110C1 Coromandel Range Mts NZ
22D4 Corona California, USA
13E2 Coronation Can
4G3 Coronation G Can
34C2 Coronda Arg
29B3 Coronel Chile
34D3 Coronel Brandsen Arg
34C3 Coronel Dorrego Arg
35C1 Coronel Fabriciano Brazil
30E4 Coronel Oviedo Par
29D3 Coronel Pringles Arg
34C3 Coronel Suárez Arg
34D3 Coronel Vidal Arg
30B2 Coropuna Mt Peru
109C3 Corowa Aust
49D3 Corps France

9D4 Corpus Christi USA
9D4 Corpus Christi,L USA
79B3 Corregidor I Phil
35A1 Corrente R Mato Grosso, Brazil
30E4 Corrientes Arg
30E4 Corrientes State, Arg
19B3 Corrigan USA
10A4 Corrigin Aust
107E2 Corringe Is Aust
109C3 Corryong Aust
52A2 Corse I Medit S
42B2 Corsewall Pt Scot
Corsica = Corse
9D3 Corsicana USA
52A2 Corte Corse
52B1 Cortina d'Ampezzo Italy
15C2 Cortland USA
23A2 Coruca da Catalan Mexico
93D1 Çoruh R Turk
60E5 Çorum Turk
31C4 Corumbá Brazil
35B1 Corumba Brazil
35B1 Corumbaiba Brazil
20B2 Corvallis USA
96A1 Corvo I Açores
43C3 Corwen Wales
23B2 Coscomatopec Mexico
53C3 Cosenza Italy
101D1 Cosmoledo Is Seychelles
34C2 Cosquín Arg
51B2 Costa Blanca Region, Spain
51C1 Costa Brava Region, Spain
50B2 Costa de la Luz Region, Spain
50B2 Costa del Sol Region, Spain
22D4 Costa Mesa USA
25D3 Costa Rica Republic, Cent America
79B4 Cotabato Phil
30C3 Cotagaita Bol
49D3 Côte d'Azur Region, France
97B4 Côte d'Ivoire Republic, Africa
46C2 Côtes de Meuse Mts France
97C4 Cotonou Benin
32B4 Cotopaxi Mt Ecuador
43C4 Cotswold Hills Upland Eng
20B2 Cottage Grove USA
56C2 Cottbus Germany
108A3 Couedic,C du Aust
20C1 Couer d'Alene L USA
46B2 Coulommiers France
15C1 Coulonge R Can
22B2 Coulterville USA
4B3 Council USA
8D2 Council Bluffs USA
58C1 Courland Lagoon Lg Lithuania/Russian Fed
47B2 Courmayeur Italy
13B3 Courtenay Can
Courtrai = Kortrijk
48B2 Coutances France
43D3 Coventry Eng
50A1 Covilhã Spain
17B1 Covington Georgia, USA
19B3 Covington Louisiana, USA
109C2 Cowal,L Aust
108B3 Cowangie Aust
15D1 Cowansville Can
108A1 Coward Springs Aust
108A2 Cowell Aust
108C3 Cowes Aust
20B1 Cowlitz R USA
109C2 Cowra Aust
30F2 Coxim Brazil
16C1 Coxsackie USA
86C2 Cox's Bazar Bang
22B2 Coyote USA

76D1	Dinh Lap Viet
22C2	Dinuba USA
97A3	Diouloulou Sen
86C1	Diphu India
99E2	Diré Dawa Eth
106A3	Dirk Hartog I Aust
95A3	Dirkou Niger
109C1	Dirranbandi Aust
99E2	Dirri Somalia
29G8	Disappointment,C South Georgia
20B1	Disappointment,L USA
106B3	Disappointment,L Aust
108B3	Discovery B Aust
103J7	Discovery Tablemount Atlantic O
47C1	Disentis Muster Switz
6E3	Disko Greenland
6E3	Disko Bugt B Greenland
6E3	Diskorjord Greenland
58D1	Disna R Belarus
35B1	Distrito Federal Federal District, Brazil
84C2	Diu India
79C4	Diuat Mts Phil
31C6	Divinópolis Brazil
61F4	Divnoye Russian Fed
93C2	Divriği Turk
22B1	Dixon California, USA
5E4	Dixon Entrance Sd Can/USA
13D1	Dixonville Can
93E3	Diyálá R Iraq
65E4	Diyarbakir Turk
90A3	Diz R Iran
98B2	Dja R Cam
96C1	Djadi R Alg
95A2	Djado,Plat du Niger
96C2	Djanet Alg
50A2	Djebel Bouhalla Mt Mor
96C1	Djelfa Alg
98C2	Djéma CAR
97B3	Djenné Mali
97B3	Djibo Burkina
99E1	Djibouti Djibouti
99E1	Djibouti Republic, E Africa
98C2	Djolu Zaire
97C4	Djougou Benin
98D2	Djugu Zaire
38C2	Djúpivogur Iceland
51C2	Djurdjura Mts Alg
60E2	Dmitrov Russian Fed
	Dnepr = Dnieper
60D4	Dneprodzerzhinsk Ukraine
60D4	Dnepropetrovsk Ukraine
60C3	Dneprovskaya Nizmennost' Region, Belarus
	Dnestr = Dniester
60D4	Dnieper R Ukraine
60B4	Dniester R Ukraine
60D2	Dno Russian Fed
98B2	Doba Chad
58C1	Dobele Latvia
34C3	Doblas Arg
71E4	Dobo Indon
54A2	Doboj Bosnia-Herzegovina
54B2	Dobreta-Turnu-Severin Rom
54C2	Dobrich Bulg
60D3	Dobrush Belarus
31C5	Doce R Brazil
87B2	Doctor R P Peña Arg
87B2	Dod India
87B2	Doda Betta Mt India
	Dodecanese = Sporádhes
9C3	Dodge City USA
99D3	Dodoma Tanz
75A1	Dōgo I Japan
97C3	Dogondoutchi Niger
93D2	Doğubayazit Turk
91B4	Doha Qatar
7C5	Dolbeau Can
49D2	Dôle France
43C3	Dolgellau Wales
49E2	Dolomitiche Mts Italy
99E2	Dolo Odo Eth
29E3	Dolores Arg
34D2	Dolores Urug
23A1	Dolores Hidalgo Mexico
4G3	Dolphin and Union Str Can
29E6	Dolphin,C Falkland Is
71E4	Dom Mt Indon
65G4	Dombarovskiy Russian Fed
38F6	Dombas Nor
46D2	Dombasle-sur-Meurthe France
54A1	Dombóvár Hung
48B2	Domfront France
27E3	Dominica I Caribbean S
27C3	Dominican Republic Caribbean S
6C3	Dominion,C Can
7E4	Domino Can
68D1	Domna Russian Fed
52A1	Domodossola Italy
78D4	Dompu Indon
29B3	Domuyo Mt Arg
109D1	Donville,Mn Aust
44C3	Don R Scot
61F4	Don R Russian Fed
45C1	Donaghadee N Ire
57C3	Donau R Germany
57C3	Donauwörth Germany
50A2	Don Benito Spain
43D3	Doncaster Eng
98B3	Dondo Angola
101C2	Dondo Mozam
87C3	Dondra Head C Sri Lanka
45B1	Donegal County, Irish Rep
40B3	Donegal Irish Rep
40B3	Donegal B Irish Rep
45B1	Donegal Mts Irish Rep
60E4	Donetsk Ukraine
73C4	Dong'an Ukraine
106A3	Dongara Aust
76D2	Dongfang China
74B2	Dongfeng China
70C4	Donggala Indon
68B3	Donggi Cona L China
74A3	Dongou China
73C5	Donghai Dao I China
72A1	Dong He R China
73C5	Dong Jiang R China
95C3	Dongola Sudan
73D5	Dongshan China
68D4	Dongsha Qundao I China
72C2	Dongsheng China
72E3	Dongtai China
73C4	Dongting Hu L China
73B5	Dongxing China
73D3	Dongzhi China
18B2	Doniphan USA
52C2	Donji Vakuf Bosnia-Herzegovina
38G5	Dönna I Nor
21A2	Donner? USA
46D2	Donnersberg Mt Germany
101G1	Donnybrook S Africa
	Donostia = San Sebastian
22B2	Don Pedro Res USA
12D1	Doonerak,Mt USA
79B4	Dopolong Phil
73A3	Do Qu R China
47B2	Dora Baltea R Italy
49D2	Dorbirn Austria
43C4	Dorchester Eng
48C2	Dordogne R France
56A2	Dordrecht Neth
13F2	Dore L Can
13F2	Dore Lake Can
97B3	Dori Burkina
46B2	Dormans France
57B3	Dornbirn Austria
44B3	Dornoch Scot
44B3	Dornoch Firth Estuary Scot
38H6	Dorotea Sweden
109D2	Dorrigo Aust
20D2	Dorris USA
43C4	Dorset County, Eng
46D1	Dorsten Germany
56B2	Dortmund Germany
98C2	Doruma Zaire
63D2	Dosatuy Russian Fed
84B1	Doshi Afghan
22B2	Dos Palos USA
95B3	Dosso Niger
65G5	Dossor Kazakhstan
11B3	Dothan USA
49C1	Douai France
98A2	Douala Cam
109D1	Double Island Pt Aust
49D2	Doubs R France
111A3	Doubtful Sd NZ
97B3	Douentza Mali
9C3	Douglas Arizona, USA
42B2	Douglas Eng
17B1	Douglas Georgia, USA
8C2	Douglas Wyoming, USA
12A1	Douglas,C USA
12D3	Douglas Chan Can
12D3	Douglas,Mt USA
46B1	Doullens France
50A1	Douro R Port
15C3	Dover Delaware, USA
43E4	Dover Eng
15D2	Dover New Hampshire, USA
16B2	Dover New Jersey, USA
14B2	Dover Ohio, USA
43D3	Dover Eng
41D3	Dover,Str of UK/France
16B3	Downington USA
42B2	Downpatrick N Ire
13C2	Downton,Mt USA
16B2	Doylestown USA
75A1	Dōzen I Japan
96A2	Dr'aa R Mor
35A2	Dracena Brazil
11B3	Dracut USA
49D3	Draguignan France
101C3	Drakensberg Mts S Africa
101G1	Drakensberg Mt S Africa
103E7	Drake Pass Pacific/Atlantic O
55B2	Dráma Greece
39G7	Drammen Nor
38A1	Drangajökull Iceland
52C1	Drava R Slovenia
13D2	Drayton Valley Can
49C2	Dreux France
57C2	Dresden Germany
48C2	Dreux France
20C2	Drewsey USA
54B2	Drin R Alb
54A2	Drina R Bosnia-Herzegovina/Serbia
58D1	Drissa R Belarus
45C2	Drogheda Irish Rep
55C3	Drogobych Ukraine
112B12	Dronning Maud Land Region, Ant
30D3	Dr P.P. Pená Par
52A2	Drumheller Can
14B1	Drummond I USA
15D1	Drummondville Can
58C2	Druskininksi Lithuania
12G3	Dry B USA
7A5	Dryden Can
27H1	Dry Harbour Mts Jamaica
76B3	Duang I Myan
91C4	Dubai UAE
5H3	Dubawnt R Can
4H3	Dubawnt L Can
45C2	Dublin County, Irish Rep
45C2	Dublin Irish Rep
17B1	Dublin USA
60E2	Dubna Russian Fed
60C3	Dubno Ukraine
15C2	Du Bois USA
13B2	Dubose,Mt Can
58D2	Dubrovica Ukraine
54A2	Dubrovnik Croatia
10A2	Dubuque USA
46D2	Dudelange Lux
1C10	Dudinka Russian Fed
43C3	Dudley Eng
97B4	Duékoué Côte d'Ivoire
50B1	Duero R Spain
44C3	Dufftown Scot
52C2	Dugi Otok I Croatia
56B2	Duisburg Germany
93E3	Dükan Iraq
99D2	Duk Faiwil Sudan
91B4	Dukhán Qatar
73A4	Dukou China
68B3	Dulan China
34C2	Dulce R Arg
78C2	Dulit Range Mts Malay
86C2	Dullabchara India
10A2	Duluth USA
94C2	Dūmā Syria
78A2	Dumai Indon
79A3	Dumaran I Phil
9C3	Dumas USA
94C2	Dumayr Syria
42C2	Dumbarton Scot
42C2	Dumfries Scot
42C2	Dumfries and Galloway Division, Scot
86B2	Dumka India
15C1	Dumoine,L Can
112C8	Dumont d'Urville Base Ant
95C1	Dumyat Egypt
54C2	Dunărea R Rom
45C2	Dunany Head Pt Irish Rep
54B2	Dunav R Bulg
32J4	Dunayevtsy Ukraine
13C3	Duncan Can
16A2	Duncannon USA
44C2	Duncansby Head Pt Scot
45C1	Dundalk Irish Rep
16A3	Dundalk USA
45C2	Dundalk B Irish Rep
6D2	Dundas Greenland
12C6	Dundas I Can
71E5	Dundas Str Aust
101H1	Dundee S Africa
44C3	Dundee Scot
44C3	Dundee City Division, Scot
108B1	Dundoo Aust
42B2	Dundrum B N Ire
111B3	Dunedin NZ
17B2	Dunedin USA
109C2	Dunedoo Aust
44C3	Dunfermline Scot
85C4	Dungarpur India
45C2	Dungarvan Irish Rep
43E4	Dungeness Eng
109D2	Dungog Aust
99C2	Dungu Zaire
95C2	Dungunab Sudan
60D4	Dunhuang China
46B1	Dunkerque France
10C2	Dunkirk USA
99D1	Dunkur Eth
97B4	Dunkwa Ghana
41B3	Dun Laoghaire Irish Rep
45B3	Dunmanway Irish Rep
26B1	Dunmore Town The Bahamas
44C2	Dunnet Head Pt Scot
42C2	Duns Scot
20B2	Dunsmuir USA

El Milagro

111A2 **Dunstan Mts** NZ
46C2 **Dun-sur-Meuse** France
72D1 **Duolun** China
18C2 **Du Quoin** USA
94B3 **Dura** Israel
49D3 **Durance** R France
24B2 **Durango** Mexico
50B1 **Durango** Spain
9C3 **Durango** USA
29E2 **Durango** Urug
9D3 **Durant** USA
94C1 **Duraykish** Syria
101H1 **Durban** S Africa
46D1 **Düren** Germany
86A2 **Durg** India
86B2 **Durgapur** India
42D2 **Durham** County, Eng
42D2 **Durham** Eng
11C3 **Durham** N Carolina, USA
16D1 **Durham** New Hampshire, USA
108B1 **Durham Downs** Aust
54A2 **Durmitor** Mt Montenegro, Yugos
44B2 **Durness** Scot
55A2 **Durrës** Alb
108B1 **Durrie** Aust
45A3 **Dursey** I Irish Rep
55C3 **Dursunbey** Turk
110B2 **D'Urville I** NZ
90D2 **Dushak** Turkmenistan
73B4 **Dushan** China
82A2 **Dushanbe** Tajikistan
111A3 **Dusky Sd** NZ
56B2 **Düsseldorf** Germany
73B4 **Duyun** China
92B1 **Düzce** Turk
60C2 **Dvina** R Latvia
85B4 **Dwarka** India
6D3 **Dyer,C** Can
11B3 **Dyersburg** USA
61F5 **Dykh Tau** Mt Russian Fed
108B1 **Dynevor Downs** Aust
68B2 **Dzag** Mongolia
63C3 **Dzamin Uüd** Mongolia
101D2 **Dzaoudzi** Mayotte
68C2 **Dzarnin Uüd** Mongolia
68B2 **Dzavhan Gol** R Mongolia
80E1 **Dzhezkazgan** Kazakhstan
61F2 **Dzerzhinsk** Russian Fed
63E2 **Dzhalinda** Russian Fed
65J5 **Dzhambul** Kazakhstan
60D4 **Dzhankoy** Ukraine
93D **Dzharkent = Panfilov**
65H4 **Dzhezkazgan** Kazakhstan
84B1 **Dzhilikul'** Tajikistan
65J5 **Dzhungarskiy Alatau** Mts Kazakhstan
59B2 **Dzierzoniow** Pol
63B3 **Dzüyl** Mongolia
82C1 **Dzungaria** Basin, China

E

7B4 **Eabamet L** Can
12F2 **Eagle** Alaska, USA
20B2 **Eagle L** California, USA
19A3 **Eagle Mountain L** USA
9C4 **Eagle Pass** USA
4E3 **Eagle Plain** Can
12E2 **Eagle River** USA
17B1 **Easley** USA
15C2 **East Aurora** USA
42B2 **East Ayrshire** Division, Scot
43E4 **Eastbourne** Eng
14A2 **East Chicago** USA
69E3 **East China Sea** China/Japan

100B4 **Eastern Cape** Province, S Africa
44B3 **East Dunbartonshire** Division, Scot
83B4 **Eastern Ghats** Mts India
29E6 **East Falkland I** Falkland Is
12E1 **East Fork** R USA
21B2 **Eastgate** USA
16C1 **Easthampton** USA
16C2 **East Hampton** USA
14A2 **East Lake** USA
14B2 **East Liverpool** USA
100B4 **East London** S Africa
44C3 **East Lothian** Division, Scot
7C4 **Eastmain** Can
7C4 **Eastmain** R Can
17B1 **Eastman** USA
15C3 **Easton** Maryland, USA
15C2 **Easton** Pennsylvania, USA
16B2 **East Orange** USA
105L4 **East Pacific Ridge** Pacific O
17B1 **East Point** USA
44B4 **East Renfrewshire** Division, Scot
42D3 **East Retford** Eng
42D3 **East Riding of Yorkshire** County Eng
11A3 **East St Louis** USA
1B7 **East Siberian S** Russian Fed
43E4 **East Sussex** County, Eng
17B1 **Eatonton** USA
10A2 **Eau Claire** USA
71F3 **Eauripik** I Pacific O
23B1 **Ebano** Nigeria
98B2 **Ebebiyin** Eq Guinea
56C2 **Ebersvalde** Germ
73A4 **Ebian** China
65K5 **Ebinur** L China
53C2 **Eboli** Italy
98B2 **Ebolowa** Cam
51B1 **Ebro** R Spain
92A1 **Eceabat** Turk
96C1 **Ech Cheliff** Alg
72D2 **Eching** China
20C1 **Echo** USA
4G3 **Echo Bay** Can
46D2 **Echternach** Lux
108B3 **Echuca** Aust
50A2 **Ecija** Spain
6D2 **Eclipse Sd** Can
32B4 **Ecuador** Republic, S America
99E1 **Ed** Eritrea
44C2 **Eday** I Scot
98C1 **Ed Da'ein** Sudan
95C3 **Ed Damer** Sudan
95C3 **Ed Debba** Sudan
44B2 **Eddrachillis B** Scot
99D1 **Ed Dueim** Sudan
109C4 **Eddystone Pt** Aust
98A2 **Edea** Cam
109C3 **Eden** Aust
42A2 **Eden** R Eng
101G1 **Edenburg** S Africa
111A3 **Edendale** NZ
46E2 **Edenkoben** Germany
46E1 **Eder** R Germany
6D3 **Edgell I** Can
64D2 **Edgeoya** I Barents S
16A3 **Edgewood** USA
94B3 **Edh Dhahiriya** Israel
55B2 **Edhessa** Greece
44C3 **Edinburgh** Scot
44C3 **Edinburgh, City of** Division, Scot
60C5 **Edirne** Turk
17B1 **Edisto** R USA
13D2 **Edith Cavell,Mt** Can
20B1 **Edmonds** USA
20B1 **Edmonton** Can
7D5 **Edmundston** Can
19A4 **Edna** USA
12H3 **Edna Bay** USA
52B1 **Edolo** Italy

94B3 **Edom** Region, Jordan
92A2 **Edremit** Turk
55C3 **Edremit Körfezi** B Turk
68B2 **Edrengiyn Nuruu** Mts Mongolia
5G4 **Edson** Can
34C3 **Eduardo Castex** Arg
12J2 **Eduni,Mt** Can
108B3 **Edward** R Aust
99C3 **Edward,L** Uganda/ Zaire
108A1 **Edwards Creek** Aust
9C3 **Edwards Plat** USA
18C2 **Edwardsville** USA
12H3 **Edziza,Mt** Can
4G2 **Eglinton I** Can
110B1 **Egmont,C** NZ
92B2 **Eğridir Gölü** L Turk
95B2 **Egypt** Republic, Africa
50B1 **Eibar** Spain
49C2 **Eibeuf** France
46D1 **Eifel** Region, Germ
44A3 **Eigg** I Scot
83B5 **Eight Degree Chan** Indian O
106B2 **Eighty Mile Beach** Aust
108C3 **Eildon,L** Aust
56B2 **Eindhoven** Neth
47C1 **Einsiedeln** Switz
94B3 **Ein Yahav** Israel
57C2 **Eisenach** Germany
57C3 **Eisenerz** Austria
46D1 **Eitorf** Germany
72A1 **Ejin qi** China
23B2 **Ejutla** Mexico
110C2 **Eketahuna** NZ
65J4 **Ekibastuz** Kazakhstan
63F2 **Ekimchan** Russian Fed
6E **Ek Mahalla el Kubra** Egypt
39H7 **Eksjo** Sweden
10B1 **Ekwen** R Can
92A3 **El'Alamein** Egypt
92B3 **El'Arish** Egypt
92B4 **Elat** Israel
95B3 **El'Atrun Oasis** Sudan
93C2 **Elazig** Turk
92C3 **El Azraq** Jordan
52B2 **Elba** I Italy
4H2 **Elira,C** Can
95C2 **El Balyana** Egypt
32C2 **El Banco** Colombia
55B2 **Elbasan** Alb
27D5 **El Baul** Ven
57C2 **Elbe** R Germany
94C1 **El Bega'a** R Leb
14A2 **Elberta** USA
8C3 **Elbert,Mt** USA
17B1 **Elberton** USA
92C2 **Elbistan** Turk
58B2 **Elblag** Pol
29B4 **El Bolson** Arg
61F5 **El'brus** Mt Russian Fed
Elburz Mts = Reshteh-ye Alborz
21B3 **El Cajon** USA
19A4 **El Campo** USA
51B2 **Elche** Spain
51B2 **Elda** Spain
32B3 **El Diviso** Colombia
96B2 **El Djouf** Desert Region Maur
18B2 **Eldon** USA
11A3 **El Dorado** Arkansas, USA
35B2 **Eldorado** Brazil
9D3 **El Dorado** Kansas, USA
24B2 **El Dorado** Mexico
33E2 **El Dorado** Ven

99D2 **Eldoret** Kenya
22C1 **Eleanor,L** USA
96B2 **El Eglab** Region, Alg
51B2 **El Escorial** Spain
93D2 **Eleskirt** Turk
11C4 **Eleuthera** I The Bahamas
92B4 **El Faiyûm** Egypt
95A3 **El Farsia** Well Mor
98C1 **El Fasher** Sudan
92B4 **El Fashn** Egypt
50A1 **El Ferrol del Caudillo** Spain
99C1 **El Fula** Sudan
96C1 **El Gassi** Alg
99D1 **El Geteina** Sudan
99D1 **El Gezira** Region, Sudan
94B3 **El Ghor** V Israel/ Jordan
10B2 **Elgin** Illinois, USA
44C3 **Elgin** Scot
92B3 **El Giza** Egypt
96C1 **El Golea** Alg
99D2 **Elgon,Mt** Uganda/ Kenya
99E2 **El Goran** Eth
23A2 **El Grullo** Mexico
96B2 **El Guettara** Well Mali
86B2 **El Hadicha** Desert Region Mali
92A4 **El Harra** Egypt
51C2 **El Harrach** Alg
99D1 **El Hawata** Sudan
23B1 **El Higo** Mexico
34A3 **El Huecu** Arg
92B4 **El'Igma** Desert Region Egypt
12B2 **Elim** USA
4H2 **Elira,C** Can
Elisabethville = Lubumbashi
39K6 **Elisenvaara** Fin
71F4 **El Iskandariya = Alexandria**
61F4 **Elista** Russian Fed
106C4 **Elizabeth** Aust
15D2 **Elizabeth** USA
11C3 **Elizabeth City** USA
17C1 **Elizabethtown** N Carolina, USA
16A2 **Elizabethtown** Pennsylvania, USA
96B1 **El Jadida** Mor
92C3 **El Jafr** Jordan
99D1 **El Jebelein** Sudan
96D1 **El Jem** Tunisia
58C2 **Elk** Pol
16B3 **Elk** R Maryland, USA
14B3 **Elk** R W Virginia, USA
95C3 **El Kamlin** Sudan
22B1 **Elk Grove** USA
El Khalil = Hebron
80B3 **El Khârga** Egypt
80B3 **El Khârga Oasis** Egypt
14A2 **Elkhart** USA
96B2 **El Khenachich** Desert Region Mali
54C2 **Elkhovo** Bulg
14C3 **Elkins** USA
8B2 **Elko** USA
16B3 **Elkton** USA
92B3 **El Khalil** Egypt
99C1 **El Lagowa** Sudan
4H2 **Ellef Ringnes I** Can
8A2 **Ellensburg** USA
16B2 **Ellenville** USA
11B2 **Ellesmere,L** Can
16A3 **Ellicott City** USA
100B4 **Elliot** S Africa
7B5 **Elliot Lake** Can
94B3 **El Lisan** Pen Jordan
112B3 **Ellsworth Land** Region Ant
95B1 **El Maghra** L Egypt
92B3 **El Mansûra** Egypt
16B3 **Elmer** USA
96B3 **El Merelé** Desert Region Maur
34B2 **El Milagro** Arg

El Mīna

94B1 El Mina Leb
92B4 El Minya Egypt
22B1 Elmira California, USA
10C2 Elmira New York, USA
96B2 El Mreiti Well Maur
56B2 Elmshorn Germany
98C1 El Muglad Sudan
96B2 El Mzereb Well Mali
79A3 El Nido Phil
99D1 El Obeid Sudan
23A2 El Oro Mexico
96C1 El Oued Alg
9C3 El Paso USA
21A2 El Porta USA
22C2 El Portal USA
50A2 El Puerto del Sta Maria Spain
El Qâhira = Cairo
El Quds = Jerusalem
94B3 El Quseima Egypt
9D3 El Reno USA
4E3 Elsa Can
25D3 El Salvador Republic, Cent America
22D4 Elsinore L USA
34B3 El Sosneade Arg
57C2 Elsterwerde Germany
El Suweis = Suez
50A1 El Teleno Mt Spain
110B1 Eltham NZ
33E2 El Tigre Ven
92B4 El Tîh Desert Region Egypt
34C2 El Tio Arg
20C1 Eltopia USA
92B4 El Tûr Egypt
87C1 Eluru India
50A2 Elvas Port
32C5 Elvira Brazil
34A2 El Volcán Chile
14A2 Elwood USA
43E3 Ely Eng
10A2 Ely Minnesota, USA
8B3 Ely Nevada, USA
14B2 Elyria USA
90B2 Emāmrūd Iran
84B1 Emām Sāheb Afghan
58B1 Eman R Sweden
61J4 Emba Kazakhstan
61J4 Emba R Kazakhstan
29C3 Embalse Cerros Colorados L Arg
51B2 Embalse de Alarcón Res Spain
50A2 Embalse de Alcántara Res Spain
50A1 Embalse de Almendra Res Spain
50A2 Embalse de Garcia de Sola Res Spain
33E2 Embalse de Guri L Ven
51B1 Embalse de Mequinenza Res Spain
50A1 Embalse de Ricobayo Res Spain
29E2 Embalse de Rio Negro Res Urug
29C3 Embalse El Chocón L Arg
29C4 Embalse Florentine Ameghino L Arg
50A1 Embalse Gabriel y Galan Res Spain
30D3 Embarcación Arg
5G4 Embarras Portage Can
47B2 Embrun France
99D3 Embu Kenya
56B2 Emden Germany
73A4 Emei China
107D3 Emerald Aust
7D4 Emeri Can
5J5 Emerson Can
21B1 Emigrant P USA
95A3 Emi Koussi Mt Chad
34B3 Emilo Mitre Arg
92B2 Emirdağ Turk
16B2 Emmaus USA
56B2 Emmen Neth

20C2 Emmett USA
16A3 Emmitsburg USA
12B2 Emmonak USA
9C4 Emory Peak Mt USA
24A2 Empalme Mexico
101H1 Empangeni S Africa
30E4 Empedrado Arg
105G1 Emperor Seamount Chain Pacific O
18A2 Emporia Kansas, USA
56B2 Ems R Germany
44B2 Enard B Scot
23A1 Encarnacion Mexico
30E4 Encarnación Par
97B4 Enchi Ghana
22D4 Encinitas USA
35C1 Encruzilhada Brazil
106B1 Endeh Indon
13D2 Enderby Can
112C11 Enderby Land Region, Ant
15C2 Endicott USA
12D1 Endicott Mts USA
47D1 Engadin Mts Switz
79B2 Engaño,C Phil
94B3 En Gedi Israel
47C1 Engelberg Switz
78A4 Enggano I Indon
41C3 England Country, UK
7E4 Englee Can
41C3 English Channel Eng/France
97B3 Enji Well Maur
39H7 Enkoping Sweden
53B3 Enna Italy
99C1 En Nahud Sudan
95B3 Ennedi Region Chad
109C1 Enngonia Aust
41B3 Ennis Irish Rep
19A3 Ennis Texas, USA
45C2 Enniscorthy Irish Rep
45C1 Enniskillen N Ire
45B2 Ennistimon Irish Rep
94B2 Enn Nâqoûra Leb
57C3 Enns R Austria
39F8 Enschede Neth
24A1 Ensenada Mexico
73B3 Enshi China
99D2 Entebbe Uganda
17A1 Enterprise Alabama, USA
20C1 Enterprise Oregon, USA
97C4 Enugu Nig
75B1 Enzan Japan
49C2 Epernay France
16A2 Ephrata Pennsylvania, USA
20C1 Ephrata Washington, USA
49D2 Épinal France
46A2 Epte R France
100A3 Epukiro Namibia
34C3 Epu pel Arg
90B3 Eqlid Iran
89D7 Equator
98A2 Equatorial Guinea Republic, Africa
47C2 Erba Italy
46D2 Erbeskopf Mt Germany
34A3 Ercilla Chile
93D2 Erciş Turk
92C2 Erciyas Daglari Mt Turk
74B2 Erdaobaihe China
72C1 Erdene Mongolia
68C2 Erdenet Mongolia
95B3 Erdi Region Chad
30F4 Erechim Brazil
92B1 Ereğli Turk
92B2 Ereğli Turk
68D2 Erenhot China
50B1 Eresma R Spain
76D1 Erft R Germany
57C2 Erfurt Germany
93C2 Ergani Turk
95A3 Erg Chech Desert Region Alg
95A3 Erg du Djourab Desert Chad
97D3 Erg Du Ténéré Desert Region Niger

92A1 Ergene R Turk
96B2 Erg Iguidi Region Alg
58D1 Ergli Latvia
98B1 Erguig R Chad
68D1 Ergun' R China/Russian Fed
63E2 Ergun Zuoqi China
95C3 Eriba Sudan
10C2 Erie USA
10B2 Erie,L Can/USA
42B2 Erin Port Eng
44A3 Eriskay I Scot
99D1 Eritrea Republic,Africa
46D1 Erkelenz Germany
57C3 Erlangen Germany
19B3 Erling,L USA
101G1 Ermelo S Africa
87B3 Ernakulam India
87B2 Erode India
108B1 Eromanga Aust
96B1 Er Rachidia Mor
99D1 Er Rahad Sudan
101C2 Errego Mozam
40B2 Errigal Mt Irish Rep
41A3 Erris Head Pt Irish Rep
99D1 Er Roseires Sudan
94B2 Er Rummān Jordan
57C2 Erzgebirge Upland Germany
93C2 Erzincan Turk
65F6 Erzurum Turk
48C3 Esara R Spain
56B1 Esbjerg Den
9C4 Escalón Mexico
10B2 Escanaba USA
25C3 Escárcega Mexico
46C2 Esch Lux
21B3 Escondido USA
24B2 Escuinapa Mexico
25C3 Escuintla Guatemala
98B2 Éséka Cam
51C1 Esera R Spain
90B3 Eşfahan Iran
101H1 Eshowe S Africa
110C1 Eskdale NZ
38C1 Eskifjörður Iceland
39H7 Eskilstuna Sweden
4E3 Eskimo L Can
7A3 Eskimo Point Can
92B2 Eskişehir Turk
50A1 Esla R Spain
29A5 Esmeralda I Chile
32B3 Esmeraldas Ecuador
26B2 Esmerelda Cuba
49C3 Espalion France
32J7 Española I Ecuador
108B4 Esperance Aust
34C2 Esperanza Arg
112C2 Esperanza Base Ant
35C1 Espirito Santo State, Brazil
101C3 Espungabera Mozam
29B4 Esquel Arg
34D2 Esquina Arg
94C2 Es Samra Jordan
96B1 Essaouira Mor
96C2 Es Semara Mor
56B2 Essen Germany
33F3 Essequibo R Guyana
43E4 Essex County, Eng
14B2 Essexville USA
57B3 Esslingen Germany
46B2 Essonne France
31D4 Estância Brazil
101G1 Estcourt S Africa
57B3 Esternay France
30D3 Esteros Par
5H5 Estevan Can
17B1 Estill USA
60B2 Estonia Republic, Europe
29B6 Estrecho de Magallanes Str Chile
50A2 Estremoz Port
59B3 Esztergom Hung
108A1 Etadunna Aust
46C2 Etam France

48C2 Étampes France
108A1 Etamunbanie,L Aust
46A1 Étaples France
85D3 Etāwah India
99D2 Ethiopia Republic, Africa
23B2 Etla Mexico
53B3 Etna Mt Italy
12H3 Etolin I US
12A2 Etolin Str USA
6C2 Eton Can
100A2 Etosha Pan L Namibia
100A2 Etosha Pan Salt L Namibia
17B1 Etowah R USA
46D2 Ettelbruck Lux
109C2 Eualabong Aust
13B2 Euclid USA
109C3 Eucumbene,L Aust
108A2 Eudunda Aust
19A2 Eufala L USA
17A1 Eufaula USA
8A2 Eugene USA
108C1 Eulo Aust
19B3 Eunice Louisiana, USA
46D1 Eupen Germany
93D3 Euphrates R Iraq
19C3 Eupora USA
48C2 Eure R France
20B2 Eureka California, USA
6B1 Eureka Can
8B3 Eureka Nevada, USA
8B2 Eureka Sd Can
108C3 Euroa Aust
100C1 Eurombah R Aust
101D3 Europa I Mozam
57B2 Euskirchen Germany
13B2 Eutsuk L Can
13D2 Evansburg Can
6B1 Evans,C Can
7C4 Evans,L Can
6B3 Evans Str Can
24A2 Evanston Illinois, USA
8B2 Evanston Wyoming, USA
11B3 Evansville Indiana, USA
101G1 Evaton S Africa
106C4 Everard,L Aust
82C3 Everest,Mt China/Nepal
8A2 Everett Washington, USA
16C1 Everett,Mt USA
11B4 Everglades,The Swamp USA
43D3 Evesham Eng
98B2 Evinayong Eq Guinea
39F7 Evje Nor
47B1 Evolène Switz
50A2 Évora Port
48C2 Évreux France
55B3 Évvoia I Greece
98B3 Ewo Congo
22C1 Excelsior Mt USA
18B2 Excelsior Springs USA
21B2 Exeter California, USA
43C4 Exeter Eng
15D2 Exeter New Hampshire, USA
43C4 Exmoor Nat Pk Eng
43C4 Exmouth Eng
50A2 Extremadura Region, Spain
25E2 Exuma Sd The Bahamas
99D3 Eyasi L Tanz
42C2 Eyemouth Scot
99E2 Eyl Somalia
108A4 Eyre Aust
106C3 Eyre Creek R Aust
106C3 Eyre,L Aust
108A3 Eyre Pen Aust
79B3 Eyte I Phil
23A1 Ezatlan Mexico
55C3 Ezine Turk

F

4G3 Faber L Can
39G7 Fåborg Den
52B2 Fabriano Italy
95A3 Fachi Niger
95B3 Fada Chad
97C3 Fada N'Gourma Burkina
52B2 Faenza Italy
6E3 Faeringehavn Greenland
98B2 Fafa R CAR
99E2 Fafan R Eth
54B1 Fågäras Rom
46C1 Fagnes Region, Belg
97B3 Faguibine,L L Mali
91C5 Fahud Oman
96A1 Faiol I Açores
4D3 Fairbanks USA
14B3 Fairborn USA
8D2 Fairbury USA
16A3 Fairfax USA
21A2 Fairfield California, USA
16C2 Fairfield Connecticut, USA
14B3 Fairfield Ohio, USA
45C1 Fair Head Pt N Ire
40C2 Fair Isle I Scot
111B2 Fairlie NZ
14B3 Fairview W Virginia, USA
13D1 Fairview Can
4E4 Fairweather,Mt USA
71F3 Fais I Pacific O
84C2 Faisalabad Pak
8C2 Faith USA
44E1 Faither,The Pen Scot
86A1 Faizäbäd India
43E3 Fakenham Eng
39G7 Fåköping Sweden
86C2 Falam Myan
24C2 Falcon Res Mexico/ USA
97A3 Falémé R Mali/Sen
39G7 Falkenberg Sweden
42C2 Falkirk Scot
44C3 Falkirk Division, Scot
29D6 Falkland Is Dependency, S Atlantic
29E6 Falkland Sd Falkland Is
22D4 Fallbrook USA
8B3 Fallon USA
15D2 Fall River USA
18A1 Falls City USA
43B4 Falmouth Eng
27H1 Falmouth Jamaica
16D2 Falmouth Massachusetts, USA
100A4 False B S Africa
24A2 Falso,C Mexico
56C2 Fålster I Den
54C1 Fålticeni Rom
39H6 Falun Sweden
92B2 Famagusta Cyprus
46C1 Famenne Region, Belg
76B2 Fang Thai
99D2 Fangak Sudan
73E5 Fang Iiao Taiwan
52B2 Fano Italy
112C3 Faraday Base Ant
94D3 Farafra Zaire
101D3 Farafangana Madag
95B2 Farafra Oasis Egypt
80E2 Farah Afghan
71F2 Farallon de Medinilla I Pacific O
97A3 Faranah Guinea
71F3 Faraulep I Pacific O
43D4 Fareham Eng
Farewell,C = Kap Farvel
107G5 Farewell,C NZ
110B2 Farewell Spit NZ
8D2 Fargo USA
94B2 Faria R Israel
10A2 Faribault USA
86B2 Faridpur Bang
90C2 Farimān Iran

18B2 Farmington Missouri, USA
9C3 Farmington New Mexico, USA
22B2 Farmington Res USA
42D2 Farne Deep N Sea
13D2 Farnham,Mt Can
12H2 Faro Can
50A2 Faro Port
39H7 Faro I Sweden
89K9 Farquhar Is Indian O
44B3 Farrar R Scot
14B2 Farrell USA
55B3 Fársala Greece
91B4 Fasä Iran
45B3 Fastnet Rock Irish Rep
60C3 Fastov Ukraine
86A1 Fatehpur India
13D1 Father Can
30F2 Fatima do Sul Brazil
101G1 Fauresmith S Africa
47B2 Faverges France
7B4 Fawn R Can
38H6 Fax R Sweden
38A2 Faxaflói B Iceland
95A3 Faya Chad
11A3 Fayetteville Arkansas, USA
11C3 Fayetteville N Carolina, USA
93E4 Faylakah I Kuwait
84C2 Fäzilka India
96A2 Fdérik Maur
11C3 Fear,C USA
21A2 Feather Middle Fork R USA
48C2 Fécamp France
34D2 Federación Arg
34D2 Federal Arg
71F3 Federated States of Micronesia Is Pacific O
56C2 Fehmarn I Germany
32C5 Feijó Brazil
73C5 Feilai Xai Bei Jiang R China
110C2 Feilding NZ
100C2 Feira Zambia
31D4 Feira de Santan Brazil
92C2 Feke Turk
57B3 Feldkirch Austria
34D2 Feliciano R Arg
41D3 Felixstowe Eng
47D1 Feltre Italy
38G6 Femund L Nor
74A2 Fengcheng China
73B4 Fengdu China
72D1 Fengning China
73B3 Fengjie China
72B3 Feng Xian China
72C2 Fen He R China
101D2 Fenoarivo Atsinanana Madag
60E5 Feodosiya Ukraine
90C3 Ferdow Iran
46B2 Fère-Champenoise France
82B2 Fergana Uzbekistan
45C1 Fermanagh County, N Ire
45B2 Fermoy Irish Rep
47D1 Fern Mt Austria
32J7 Fernandina I Ecuador
17B1 Fernandina Beach USA
103G5 Fernando de Noronha I Atlantic O
35A2 Fernandópolis Brazil
20B1 Ferndale USA
21B2 Fernley USA
32B5 Ferreñafe Peru
19B3 Ferriday USA
96B1 Fès Mor
18B2 Festus USA
54C2 Feteşti Rom
92A2 Fethiye Turk
61H5 Fetisovo Kazakhstan
44E1 Fetlar I Scot
84C1 Feyzabad Afghan

101D3 Fianarantsoa Madag
99D2 Fiché Eth
101G1 Ficksburg S Africa
47D2 Fidenza Italy
55A2 Fier Alb
47D1 Fiera Di Primeiro Italy
48C3 Figeac France
44C3 Fife Region, Scot
44C3 Fife Ness Pt Scot
50A1 Figueira da Foz Port
51C1 Figueras Spain
Figueras = Figueras
96B1 Figuig Mor
105G4 Fiji Is Pacific O
30D3 Filadelfia Par
54B2 Fîliaşi Rom
55B3 Filiatrá Greece
53B3 Filicudi I Italy
21A2 Fillmore California, USA
44B3 Findhorn R Scot
44B3 Findlay,Mt Can
15C2 Finger Lakes USA
101C2 Fingoè Mozam
92B2 Finike Turk
106C3 Finke R Aust
108A1 Finke Flood Flats Aust
64D3 Finland Republic, N Europe
39J7 Finland,G of N Europe
5F4 Finlay R Can
5F4 Finlay Forks Can
108C3 Finley Aust
38H5 Finnsnes Nor
71F4 Finschhafen PNG
47C1 Finsteraarhorn Mt Switz
56C2 Finsterwalde Germany
45C1 Fintona N Ire
111A3 Fiordland Nat Pk NZ
94B2 Fiq Syria
93C2 Firat R Turk
22B2 Firebaugh USA
52B2 Firenze Italy
34C2 Firmat Arg
85D3 Fîrozäbäd India
84C2 Firozpur India
39H7 Firspång Sweden
44C3 Firth of Clyde Estuary Scot
44C3 Firth of Forth Estuary Scot
44A3 Firth of Lorn Estuary Scot
40C2 Firth of Tay Estuary Scot
91B4 Fîrüzäbäd Iran
100A3 Fish R Namibia
22C2 Fish Camp USA
16C2 Fishers I USA
6B3 Fisher Str Can
43B4 Fishguard Wales
6E3 Fiskenaesset Greenland
47B2 Fismes France
15D2 Fitchburg USA
44E2 Fitful Head Pt Scot
17B1 Fitzgerald USA
106B2 Fitzroy R Aust
106B2 Fitzroy Crossing Aust
14B1 Fitzwilliam I Can
Fiume = Rijeka
99C3 Fizi Zaire
9B3 Flagstaff USA
42D2 Flamborough Head C Eng
8C2 Flaming Gorge Res USA
44A2 Flannan Isles Is Scot
12J2 Flat R Can
13E3 Flathead R USA
8B2 Flathead L USA
18B2 Flat River USA
8A2 Flattery,C USA
56B2 Flensburg Germany

47B1 Fleurier Switz
106C4 Flinders I Aust
107D4 Flinders I Aust
107D2 Flinders R Aust
106C4 Flinders Range Mts Aust
5H4 Flin Flon Can
11B2 Flint USA
42C3 Flint Wales
11B3 Flint R USA
42C3 Flintshire County Wales
46B1 Flixecourt France
17A1 Florala USA
Florence = Firenze
11B3 Florence Alabama, USA
18A2 Florence Kansas, USA
20B2 Florence Oregon, USA
11C3 Florence S Carolina, USA
32B3 Florencia Colombia
46C2 Florenville Belg
25D3 Flores Guatemala
96A1 Flores I Açores
106B1 Flores I Indon
34D3 Flores R Arg
70C4 Flores S Indon
31C3 Floriano Brazil
30G4 Florianópolis Brazil
25D2 Florida State, USA
29E2 Florida Urug
17B2 Florida B USA
17B2 Florida City USA
107E1 Florida Is Solomon Is
11B4 Florida Keys Is USA
11B4 Florida,Strs of USA
55B2 Flórina Greece
38F6 Florø Nor
47D1 Fluchthorn Mt Austria
54C1 Focsani Rom
52B2 Fogia Italy
97A4 Fogo I Cape Verde
48C3 Foix France
6C3 Foley I Can
52B2 Foligno Italy
43E4 Folkestone Eng
17B1 Folkston USA
52B2 Follonica Italy
22B1 Folsom USA
22B1 Folsom L USA
5H4 Fond-du-Lac Can
10B2 Fond du Lac USA
48C2 Fontainebleau France
18B2 Fontenac USA
48B2 Fontenay-le-Comte France
52C1 Fonyód Hung
Foochow = Fuzhou
12D2 Foraker,Mt USA
46D2 Forbach France
109C2 Forbes Aust
97C4 Forcados Nig
38F6 Forde Nor
108C1 Fords Bridge Aust
19B3 Fordyce USA
97A4 Forécariah Guinea
6G3 Forel,Mt Greenland
14B2 Forest USA
17B1 Forest Park USA
22A1 Forestville USA
44C3 Forfar Scot
46A2 Forges-les-Eaux France
20B1 Forks USA
52B2 Forlì Italy
51C2 Formentera I Spain
53B2 Formia Italy
96A1 Formigas I Açores
Formosa = Taiwan
30E4 Formosa Arg
31B5 Formosa Brazil
30D3 Formosa State, Arg
73D5 Formosa Str Taiwan/ China
47D2 Fornovo di Taro Italy
38D3 Føroyar Is N Atlantic O
44C3 Forres Scot
106B4 Forrest Aust

Forrest City

11A3 Forrest City USA
107D2 Forsayth Aust
39J6 Forssa Fin
109D2 Forster Aust
18B2 Forsyth Missouri, USA
84C3 Fort Abbas Pak
7B4 Fort Albany Can
31D2 Fortaleza Brazil
44B3 Fort Augustus Scot
100B4 Fort Beaufort S Africa
21A2 Fort Bragg USA
8C2 Fort Collins USA
15C1 Fort Coulogne Can
27E4 Fort de France Martinique
17A1 Fort Deposit USA
10A2 Fort Dodge USA
106A3 Fortescue R Aust
7A5 Fort Frances Can
4F3 Fort Franklin Can
4F3 Fort Good Hope Can
108B1 Fort Grey Aust
44B3 Forth R Scot
7B4 Fort Hope Can
3A83 Fortin Uno Arg
4F3 Fort Laird Can
96C1 Fort Lallemand Alg
Fort Lamy = Ndjamena
11B4 Fort Lauderdale USA
4F3 Fort Liard Can
5G4 Fort Mackay Can
5G4 Fort Macleod Can
5G4 Fort McMurray Can
4E3 Fort McPherson Can
18B2 Fort Madison USA
11B4 Fort Myers USA
5F4 Fort Nelson Can
4F3 Fort Norman Can
17A1 Fort Payne USA
8C2 Fort Peck Res USA
11B4 Fort Pierce USA
4G3 Fort Providence Can
5G3 Fort Resolution Can
98B3 Fort St James Can
5F4 Fort St John Can
13C1 Fort St John Can
13E2 Fort Saskatchewan Can
18B2 Fort Scott USA
4E3 Fort Selkirk USA
7B4 Fort Severn Can
61H5 Fort Shevchenko Kazakhstan
4F3 Fort Simpson Can
5G3 Fort Smith Can
4G3 Fort Smith Region, Can
11A3 Fort Smith USA
9C3 Fort Stockton USA
20B2 Fortuna California, USA
5G4 Fort Vermillion Can
17A1 Fort Walton Beach USA
10B2 Fort Wayne USA
44B3 Fort William Scot
9C3 Fort Worth USA
12F2 Fortymile R USA
12E1 Fort Yukon USA
73C5 Foshan China
47B2 Fossano Italy
12C3 Foster Mt USA
98B3 Fougamou Gabon
48B2 Fougères France
44D1 Foula I Scot
43C4 Foulness I Eng
111B2 Foulwind,C NZ
98B2 Foumban Cam
49C1 Fourmies France
55C3 Fournoí I Greece
97A3 Fouta Djallon Mts Guinea
111B3 Foveaux Str NZ
43B4 Fowey Eng
13D2 Fox Creek Can
6B3 Foxe Basin G Can
6B3 Foxe Chan Can
6C3 Foxe Pen Can
110C2 Foxton NZ
13F2 Fox Valley Can

45B2 Foynes Irish Rep
100A2 Foz do Cuene Angola
30F4 Foz do Iguaçu Brazil
16A2 Frackville USA
34B2 Fraga Arg
16D1 Framingham USA
31B6 Franca Brazil
49C2 France Republic, Europe
10A2 Frances R Can
12J2 Frances R Can
98B3 Franceville Gabon
49D2 Franche Comté Region, France
100B3 Francistown Botswana
13B2 François L Can
14A2 Frankfort Indiana, USA
11B3 Frankfort Kentucky, USA
10G1 Frankfort S Africa
57B2 Frankfurt Germany
46E1 Frankfurt am Main Germany
56C2 Frankfurt-an-der-Oder Germany
57C3 Fränkischer Alb Upland Germany
14A3 Franklin Indiana, USA
19B4 Franklin Louisiana, USA
16D1 Franklin Massachusetts, USA
16B2 Franklin New Jersey, USA
14C2 Franklin Pennsylvania, USA
4F2 Franklin B Can
20C1 Franklin D Roosevelt L USA
4F3 Franklin Mts Can
4J2 Franklin Str Can
111B2 Franz Josef Glacier NZ
Franz-Joseph-Land = Zemlya Frantsa Iosifa
5F5 Fraser R Can
44C3 Fraserburgh Scot
107E3 Fraser I Aust
13B2 Fraser L Can
47B1 Frasne France
47C1 Frauenfeld Switz
34D2 Fray Bentos Urug
40C2 Frazerburgh Scot
16B3 Frederica USA
56B1 Fredericia Den
16C3 Frederick Maryland, USA
15C3 Fredericksburg Virginia, USA
12H3 Frederick Sd USA
18B2 Fredericktown USA
7D5 Fredericton Can
6E3 Frederikshåb Greenland
39G7 Frederikshavn Den
15C2 Fredonia USA
39G7 Fredrikstad Nor
16B2 Freehold USA
26B1 Freeport The Bahamas
101G1 Free State Province S Africa
19A4 Freeport Texas, USA
97A4 Freetown Sierra Leone
57B3 Freiburg Germany
57C3 Freistadt Austria
106A4 Fremantle Aust
22B2 Fremont California, USA
18A1 Fremont Nebraska, USA
14B2 Fremont Ohio, USA
33G3 French Guiana Dependency, S America
109C4 Frenchmans Cap Mt Aust
105J4 French Polynesia Is Pacific O
24B2 Fresnillo Mexico

8B3 Fresno USA
22C2 Fresno R USA
47A1 Fretigney France
46B1 Frévent France
109C4 Freycinet Pen Aust
97A3 Fria Guinea
22C2 Friant USA
22C2 Friant Dam USA
52A1 Fribourg Switz
57B3 Friedrichshafen Germany
6D3 Frobisher B Can
6D3 Frobisher Bay Can
5H4 Frobisher L Can
61F4 Frolovo Russian Fed
43C4 Frome Eng
108A1 Frome R Aust
43C4 Frome,L Aust
25C3 Frontera Mexico
15C3 Front Royal USA
53B2 Frosinone Italy
73C5 Fuchuan China
73E4 Fuding China
24B2 Fuerte R Mexico
30E3 Fuerte Olimpo Par
96A2 Fuerteventura I Canary Is
72C2 Fugu China
68A2 Fuhai China
91C5 Fujairah UAE
75B1 Fuji Japan
73D4 Fujian Province, China
69F2 Fujin China
75B1 Fujinomiya Japan
74D3 Fuji-san Mt Japan
75B1 Fujisawa Japan
75B1 Fuji-Yoshida Japan
63A3 Fukang China
74C3 Fukuchiyima Japan
74D3 Fukui Japan
74C4 Fukuoka Japan
74C3 Fukushima Japan
74C4 Fukuyama Japan
57B2 Fulda Germany
57B2 Fulda R Germany
73B4 Fuling China
27L1 Fullarton Trinidad
22D4 Fullerton USA
18C2 Fulton Kentucky, USA
15C2 Fulton New York, USA
46C1 Fumay France
75C1 Funabashi Japan
96A1 Funchal Madeira
35C1 Fundão Brazil
7D5 Fundy,B of Can
101C3 Funhalouro Mozam
73B5 Funing China
72B3 Funing China
97C3 Funtua Nig
73D4 Fuqing China
101C2 Furancungo Mozam
91C4 Fürg Iran
47C1 Furka P Switz
107D5 Furneaux Group Is Aust
56C2 Fürstenwalde Germany
57C3 Fürth Germany
74D3 Furukawa Japan
6B3 Fury and Hecla St Can
74A2 Fushun Liaoning, China
73A4 Fushun Sichuan, China
74B2 Fusong China
57C3 Füssen Germany
72E2 Fu Xian China
72E1 Fuxin China
72D3 Fuyang China
72E1 Fuyuan Liaoning, China
73A4 Fuyuan Yunnan, China
68A2 Fuyun China
73D4 Fuzhou China
56C1 Fyn I Den

G

99E2 Gaalkacyo Somalia

21B2 Gabbs USA
100A2 Gabela Angola
96D1 Gabe's Tunisia
Gabian Range Mts =
98B3 Gabon Republic, Africa
100B3 Gaborone Botswana
54C2 Gabrovo Bulg
91B3 Gach Sārān Iran
17A1 Gadsden Alabama, USA
10A1 Gads L Can
53B2 Gaeta Italy
71F3 Gaferut I Pacific O
96C1 Gafsa Tunisia
60D2 Gagarin Russian Fed
97B4 Gagnoa Côte d'Ivoire
7A4 Gagnon Can
61F5 Gagra Georgia
86B1 Gaibandha India
29C4 Gaimán Arg
17B2 Gainesville Florida, USA
17B1 Gainesville Georgia, USA
19A3 Gainesville Texas, USA
42D3 Gainsborough Eng
108A2 Gairdner,L Aust
44B3 Gairloch Scot
16A3 Gaithersburg USA
87B1 Gajendragarh India
73D4 Ga Jiang R China
99D3 Galana R Kenya
103D5 Galapagos Is Pacific O
42C2 Galashiels Scot
54C1 Galaţi Rom
22B2 Galena Alaska, USA
18B2 Galena Kansas, USA
27L1 Galeota Pt Trinidad
27L1 Galera Pt Trinidad
15C2 Galeton USA
61F2 Galich Russian Fed
50A1 Galicia Region, Spain
Galilee,S of = Tiberias,L
27J1 Galina Pt Jamaica
99D1 Galladi Somalia
47C2 Gallarate Italy
87C3 Galle Sri Lanka
51B1 Gállego R Spain
Gallipoli = Gelibolu
55A2 Gallipoli Italy
38J5 Gällivare Sweden
42B2 Galloway Region Scot
42B2 Galloway,Mull of C Scot
8C3 Gallup USA
47C2 Galt Italy
96A2 Galtat Zemmour Mor
25C2 Galveston USA
11A4 Galveston B USA
34C2 Gálvez Arg
45B2 Galway County, Irish Rep
41B3 Galway Irish Rep
41B3 Galway B Irish Rep
86B1 Gamba China
97B3 Gambaga Ghana
4A3 Gambell USA
97A3 Gambia R The Gambia/Sen
97A3 Gambia,The Republic, Africa
105K5 Gambier, Is Pacific O
98B3 Gamboma Congo
100A2 Gambos Angola
87C3 Gampola Sri Lanka
99E2 Ganale Dorya R Eth
15C2 Gananoque Can
Gand = Gent
100A2 Ganda Angola
98C3 Gandajika Zaïre
84B3 Gandava Pak
7E5 Gander Can
85C4 Gändhidham India
85C4 Gandhinagar India
51B2 Gandia Spain
86B2 Ganga R India
85C3 Ganganar India

86C2 Gangaw Myan
72A2 Gangca China
82C2 Gangdise Shan Mts
China
Ganges = Ganga
86B1 Gangtok India
72B3 Gangu China
8C2 Garnett Peak Mt
USA
72B2 Ganquan China
108A3 Gantheaume C
Aust
39K8 Gantsevichi Belarus
73D4 Ganzhou China
97C3 Gao Mali
72A2 Gaolan China
72C2 Gaoping China
97B3 Gaoua Burkina
97A3 Gaoual Guinea
72D3 Gaoyou Hu L China
73C5 Gaozhou China
43D5 Gap France
79B2 Gapan Phil
84D2 Gar China
109C1 Garah Aust
21A3 Garanhuns Brazil
21A1 Garberville USA
35B2 Garça Brazil
35A2 Garcias Brazil
47D2 Garda Italy
9C3 Garden City USA
14A1 Garden Pen USA
34D3 Gardey Arg
84B2 Gardez Afghan
16C2 Gardiners I USA
16D1 Gardner USA
47D2 Gardone Italy
47D2 Gargano Italy
85B3 Garhákota India
61K2 Gari Russian Fed
100A4 Garies S Africa
99D3 Garissa Kenya
19A3 Garland USA
57C3 Garmisch-
Partenkirchen
Germany
90B2 Garmsar Iran
18A2 Garnett USA
8B2 Garnett Peak Mt
USA
48C3 Garonne R France
31A5 Garry R Scot
78B4 Garut Indon
86A2 Garwa India
14A2 Gary USA
82C2 Garyarsa China
4H3 Gary L Can
19A3 Garza-Little Elm Res
USA
90B2 Gasan Kuli
Turkmenistan
48B3 Gascogne Region,
France
18B2 Gasconade R USA
106A3 Gascoyne R Aust
18B2 Gashaka Nig
91D3 Gashua Nig
10D2 Gaspé Can
10D2 Gaspé,C de Can
94A1 Gata,C Cyprus
60C2 Gatchina
Russian Fed
42D2 Gateshead Eng
19A3 Gatesville USA
15C1 Gatineau Can
15C1 Gatineau R Can
109D1 Gatton Aust
86C1 Gauhati India
52F1 Gauja R Latvia
86A1 Gauri Phanta India
100B3 Gauteng Province,
S Africa
22B3 Gaviota USA
39H6 Gävle Sweden
108A2 Gawler Ranges Mts
Aust
72A1 Gaxun Nur L China
86A2 Gaya India
97C3 Gaya Niger
14B1 Gaylord USA
109D1 Gayndah Aust
61H1 Gayny Russian Fed
60C4 Gaysin Ukraine
94B3 Gaza Israel

94B3 Gaza
Autonomous Region
S W Asia
92C2 Gaziantep Turk
97B4 Gbaringa Lib
58B2 Gdańsk Pol
58B2 Gdańsk,G of Pol
39K7 Gdov Russian Fed
58B2 Gdynia Pol
94A3 Gebel Halâl Mt
Egypt
92B4 Gebel Katherina Mt
Egypt
94A3 Gebel Libni Mt
Egypt
94A3 Gebel Maghâra Mt
Egypt
99D1 Gedaref Sudan
55C3 Gediz R Turk
56C2 Gedser Den
46C1 Geel Belg
108B3 Geelong Aust
109C4 Geeveston Aust
97D3 Geidam Nig
46D1 Geilenkirchen
Germany
99D3 Geita Tanz
73A5 Gejiu China
53B3 Gela Italy
99E2 Geladi Eth
46D1 Geldern Germany
55C2 Gelibolu Turk
92B2 Gelidonya Burun
Turk
46D1 Gelsenkirchen
Germany
39F8 Gelting Germany
77C5 Gemas Malay
46C1 Gembloux Belg
98B2 Gemena Zaïre
92C2 Gemerek Turk
92A1 Gemlik Turk
52B1 Gemona Italy
100B3 Gemsbok Nat Pk
Botswana
98C1 Geneina Sudan
34C3 General Acha Arg
34C3 General Alvear
Buenos Aires, Arg
34B2 General Alvear
Mendoza, Arg
34C2 General Arenales Arg
34D3 General Belgrano
Arg
112B2 General Belgrano
Base Ant
112C2 General Bernardo
O'Higgins Base Ant
34D3 General Conesa
Buenos Aires, Arg
30D3 General Eugenio A
Garay Par
34D3 General Guido Arg
34C3 General La Madrid
Arg
34C2 General Levalle Arg
30C4 General Manuel
Belgrano Mt Arg
34D3 General Paz
Buenos Aires, Arg
34C3 General Pico Arg
34C2 General Pinto Arg
34D3 General Pirán Arg
29C3 General Roca Arg
112C3 General San Martin
Base Ant
79C4 General Santos Phil
34C3 General Viamonte
Arg
34C3 General Villegas Arg
15C2 Genesee R USA
15C2 Geneseo USA
18A1 Geneva Nebraska,
USA
15C2 Geneva New York,
USA
Geneva,L of =
LeLéman
52A1 Genève Switz
50B2 Genil R Spain
Genoa = Genova
109C3 Genoa Aust
52A2 Genova Italy

32J7 Genovesa I Ecuador
46B1 Gent Belg
78B4 Genteng Indon
56C2 Genthin Germany
93E1 Geokchay Azerbaijan
100B4 George S Africa
7D4 George R Can
109C2 George,L Aust
17B2 George,L Florida,
USA
15D2 George,L New York,
USA
111A2 George Sd NZ
109C4 George Town Aust
15C3 Georgetown
Delaware, USA
33F2 Georgetown Guyana
14B3 Georgetown
Kentucky, USA
77C4 George Town Malay
27N2 Georgetown
St Vincent and the
Grenadines
17C1 Georgetown S
Carolina, USA
19A3 Georgetown Texas,
USA
97A3 Georgetown The
Gambia
112C8 George V Land
Region, Ant
65F5 Georgia Republic,
Europe
112C12 Georg Forster Base
Ant
17B1 Georgia State, USA
14B1 Georgian B Can
13C3 Georgia,Str of Can
106C3 Georgina R Aust
61F5 Georgiyevsk
Russian Fed
57C2 Gera Germany
46C1 Geraardsbergen Belg
111B2 Geraldine NZ
106A3 Geraldton Aust
10B2 Geraldton Can
94B3 Gerar R Israel
4C3 Gerdine,Mt USA
12E2 Gerdova Peak Mt
USA
77C4 Gerik Malay
60B4 Gerlachovský Štit Mt
Pol
13C1 Germansen Lodge
Can
56C2 Germany
Republic, Europe
101G1 Germiston S Africa
46D1 Gerolstein Germany
51C1 Gerona Spain
46D1 Gerona Germany
99E2 Gestro R Eth
50B1 Getafe Spain
16A3 Gettysburg
Pennsylvania, USA
93D2 Gevas Turk
55B2 Gevgelija Macedonia
47B1 Gex France
94C2 Ghabaghib Syria
96C1 Ghadamis Libya
90B2 Ghaem Shahr Iran
86A1 Ghâghara R India
97B4 Ghana Republic,
Africa
100B3 Ghanzi Botswana
96C1 Ghardaïa Alg
95A1 Gharyan Libya
95A2 Ghät Libya
86A2 Ghätsila India
84C3 Ghazi Khan Pak
84B2 Ghazni Afghan
54C1 Gheorgheni Rom
86E4 Ghudamis Alg
90D3 Ghurian Afghan
95B2 Gialo Libya
99E2 Giamame Somalia
53C3 Giarre Italy
100A3 Gibeon Namibia
50A2 Gibraltar Colony,
SW Europe
50A2 Gibraltar,Str of
Spain/Africa
106B3 Gibson Desert Aust
20B1 Gibsons Can

87B1 Giddalür India
99D2 Gidolē Eth
57B2 Giessen Germany
17B2 Gifford USA
74D3 Gifu Japan
42B2 Gigha I Scot
52B2 Giglio I Italy
50A1 Gijón Spain
107D2 Gilbert R Aust
13C2 Gilbert,Mt Can
101C2 Gile Mozam
94B2 Gilead Region,
Jordan
95B2 Gilf Kebir Plat Egypt
109C2 Gilgandra Aust
84C1 Gilgit Pak
84C1 Gilgit R Pak
108C2 Gilgunnia Aust
7A4 Gillam Can
108A2 Gilles L Aust
13B2 Gill I Can
14A1 Gills Rock USA
14A2 Gilman USA
22B2 Gilroy USA
8D1 Gimli Can
101H1 Gingindlovu S Africa
79C4 Gingoog Phil
99E2 Ginir Eth
55B3 Gióna Mt Greece
109C3 Gippsland Mts Aust
14B2 Girard USA
32C3 Girardot Colombia
44C3 Girdle Ness Pen
Scot
93C1 Giresun Turk
85C4 Gir Hills India
98B2 Giri R Zaïre
86B2 Giridih India
Girona = Gerona
48B2 Gironde R France
42B2 Girvan Scot
111C2 Gisborne NZ
46A2 Gisors France
46H2 Gisenyi Zaïre
99C3 Gitega Burundi
54C2 Giubiu,R = Juba,R
54C2 Giurgiu Rom
58C2 Gizycko Pol
55B2 Gjirokastër Alb
4J3 Gjoatlaven Can
39G6 Gjøvik Nor
7D5 Glace Bay Can
12G3 Glacier Bay Nat Mon
USA
13E3 Glacier Nat Pk USA/
Can
20B1 Glacier Peak Mt
USA
6B2 Glacier Str Can
107E3 Gladstone
Queensland, Aust
108A2 Gladstone S Aust,
Aust
109C4 Gladstone Tasmania,
Aust
14A1 Gladstone USA
38A1 Gláma R Iceland
39G6 Gláma R Nor
46D2 Glan R Germany
47C1 Glarner Mts Switz
47C1 Glarus Switz
18A2 Glasco USA
8C2 Glasgow Montana,
USA
42B2 Glasgow Scot
42B2 Glasgow, City of
Division, Scot
16B3 Glassboro USA
43C4 Glastonbury Eng
61H2 Glazov Russian Fed
59B3 Gleisdorf Austria
110C1 Glen Afton NZ
16A3 Glen Burnie USA
101H1 Glencoe S Africa
9B3 Glendale Arizona,
USA
22C3 Glendale California,
USA
12E2 Glenhallen USA
109D1 Glen Innes Aust
109C1 Glenmorgan Aust
109D2 Glenreagh Aust
16A3 Glen Rock USA
19A3 Glen Rose USA

Glenrothes

Gunung Besar

110C1	Hastings NZ
108B2	Hatfield Aust
12B1	Hatham Inlet USA
85D3	Hāthras India
78D2	Ha Tinh Viet
108B2	Hattah Aust
11C3	Hatteras,C USA
19C3	Hattiesburg USA
59B3	Hatvan Hung
76D3	Hau Bon Viet
99E2	Haud Region, Eth
39F7	Haugesund Nor
110C1	Hauhungaroa Range Mts NZ
13F1	Haultain R Can
110B1	Hauraki G NZ
111A3	Hauroko,L NZ
47C1	Hausstock Mt Switz
96B1	Haut Atlas Mts Mor
98C2	Haute Kotto Region, CAR
46C1	Hautes Fagnes Mts Belg
46B1	Hautmont Belg
96B1	Hauts Plateaux Mts Alg
90D3	Hauzdar Iran
18B1	Havana USA
	Havana = Habana
87B3	Havankulam Sri Lanka
110C1	Havelock North NZ
43B4	Haverfordwest Wales
16D1	Haverhill USA
87B2	Hāveri India
16C2	Haverstraw USA
59B3	Havlíčkův Brod Czech Republic
8C2	Havre USA
16A3	Havre de Grace USA
7D4	Havre-St-Pierre Can
54C2	Havsa Turk
21C4	Hawaii / Hawaiian Is
21C4	Hawaii Volcanoes Nat Pk Hawaiian Is
111A2	Hawea,L NZ
110B1	Hawera NZ
42C2	Hawick Scot
111A2	Hawkdun Range Mts NZ
110C1	Hawke B NZ
109C2	Hawke,C Aust
108A2	Hawker Aust
76B1	Hawng Luk Myan
93D3	Hawr al Habbaniyah L Iraq
93E3	Hawr al Hammār L Iraq
21B2	Hawthorne USA
108B2	Hay Aust
5G3	Hay R Can
46D2	Hayange France
4B3	Haycock USA
7A4	Hayes R Can
6D2	Hayes Halvo Region Greenland
12E2	Hayes,Mt USA
5G3	Hay River Can
18A2	Haysville USA
22A2	Hayward California, USA
86B2	Hazārībāg India
46B1	Hazebrouck France
19B3	Hazelhurst USA
4G2	Hazel Str Can
5F4	Hazelton Can
13B1	Hazelton Mts Can
6C1	Hazen L Can
94B3	Hazeva Israel
16B2	Hazleton USA
22A1	Healdsburg USA
108C3	Healesville Aust
12E2	Healy USA
104B6	Heard I Indian O
19A3	Hearne USA
10B2	Hearst Can
72D2	Hebei Province, China
109C1	Hebel Aust
72C2	Hebi China
72C2	Hebian China
7D4	Hebron Can
94B3	Hebron Israel
18A1	Hebron Nebraska, USA
5E4	Hecate Str Can
12H3	Hecela I USA
73B5	Hechi China
4G2	Hecla and Griper B Can
111C2	Hector,Mt NZ
38G6	Hede Sweden
39H6	Hedemora Sweden
20C1	He Devil Mt USA
56B2	Heerenveen Neth
46C1	Heerlen Neth
	Hefa = Haifa
73D3	Hefei China
73B4	Hefeng China
65F2	Hegang China
73B5	Hegura-jima I Japan
54B3	Heidan R Jordan
101G1	Heidelberg Transvaal, S Africa
57B3	Heidelberg Germany
63E2	Heihe China
101G1	Heilbron S Africa
57B3	Heilbronn Germany
57C3	Heiligenstadt Germany
38K6	Heinola Fin
73B4	Hejiang China
6J3	Hekla Mt Iceland
76C1	Hekou Viet
73A5	Hekou Yaozou Zizhixian China
72B2	Helan China
72B2	Helan Shan Mt China
19B3	Helena Arkansas, USA
8B2	Helena Montana, USA
22D3	Helendale USA
71E3	Helen Reef / Pacific O
44B3	Helensburgh Scot
91B4	Helleh R Iran
51B2	Hellin Spain
20C1	Hells Canyon R USA
46D1	Hellweg Region, Germany
22B2	Helm USA
80E2	Helmand R Afghan
100A3	Helmeringhausen Namibia
46C1	Helmond Neth
44C2	Helmsdale Scot
74B2	Helong China
39G7	Helsingborg Sweden
	Helsingfors = Helsinki
56C1	Helsingor Den
38J6	Helsinki Fin
43B4	Helston Eng
92B4	Helwân Egypt
19A3	Hempstead USA
39H7	Hemse Sweden
72A3	Henan China
72C3	Henan Province, China
110B1	Hen and Chicken Is NZ
14A3	Henderson Kentucky, USA
9B3	Henderson Nevada, USA
19B3	Henderson Texas, USA
73E5	Heng-ch'un Taiwan
68B4	Hengduan Shan Mts China
56B2	Hengelo Neth
72B2	Hengshan China
72D2	Hengshui China
76D1	Heng Xian China
73C4	Hengyang China
77A4	Henhoaha Nicobar Is India
43D4	Henley-on-Thames Eng
16B3	Henlopen,C USA
7B4	Henrietta Maria,C Can
18A2	Henryetta USA
112C2	Henryk Arctowski Base Ant
6D3	Henry Kater Pen Can
68C2	Hentiyn Nuruu Mts Mongolia
76B2	Henzada Myan
73B5	Hepu China
80E2	Herat Afghan
5H4	Herbert Can
110C2	Herbertville NZ
46E1	Herborn Germany
26A4	Heredia Costa Rica
43C3	Hereford Eng
43C3	Hereford & Worcester County, Eng
46C1	Herentals Belg
47B1	Héricourt France
18A2	Herington USA
111A3	Heriot NZ
47C1	Herisau Switz
15C2	Herkimer USA
44E1	Herma Ness Pen Scot
109C2	Hermidale Aust
111B2	Hermiston USA
112B2	Hermon,Mt = Jebel ash Shaykh
24A2	Hermosillo Mexico
16A2	Herndon Pennsylvania, USA
22C2	Herndon California, USA
46D1	Herne Germany
56C1	Herning Den
90A2	Herowābad Iran
52A2	Herrera del Duque Spain
16A2	Hershey USA
43D4	Hertford County, Eng
94B2	Herzliyya Israel
46C1	Hesbaye Region, Belg
46B1	Hesdin France
72B2	Heshui China
22D3	Hesperia USA
12H2	Hess R Can
57B2	Hessen State, Germ
22C2	Hetch Hetchy Res USA
42C2	Hexham Eng
73C5	He Xian China
73C5	Heyuan China
108B3	Heywood Aust
72D2	Heze China
17B2	Hialeah USA
10A2	Hibbing USA
111C2	Hicks Bay NZ
109C3	Hicks,Pt Aust
23B1	Hidalgo State, Mexico
24B2	Hidalgo del Parral Mexico
35B1	Hidrolândia Brazil
96A2	Hierro / Canary Is
75C1	Higashine Japan
74B4	Higashi-suidō Str Japan
28D2	High Desert USA
19B4	High Island USA
43D4	Highland Division, Scot
22D3	Highland USA
22C1	Highland Peak Mt USA
16B2	Highlands Falls USA
11B3	High Point USA
13D1	High Prairie Can
5G4	High River Can
16B2	High Springs USA
16B2	Hightstown USA
43D4	High Wycombe Eng
39J7	Hiiumaa / Estonia
80B3	Hijāz Region, S Arabia
75B2	Hikigawa Japan
75B1	Hikone Japan
110B1	Hikurangi NZ
56B2	Hildesheim Germany
27R3	Hillaby,Mt Barbados
56C1	Hillerod Den
14B3	Hillsboro Ohio, USA
20B1	Hillsboro Oregon, USA
19A3	Hillsboro Texas, USA
108C2	Hillston Aust
44E1	Hillswick Scot
21C4	Hilo Hawaiian Is
93C2	Hilvan Turk
56B2	Hilversum Neth
84D2	Himachal Pradesh State, India
82B3	Himalaya Mts Asia
85C4	Himatnagar India
74C4	Himeji Japan
84D3	Himi Japan
92C3	Hims Syria
11C3	Hinchinbrook Entrance USA
12E2	Hinchinbrook I USA
85D3	Hindaun India
84B1	Hindu Kush Mts Afghan
87B2	Hindupur India
13D1	Hines Creek Can
85D4	Hinganghāt India
69E2	Hinggan Ling Upland China
85B3	Hingoli India
38H5	Hinnoya I Nor
16C1	Hinsdale USA
13D2	Hinton Can
34B2	Hipolito Itrogoyen Arg
86A2	Hīrakud Res India
92B2	Hīrfanli Baraji Res Turk
87B2	Hirihar India
74E2	Hirosaki Japan
74C4	Hiroshima Japan
46C2	Hirson France
54C2	Hîrsova Rom
56B1	Hirtshals Den
84D3	Hisār India
24C3	Hispaniola / Caribbean S
94C3	Hisyah Syria
93D3	Hit Iraq
74E3	Hitachi Japan
75C1	Hitachi-Ota Japan
43D4	Hitchin Eng
38F6	Hitra I Nor
75A2	Hiuchi-nada B Japan
75A2	Hivasa Japan
56B1	Hjørring Den
76B1	Hka R Myan
97C4	Ho Ghana
76D1	Hoa Binh Viet
76D3	Hoa Da Viet
109C4	Hobart Aust
9C3	Hobbs USA
56B1	Hobro Den
13C2	Hobson L Can
99E2	Hobyo Somalia
76D3	Ho Chi Minh Viet
57C3	Hochkönig Mt Austria
54B1	Hódmezö'hely Hung
59B3	Hodonín Czech Republic
74B2	Hoeryong N Korea
57C2	Hof Germany
38B2	Hofsjökull Mts Iceland
74C4	Höfu Japan
96C2	Hoggar Upland Alg
46D1	Hohe Acht Mt Germany
72C1	Hohhot China
6J3	Höhn Iceland
68B3	Hoh Sai Hu L China
82C2	Hoh Xil Shan Mts China
99D2	Hoima Uganda
86C1	Hojāi India
75A2	Hojo Japan
110B1	Hokianga Harbour B NZ
111B2	Hokitika NZ
74E2	Hokkaidō Japan
74E2	Hokmābād Iran
109C3	Holbrook Aust
9B3	Holbrook USA
19A2	Holdenville USA
87B2	Hole Narsipur India
27R3	Holetown Barbados
26B2	Holguín Cuba
111B2	Holitika NZ
12C2	Holitna USA

59B3	Hollabrunn Austria
14A2	Holland USA
22B2	Hollister USA
19C3	Holly Springs USA
22C3	Hollywood California, USA
17B2	Hollywood Florida, USA
4G2	Holman Island Can
38J6	Holmsund Sweden
94B2	Holon Israel
56B1	Holstebro Den
6E3	Holsteinborg Greenland
14B2	Holt USA
18A2	Holton USA
12C2	Holy Cross USA
42B3	Holyhead Wales
42D2	Holy I Eng
43B3	Holy I Wales
16C1	Holyoke Massachusetts, USA
86C2	Homalin Myan
6D3	Home B Can
12D3	Homer Alaska, USA
19B3	Homer Louisiana, USA
111A2	Homer Tunnel NZ
17B1	Homerville USA
21C3	Homestead USA
17A1	Homewood USA
87B1	Homnābād India
101C3	Homoine Mozam
25D3	Hondo R Mexico
25D3	Hondo R USA
25D3	Honduras Republic, Cent America
25D3	Honduras,G of Honduras
39G6	Hønefoss Nor
15C2	Honesdale USA
21A1	Honey L USA
76C1	Hong R Viet
76D1	Hon Gai Viet
73A4	Hongguo China
73C4	Hong Hu L China
72B2	Hongshui China
73C4	Hongjiang China
68D2	Hong Kong Colony, S E Asia
68D2	Hongor Mongolia
73B5	Hongshui He R China
72A3	Hongyuan China
72D3	Hongze Hu L China
107E1	Honiara Solomon Is
77C4	Hon Khoai I Camb
76D3	Hon Lan I Viet
38K4	Hønningsvåg Nor
21C4	Honolulu Hawaiian Is
77C4	Hon Panjang I Viet
74D3	Honshu I Japan
20B1	Hood,Mt USA
20B1	Hood River USA
45C2	Hook Head C Irish Rep
12G3	Hoonah USA
12A2	Hooper Bay USA
101G1	Hoopstad S Africa
56A2	Hoorn Neth
9B3	Hoover Dam USA
12E2	Hope Alaska, USA
19B3	Hope Arkansas, USA
13C3	Hope Can
7D4	Hopedale Can
64D2	Hopen I Barents S
6D3	Hopes Advance,C Can
108B3	Hopetoun Aust
100B3	Hopetown S Africa
18C2	Hopkinsville USA
20B1	Hoquiam USA
93D1	Horasan Turk
99F1	Hordiyo Somalia
47C1	Horgen Switz
105H5	Horizon Depth Pacific O
91C4	Hormuz,Str of Oman/ Iran
59B3	Horn Austria
6H3	Horn C Iceland
38H5	Hornavan L Sweden
19B3	Hornbeck USA
20B2	Hornbrook USA
111B2	Hornby NZ
7B5	Hornepayne Can
4F3	Horn Mts Can
42D3	Hornsea Eng
72B1	Horn Uul Mt Mongolia
30E3	Horqueta Par
15C2	Horseheads USA
56C1	Horsens Den
20B1	Horseshoe Bay Can
108B3	Horsham Aust
43D4	Horsham Eng
39G7	Horten Nor
4F3	Horton R Can
78C2	Hose Mts Malay
85D4	Hoshangābād India
84D2	Hoshiārpur India
87B1	Hospet India
29C7	Hoste I Chile
82B2	Hotan China
19B3	Hot Springs Arkansas, USA
8C2	Hot Springs S. Dakota, USA
4G3	Hottah Can
46D2	Houdan France
72C2	Houma China
19B4	Houma China
16C2	Housatonic R USA
13B2	Houston Can
19C3	Houston Mississippi, USA
19A4	Houston Texas, USA
106A3	Houtman Is Aust
68B2	Hovd Mongolia
68C1	Hövsgöl Nuur L Mongolia
12C1	Howard City USA
12C1	Howard P USA
109C3	Howe,C Aust
101H1	Howick S Africa
44C2	Hoy I Scot
39F6	Høyanger Nor
59B2	Hradec-Králové Czech Republic
59B3	Hranice Czech Republic
59B3	Hron R Slovakia
73E5	Hsin-chu Taiwan
73C5	Hsüeh Shan Mt Taiwan
72B2	Huachi China
72C1	Huade China
72D3	Huaibei China
72D3	Huaibin China
72D3	Huai He R China
73C4	Huaihua China
72D3	Huainan China
69E4	Hua-lien Taiwan
72D3	Huallaga R Peru
32B5	Huallanca Peru
32B5	Huamachuco Peru
100A2	Huambo Angola
30C2	Huanay Bol
32B5	Huancabamba Peru
32B6	Huancavelica Peru
32B6	Huancayo Peru
72D2	Huang He R China
72B2	Huangling China
76D2	Huangliu China
72C3	Huangpi China
72D3	Huangshan China
72D3	Huangshi China
34C3	Huanguelén Arg
72E4	Huangyan China
72C3	Huanren China
32B5	Huánuco Peru
30C2	Huanuni Bol
72B2	Huan Xian China
32B5	Huaráz Peru
32B5	Huarmey Peru
32B5	Huascarán Mt Peru
30B4	Huasco Chile
23B2	Huatusco Mexico
23B1	Huauchinango Mexico
23B2	Huautla Mexico
72B3	Hua Xian China
24B2	Huayapan R Mexico
73C3	Hubei Province, China
87B1	Hubli India
34C3	Hucal Arg
78A2	Huch'ang N Korea
42D3	Huddersfield Eng
39H6	Hudiksvall Sweden
17B2	Hudson Florida, USA
14B2	Hudson Michigan, USA
16C1	Hudson New York, USA
12B2	Hudson R USA
5H4	Hudson Bay Can
13C1	Hudson's Hope Can
6C3	Hudson Str Can
76D2	Hue Viet
11B1	Huelati Mexico
50A2	Huelva Spain
23A2	Hueramo Mexico
51B2	Huércal Overa Spain
51B1	Huesca Spain
23B2	Huexotla Hist Site Mexico
10D3	Hughenden Aust
12D1	Hughes USA
86B2	Hugli R India
19A3	Hugo USA
73D4	Hui'an China
110C1	Huiarau Range Mts NZ
74B2	Huich'ŏn N Korea
74B2	Huifa He R China
32B3	Huila Mt Colombia
73D5	Huilai China
73A4	Huili China
74B2	Huinan China
34C2	Huinca Renancó Arg
25C3	Huixtla Mexico
23A4	Huize China
73C5	Huizhou China
23B2	Hujuápan de León Mexico
69F2	Hulin China
15C1	Hull Can
42D3	Hull Eng
58B1	Hultsfred Sweden
63D3	Hulun Nur L China
69E1	Huma China
33E5	Humaitá Brazil
100B4	Humansdorp S Africa
42D3	Humber R Eng
5H4	Humboldt Can
20B2	Humboldt B USA
6D2	Humboldt Gletscher Gl Greenland
21B2	Humboldt R USA
108C1	Humeburn Aust
109C3	Hume,L Aust
100A2	Humpata Angola
22C2	Humphreys USA
38A1	Húnaflói B Iceland
72C2	Hunan Province, China
74C2	Hunchun China
13C2	Hundred Mile House Can
54B1	Hunedoara Rom
59B3	Hungary Republic, Europe
108B1	Hungerford Aust
74B3	Hüngnam N Korea
74B2	Hunjiang China
46D2	Hunsrück Mts, Germany
109D2	Hunter R Aust
13B2	Hunter I Can
109C4	Hunter Is Aust
12D2	Hunter,Mt USA
14A3	Huntingburg USA
43D3	Huntingdon Eng
14A2	Huntingdon Indiana, USA
14B3	Huntington W Virginia, USA
22C4	Huntington Beach USA
22C2	Huntington L USA
110C1	Huntly NZ
44C3	Huntly Scot
12J2	Hunt,Mt USA
108A1	Hunt Pen Aust
17A1	Huntsville Alabama, USA
15C1	Huntsville Can
19A3	Huntsville Texas, USA
76D2	Huong Khe Viet
71F4	Huon Peninsula Pen PNG
109C4	Huonville Anst
14B1	Hurd,C USA
80B3	Hurghada Egypt
8D2	Huron S. Dakota, USA
14B1	Huron,L Can/USA
34A2	Hurtado Chile
111B2	Hurunui R NZ
38B1	Húsavík Iceland
54C1	Huşi Rom
39G7	Huskvarna Sweden
12C1	Huslia USA
94B2	Husn Jordan
56B2	Husum Germany
109C1	Hutton,Mt USA
72D2	Hutuo He R China
46C1	Huy Belg
72A2	Huzhu China
52C2	Hvar I Croatia
100B2	Hwange Zim
100B2	Hwange Nat Pk Zim
15D2	Hyannis USA
68B2	Hyaryas Nuur L Mongolia
5E4	Hydaburg Can
16C2	Hyde Park USA
87B1	Hyderābād India
85B3	Hyderabad Pak
49D3	Hyères France
12J2	Hyland R Can
72D2	Hyndman Peak Mt USA
38K6	Hyrynsalmi Fin
13D1	Hythe Can
74C4	Hyūga Japan
39J6	Hyvikää Fin

I

31C4	Iaçu Brazil
54C2	Ialomiţa R Rom
54C1	Iaşi Rom
97C4	Ibadan Nig
32B3	Ibagué Colombia
32B3	Ibarra Ecuador
35B1	Ibiá Brazil
30E4	Ibicuí R Brazil
34D2	Ibicuy Arg
51C2	Ibiza Spain
51C2	Ibiza I Spain
10D2	Ibo Mozam
31C4	Ibotirama Brazil
91C5	'Ibri Oman
31C4	Içá R Brazil
32D3	Içana Brazil
38A1	Iceland Republic, N Atlantic O
13C2	Ice Mt Can
87A1	Ichalkaranji India
74E3	Ichihara Japan
75B1	Ichinomiya Japan
74E3	Ichinoseki Japan
12F3	Icy B USA
4B2	Icy C USA
19B3	Idabell USA
8B2	Idaho Falls USA
20B2	Idanha USA
46D2	Idar Oberstein Germany
95A2	Idehan Marzūg Desert Libya
95A2	Idehan Ubari Desert Libya
96C2	Idelès Alg
68B2	Iderlym Gol R Mongolia
95C2	Idfu Egypt
55B3	Idhi Oros Mt Greece
55B3	Ídhra I Greece
98B3	Idiofa Zaire
12D2	Iditarod R USA
92C2	Idlib Syria
39K7	Idritsa Russian Fed
100B4	Idutywa S Africa
55C3	Ierápetra Greece
46B1	Ieper Belg

Isla Magdalena

24A2 Isla Magdalena / Mexico
27E4 Isla Margarita Ven
34A3 Isla Mocha Chile
17B2 Islamorada USA
10A1 Island L Can
108A2 Island Lg Aust
110B1 Islands,B of NZ
32A4 Isla Puná / Ecuador
103D6 Isla San Ambrosia / Pacific O
103D6 Isla San Felix / Pacific O
24A2 Isla Santa Margarita / Mexico
34A3 Isla Santa Maria / Chile
51C2 Islas Baleares Is Spain
96A2 Islas Canarias Is Atlantic O
51C2 Islas Columbretes Is Spain
25D3 Islas de la Bahia Is Honduras
26A4 Islas del Maíz Is Caribbean S
33E1 Islas de Margarita Is Ven
29C7 Islas Diego Ramírez Is Chile
32J7 Islas Galapagos Is Pacific O
30H6 Islas Juan Fernández Chile
32D1 Islas los Roques Is Ven
Islas Malvinas = Falkland Is
105L3 Islas Revilla Gigedo Is Pacific O
29C7 Islas Wollaston Is Chile
97A3 Isla Tidra / Maur
29C7 Isla Wellington / Chile
48C2 Isle R France
104B5 Isle Amsterdam / Indian O
43D4 Isle of Wight / Eng
10B2 Isle Royale / USA
104B5 Isle St Paul / Indian O
104A6 Isles Crozet / Indian O
105J4 Isles de la Société Pacific O
105K5 Isles Gambier Is Pacific O
101D2 Isles Glorieuses / Madag
104B6 Isles Kerguelen Is Indian O
105K4 Isles Marquises Is Pacific O
105J4 Isles Tuamotu Is Pacific O
105J5 Isles Tubaï Is Pacific O
22B1 Isleton USA
92B3 Ismâ'ilîya Egypt
101D3 Isoanala Madag
101C2 Isoka Zambia
53B3 Isola Egadi / Italy
52B2 Isola Ponziane / Italy
52C2 Isole Lipari Is Italy
52C2 Isoles Tremiti Is Italy
75B1 Isosaki Japan
92B2 Isparta Turk
94B2 Israel Republic, S W Asia
51C1 Isser R Alg
48C2 Issoire France
47A2 Issoudun France
92A1 Istanbul Turk
55B3 Istiáia Greece
25C3 Istmo de Tehuantepec Isthmus Mexico
17B2 Istokpoga,L USA
52B1 Istra Pen Croatia
35B1 Itaberai Brazil
35C1 Itabira Brazil
35C2 Itabirito Brazil

31D4 Itabuna Brazil
33F4 Itacoatiara Brazil
32B2 Itagui Colombia
33F4 Itaituba Brazil
30G4 Itajaí Brazil
35B2 Itajuba Brazil
52B2 Italy Republic, Europe
35D1 Itamaraju Brazil
35C1 Itamarandiba Brazil
35C1 Itambacuri Brazil
35C1 Itambe Mt Brazil
86C1 Itãnagar India
35B2 Itanhaém Brazil
35C1 Itanhém Brazil
35C1 Itanhém R Brazil
35C1 Itaobim Brazil
35B2 Itapecerica Brazil
31D5 Itapesrua Brazil
35B2 Itapetinga Brazil
31C5 Itapetininga Brazil
35B2 Itapeva Brazil
31D2 Itapipoca Brazil
35B2 Itapuranga Brazil
30E4 Itaqui Brazil
35C1 Itarantim Brazil
35B2 Itararé Brazil
35B2 Itararé R Brazil
35C2 Itaúna Brazil
33E6 Iténez R Brazil/Bol
15C2 Ithaca USA
48D2 Itimbiri R Zaire
35C1 Itinga Brazil
6E3 Ithrdeq Greenland
75B2 Ito Japan
74D3 Itoigawa Japan
33E6 Itonomas R Bol
35B2 Itu Brazil
35B1 Itumbiara Brazil
35A1 Iturama Brazil
30C3 Iturbe Arg
35B1 Iturutaba Brazil
58B2 Itzehoe Germany
58D2 Ivacevichi Belarus
35A2 Ivai R Brazil
54A5 Ivalo Fin
Ivangrad = Montenegro, Yugos
108B2 Ivanhoe Aust
59C3 Ivano-Frankovsk Ukraine
61F2 Ivanovo Russian Fed
61F2 Ivanovo Division, Russian Fed
65H3 Ivdel' Russian Fed
98B2 Ivindo R Gabon
101D3 Ivohibe Madag
101D2 Ivongo Soanierana Madag
Ivory Coast = Côte d'Ivoire
52A1 Ivrea Italy
6C3 Ivujivik Can
74C4 Iwaki Japan
74E2 Iwanai Japan
97C4 Iwo Nig
69G4 Iwo Jima / Japan
23B1 Ixmiquilpa Mexico
23A2 Ixtapa Mexico
23A1 Ixtlan Mexico
60C4 Izanul' Ukraine
92A2 Izmir Turk
92A1 Izmir Körfezi R Turk
92A1 Iznik Turk
92A1 Iznik Golü L Turk
94C2 Izra' Syria
23B2 Izúcar de Matamoros Mexico
75B2 Izumi-sano Japan
75A1 Izumo Japan
74D4 Izu-shotõ Is Japan

J

95B1 Jabal al Akhdar Mts Libya
94C2 Jabal al 'Arab Syria
94C2 Jabal as Sawdã Mts Libya

91B5 Jabal az Zannah UAE
94C1 Jabal Halîmah Mt Leb/Syria
83B3 Jabalpur India
59B2 Jablonec nad Nisou Czech Republic
31D3 Jaboatão Brazil
35B2 Jaboticabal Brazil
51B1 Jaca Spain
23B1 Jacala Mexico
33F5 Jacareacanga Brazil
35B2 Jacareí Brazil
30F3 Jacarezinho Brazil
94B3 Jadaf Mt Iraq
35C1 Jacinto Brazil
13F2 Jackfish L Can
109C1 Jackson Aust
22B1 Jackson California, USA
14B2 Jackson Michigan, USA
19B3 Jackson Mississippi, USA
18C2 Jackson Missouri, USA
14B3 Jackson Ohio, USA
11B3 Jackson Tennessee, USA
111B2 Jackson,C NZ
111A2 Jackson Head Pt NZ
19B3 Jacksonville Arkansas, USA
17B1 Jacksonville Florida, USA
18B2 Jacksonville Illinois, USA
17C1 Jacksonville N Carolina, USA
19A3 Jacksonville Texas, USA
17B1 Jacksonville Beach USA
26C3 Jacmel Haiti
84B3 Jacobabad India
31C4 Jacobina Brazil
23A2 Jacona Mexico
32B5 Jaén Peru
50B2 Jaén Spain
Jaffa = Tel Aviv Yafo
108A3 Jaffa,C Aust
87B3 Jaffna Sri Lanka
86B2 Jagannathganj Ghat Bang
87C1 Jagdalpur India
91C4 Jagin R Iran
87B1 Jagtial India
29F2 Jaguarão R Brazil
35B1 Jahrom Iran
85D5 Jaina India
72A2 Jaina China
85D3 Jaipur India
85C3 Jaisalmer India
90C2 Jajarm Iran
52C2 Jajce Bosnia-Herzegovina
70B4 Jakarta Indon
6E3 Jakobshavn Greenland
38J6 Jakobstad Fin
23B2 Jalaca Mexico
84B2 Jalai-Kut Afghan
84D2 Jalandhar India
23B2 Jalapa Mexico
35A2 Jales Brazil
86B1 Jaleswar Nepal
85D4 Jalgaon India
97D4 Jalingo Nig
51B1 Jalón R Spain
85C3 Jalor India
23A1 Jalostotitlan Mexico
86B1 Jalpäiguri India
23B1 Jalpan Mexico
95B2 Jalü Oasis Libya
32A4 Jama Ecuador
26B3 Jamaica / Caribbean S
26B3 Jamaica Chan Caribbean S
86B2 Jamalpur Bang
78A3 Jambi Indon
85C4 Jambusar India
7B4 James B Can
5J5 Jameston USA

108A2 Jamestown Aust
8D2 Jamestown N. Dakota, USA
15C2 Jamestown New York, USA
16D2 Jamestown Rhode Island, USA
23J2 Jamiltepec Mexico
87B1 Jamkhandi India
84C2 Jammu India
84D2 Jammu and Kashmir State, India
85B4 Jamnagar India
84C3 Jampur Pak
86B3 Jämsä Fin
86B2 Jamshedpur India
90B3 Jandaq Iran
86B1 Janakpur Nepal
35C1 Janaüba Brazil
90B3 Jandaq Iran
100D1 Jandowae Aust
1B1 Jan Mayen / Norwegian S
35C1 Januária Brazil
85D4 Jaora India
51 Japan Empire, E Asia
74C3 Japan,S of S E Asia
104F2 Japan Trench Pacific O
32D4 Japurá R Brazil
93C2 Jarãbulus Syria
33B3 Jaraguá Brazil
51B1 Jarama R Spain
94B2 Jarash Jordan
30E3 Jardim Brazil
51B2 Jardin R Spain
26B2 Jardines de la Reina Is Cuba
Jargalant = Hovd
86C1 Jaria Jhãnjail Bang
46C2 Jarny France
58B2 Jarocin Pol
59C2 Jaroslaw Pol
38G6 Järpen Sweden
72B2 Jartai China
85C4 Jasdan India
97C4 Jasikan Ghana
91C4 Jãsk Iran
59C3 Jaslo Pol
29D6 Jason Is Falkland Is
18B2 Jasper Arkansas, USA
13D2 Jasper Can
17B1 Jasper Florida, USA
14A3 Jasper Indiana, USA
19B3 Jasper Texas, USA
13D2 Jasper Nat Pk Can
35B1 Jataí Brazil
35A1 Jataí Brazil
51B2 Jativa Spain
35B2 Jaú Brazil
32B6 Jauja Peru
86A1 Jaunpur India
Java = Jawa
87B2 Javadi Hills India
70B4 Java S Indon
106A2 Java Trench Indon
78B4 Jawa / Indon
71F4 Jayapura Indon
94C2 Jayrüd Syria
96B2 Jbel Ouarkziz Mts Mor
51B1 Jbel Sarhro Mt Mor
1984 Jeanerette USA
97C4 Jebba Nig
93D2 Jebel 'Abd al 'Aziz Mt Syria
91C5 Jebel Akhdar Mt Oman
92C4 Jebel al Lawz Mt S Arabia
94B2 Jebel ash Shaykh Mt Syria
95C2 Jebel Asoteriba Mt Sudan
94B3 Jebel Ed Dabab Mt Jordan
94B3 Jebel al Ata'ita Mt Jordan
94B3 Jebel esh Sharqi Mts Leb/Syria

Kaiwi Chan

94C3 Jebel Ithriyat *Mt* Jordan
91C5 Jebel Ja'lan *Mt* Oman
94B2 Jebel Liban *Mts* Leb
94C2 Jebel Ma'lūlā *Mt* Syria
98C1 Jebel Marra *Mt* Sudan
94C3 Jebel Mudeisisat *Mt* Jordan
95C2 Jebel Oda *Mt* Sudan
94B3 Jebel Qasr ed Deir *Mt* Jordan
94B2 Jebel Um ed Daraj *Mt* Jordan
95B2 Jebel Uweinat *Mt* Sudan
42C2 Jedburgh Scot
Jedda = Jiddah
59C2 Jedrzejów Pol
19B3 Jefferson Texas, USA
11A3 Jefferson City USA
8B3 Jefferson,Mt USA
14A3 Jeffersonville USA
60C2 Jekabpils Latvia
59B2 Jelena Góra Pol
60B2 Jelgava Latvia
78C4 Jember Indon
57C2 Jena Germany
57B2 Jenaja *I* Indon
47D1 Jenbach Austria
94B3 Jenin Israel
19B3 Jennings USA
59B2 Jeseníky *Upland* Czech Republic
6F3 Jensen Nunatakker *Mt* Greenland
6B3 Jens Munk *I* Can
108B3 Jeparit Aust
31D4 Jequié Brazil
35C1 Jequitaí *R* Brazil
35C1 Jequitinhonha Brazil
31C5 Jequitinhonha *R* Brazil
50A2 Jerez de la Frontera Spain
50A2 Jerez de los Caballeros Spain
94B3 Jericho Israel
108C3 Jerilderie Aust
48B2 Jersey *I* UK
15C2 Jersey City USA
16C2 Jersey Shore USA
13B8 Jerseyville USA
92C3 Jerusalem Israel
109D3 Jervis B Aust
13C2 Jervis Inlet *Sd* Can
52B1 Jesenice Slovenia
86B2 Jessore Bang
11B3 Jesup USA
34A2 Jesús María Arg
16D2 Jewett City USA
54A2 Jezerce *Mt* Alb
58C2 Jezioro Mamry *L* Pol
58C2 Jezioro Sniardwy *L* Pol
84C2 Jezzine Leb
85C4 Jhābua India
85D4 Jhālāwār India
84C2 Jhang Maghiana Pak
85D3 Jhānsi India
86A2 Jhārsuguda India
84C2 Jhelum Pak
84C2 Jhelum *R* Pak
11C3 J H Kerr L USA
84D3 Jhunjhunūn India
69F2 Jiamusi China
73C4 Ji'an Jiangxi, China
74B2 Ji'an Jilin, China
73D4 Jiande China
73B4 Jiang'an China
73A5 Jiangcheng China
73B3 Jiang Jiang *R* China
73C5 Jiangmen China
72D3 Jiangsu Province, China
73C4 Jiangxi Province, China
73A3 Jiangyou China
72D1 Jianping China
73A5 Jianshui China

73D4 Jian Xi *R* China
73D4 Jianyang China
72E2 Jiaonan China
72E2 Jiao Xian China
72E2 Jiaozhou Wan *B* China
72C2 Jiaozuo China
73E3 Jiaxiang China
68B3 Jiayuguan China
81B3 Jiddah S Arabia
72D3 Jieshou China
72C2 Jiexiu China
72A3 Jigzhi China
59B3 Jihlava Czech Republic
99E2 Jilib Somalia
69E2 Jilin China
51B1 Jiloca *R* Spain
99D2 Jima Eth
9C4 Jiménez Coahuila, Mexico
72D2 Jinan China
84D3 Jind India
72B2 Jingbian China
73D4 Jingdezhen China
76C1 Jinghong China
73C3 Jingmen China
72B2 Jingning China
73B4 Jing Xiang China
73D4 Jinhua China
72C1 Jining Nei Monggol, China
72D2 Jining Shandong, China
99D2 Jinja Uganda
76C1 Jinping China
73A4 Jinsha Jiang *R* China
73D4 Jinshi China
72E1 Jinxi China
72E2 Jin Xian China
72E1 Jinzhou China
33E5 Jiparaná *R* Brazil
32A4 Jipijapa Ecuador
23A2 Jiquilpan Mexico
91C4 Jiroft Iran
99E2 Jirriban Somalia
73B4 Jishou China
92C2 Jisr ash Shughūr Syria
54B2 Jiu *R* Rom
73D4 Jiujiang China
73A4 Jiulong China
73D4 Jiulong Jiang *R* China
69F2 Jixi China
84B3 Jiza Jordan
81C4 Jizan S Arabia
97A3 Joal Sen
35C1 João Monlevade Brazil
31E3 João Pessoa Brazil
35B1 João Pirheiro Brazil
34B2 Jocoli Arg
85C3 Jodhpur India
38K6 Joensuu Fin
46C2 Joeuf France
13D2 Joffre,Mt Can
86B1 Jogbani India
87A2 Jog Falls India
101G1 Johannesburg S Africa
21B2 Johannesburg USA
6C2 Johan Pen Can
12D1 John *R* USA
20C2 John Day USA
20B1 John Day *R* USA
44C2 John O'Groats Scot
18A2 John Redmond Res USA
11B3 Johnson City Tennessee, USA
17B1 Johnston USA
27N2 Johnston Pt St Vincent and the Grenadines
15C2 Johnstown Pennsylvania, USA
77C5 Johor Bharu Malay
49C2 Joigny France
30G4 Joinville Brazil
61H3 Jokk *R* Russian Fed
38H5 Jokkmokk Sweden
93E2 Jolfa Iran
10B2 Joliet USA

7C5 Joliette Can
79B4 Jolo Phil
79B4 Jolo *I* Phil
82D2 Joma *Mt* China
58C1 Jonava Lithuania
72A3 Jonê China
11A3 Jonesboro Arkansas, USA
19B3 Jonesboro Louisiana, USA
6B2 Jones Sd Can
58C1 Joniškis Lithuania
39G7 Jönköping Sweden
92C3 Jordan Kingdom, S W Asia
94B2 Jordan *R* Israel
20C2 Jordan Valley USA
86C1 Jorhāt India
38J5 Jörn Sweden
78C3 Jorong Indon
39F7 Jørpeland Nor
79B3 Jose Pañganiban Phil
106B2 Joseph Bonaparte G Aust
64B3 Jotunheimen *Mt* Nor
92B3 Jounié Leb
86C1 Jowai India
99E2 Jowhar Somalia
12H2 Joy,Mt Can
5F5 Juan de Fuca,Str of Can/USA
101D2 Juan de Nova *I* Mozam Chan
34D3 Juárez Arg
31C3 Juazeiro Brazil
31D3 Juazeiro do Norte Brazil
99D2 Juba Sudan
99E2 Juba *R* Somalia
94B1 Jubail Leb
93D3 Jubbah S Arabia
96A2 Juby,C Mor
51B2 Júcar *R* Spain
23B2 Juchatengo Mexico
23A1 Juchipila *R* Mexico
23A1 Juchitán Mexico
57C3 Judenburg Austria
30B2 Juilaca Peru
73C4 Juiling Shan *Hills* China
31C6 Juiz de Fora Brazil
30C3 Jujuy State, Arg
30C2 Juli Peru
33F3 Julianatop *Mt* Surinam
6F3 Julianehåb Greenland
46D1 Jülich Germany
84B1 Jumla Nepal
84B3 Jum Suwwāna *Mt* India
85C4 Jūnagadh India
72D2 Junan China
9D3 Junction City USA
31B6 Jundiaí Brazil
4E4 Juneau USA
107D4 Junee Aust
22C2 June Lake USA
52A1 Jungfrau *Mt* Switz
16A2 Juniata *R* USA
29D2 Junín Arg
73A4 Junlian China
31B2 Juquiá Brazil
99C2 Jur *R* Sudan
42B2 Jura *I* Scot
49D2 Jura *Mts* France
44B3 Jura,Sound of *Chan* Scot
94B3 Jurf ed Darāwish Jordan
65K4 Jurga Russian Fed
60B2 Jūrmala Latvia
32D4 Juruá *R* Brazil
33F6 Juruena *R* Brazil
94B2 Jūsīyah Syria
34B2 Justo Daract Arg
32D4 Jutaí *R* Brazil
25D3 Juticalpa Honduras
Jutland = Jylland
90C3 Jūymand Iran
88K6 Juzur al Halaniyat *Is* Oman

56B1 Jylland *Pen* Den
38K6 Jyväskylä Fin

K

82B2 K2 *Mt* China/India
90C2 Kaakhka Turkmenistan
101H1 Kaapmuiden S Africa
71D4 Kabaena *I* Indon
97A4 Kabala Sierra Leone
99D3 Kabale Uganda
98C3 Kabalo Zaïre
98C3 Kabambare Zaïre
61F5 Kabardino-Balkariya Division, Russian Fed
99D2 Kabarole Uganda
98C3 Kabinda Zaïre
90A3 Kabīr Kuh *Mts* Iran
100B2 Kabompo Zambia
100B2 Kabompo *R* Zambia
98C3 Kabongo Zaïre
84B2 Kabul Afghan
85B4 Kachchh,G of India
61J2 Kachkanar Russian Fed
63C2 Kachug Russian Fed
76B3 Kadan Myan
78D3 Kadapongan *I* Indon
85C4 Kadi India
108A2 Kadina Aust
92B2 Kadinhani Turk
87B2 Kadiri India
60E4 Kadiyevka Ukraine
100B2 Kadoma Zim
99C1 Kadugli Sudan
97C3 Kaduna Nig
97C3 Kaduna *R* Nig
87B2 Kadūr India
97A3 Kaffrine Sen
94C1 Kafrūn Bashir Syria
100B2 Kafue Zambia
100B2 Kafue *R* Zambia
100B2 Kafue Nat Pk Zambia
74D3 Kaga Japan
65H6 Kagan Kazakhstan
93D1 Kağizman Turk
74C4 Kagoshima Japan
90C2 Kāhak Iran
99D3 Kahama Tanz
84B3 Kahan Pak
98C3 Kahemba Zaïre
46E1 Kahler Asten *Mt* Germany
91C4 Kahnūji Iran
18B4 Kahoka USA
21C4 Kahoolawe *I* Hawaiian Is
92C2 Kahramanmaraş Turk
21C4 Kahuku Pt Hawaiian Is
111B2 Kaiapoi NZ
33F2 Kaieteur Fall Guyana
72C3 Kaifeng China
111B2 Kaikohe NZ
111B2 Kaikoura NZ
111B2 Kaikoura Pen NZ
111B2 Kaikoura Range *Mts* NZ
73B4 Kaili China
21C4 Kailua Hawaiian Is
71E4 Kaimana Indon
75B2 Kainan Japan
97C3 Kainji Res Nig
110B1 Kaipara Harbour *B* NZ
73C5 Kaiping China
96D1 Kairouan Tunisia
22C2 Kaiser Peak *Mt* USA
57B3 Kaiserslautern Germ
74B2 Kaishantun China
58D2 Kaisiadorys Lithuania
110B1 Kaitaia NZ
111A3 Kaitangata NZ
84D3 Kaithal India
21C4 Kaiwi Chan Hawaiian Is

73B3	Kai Xian China
73A5	Kaiyuan Liaoning, China
74A2	Kaiyuan Yunnan, China
12C2	Kaiyuh Mts USA
38K6	Kajaani Fin
81D2	Kajaki Afghan
89D2	Kajiado Kenya
84B1	Kajran Afghan
99D2	Kaka Sudan
99D2	Kakamega Kenya
75A2	Kake Japan
12I3	Kake USA
12D3	Kakhonak USA
65E5	Kakhovskoye Vodokhranilishche Res Ukraine
91B4	Kākī Iran
87C1	Kākināda India
75A2	Kakogawa Japan
12D2	Kaktovik USA
75C1	Kakuda Japan
	Kalaallit Nunaat = Greenland
55B3	Kalabáka Greece
78D1	Kalabakan Malay
100B2	Kalabo Zambia
61F3	Kalach Russian Fed
61F4	Kalach-na-Donu Russian Fed
86C2	Kaladan R Myan
21C4	Ka Lae C Hawaiian Is
100B3	Kalahari Desert Botswana
38J6	Kalajoki Fin
63D2	Kalakan Russian Fed
70A3	Kalakepen Indon
84B1	Kalam Pak
84A3	Kalámai Greece
10B2	Kalamazoo USA
84B3	Kalat Pak
92B1	Kalecik Turk
78D3	Kalembau I Indon
99C3	Kalémié Zaïre
38L5	Kalevala Russian Fed
86C2	Kalewa Myan
12D2	Kalgin I USA
108B4	Kalgoorlie Aust
78B4	Kalianda Indon
79B3	Kalibo Phil
98C3	Kalima Zaïre
78C3	Kalimantan Province, Indon
55C3	Kálimnos I Greece
86B1	Kálimpang India
60B3	Kaliningrad Russian Fed
60C3	Kalinkovichi Belarus
8B2	Kalispell USA
58B2	Kalisz Pol
99D3	Kaliua Tanz
39J5	Kalix R Swed
100A3	Kalkfeld Namibia
100A3	Kalkrand Namibia
108A1	Kallakoopah R Aust
38K6	Kallavesi L Fin
55B3	Kallonis Kólpos B Greece
39H7	Kalmar Swed
61G4	Kalmykia-Khalmg Tangch Division, Russian Fed
100B2	Kalomo Zambia
18B1	Kalona USA
13B2	Kalone Peak Mt Can
87A2	Kalpeni I India
85D3	Kālpi India
53A3	Kalsat Khasba Tunisia
12B2	Kalskag USA
12C2	Kaltag USA
60E3	Kaluga Russian Fed
60E3	Kaluga Division, Russian Fed
39G7	Kalundborg Den
59C3	Kalush Ukraine
87B2	Kalyandurg India
61J2	Kalyazin Russian Fed
61H1	Kama R Russian Fed
74E3	Kamaishi Japan
84C2	Kamalia Pak
110C1	Kamanawa Mts NZ
100A2	Kamanjab Namibia
84D2	Kamat Mt India
87B3	Kamban India
61H2	Kambarka Russian Fed
97A4	Kambia Sierra Leone
59D3	Kamenets Podolskiy Ukraine
61F3	Kamenka Russian Fed
65K4	Kamen-na-Obi Russian Fed
61K2	Kamensk-Ural'skiy Russian Fed
5H3	Kamilukuak L Can
98C3	Kamina Zaïre
7A3	Kaminak L Can
75C1	Kaminoyama Japan
5F4	Kamloops Can
93E1	Kamo Armenia
75C1	Kamogawa Japan
99D2	Kampala Uganda
77C5	Kampar Malay
78A2	Kampar R Indon
56B2	Kampen Neth
76B2	Kamphaeng Phet Thai
77C3	Kampot Camb
91D4	Kamsaptar Iran
61J2	Kamskoye Vodokhranilishche Res Russian Fed
85D4	Kämthi India
61G3	Kamyshin Russian Fed
61K2	Kamyshlov Russian Fed
7C4	Kanaaupscow R Can
61G2	Kanash Russian Fed
75B1	Kanayama Japan
74D3	Kanazawa Japan
4C3	Kanbisha USA
87B2	Kānchipuram India
84B2	Kandahar Afghan
64E3	Kandalaksha Russian Fed
38L5	Kandalakshskaya Guba B Russian Fed
97C3	Kandé Benin
109C2	Kandos Aust
87C3	Kandy Sri Lanka
15C2	Kane USA
6C1	Kane Basin B Can
98B1	Kanem Region Chad
92C2	Kangal Turk
6E2	Kangâmiut Greenland
91B4	Kangān Iran
77C4	Kangar Malay
106C4	Kangaroo I Aust
6E2	Kangâtsiaq Greenland
90A3	Kangavar Iran
72C1	Kangbao China
82C3	Kangchenjunga Mt Nepal
73A4	Kangding China
6G3	Kangerdlugssuaq B Greenland
6G3	Kangerdlugssvatsaiq B Greenland
99D2	Kangetet Kenya
74B2	Kanggye N Korea
6C3	Kangiqsualujjuaq Can
6C3	Kangiqsujuaq Can
72C1	Kangirsuk Can
73A4	Kangnung S Korea
98B2	Kango Gabon
68B4	Kangto Mt China
72B3	Kang Xian China
77D4	Kanh Hung Viet
98C3	Kaniama Zaïre
87B1	Kani Giri India
39J6	Kankaanpää Fin
14A2	Kankakee USA
14A2	Kankakee R USA
97B3	Kankan Guinea
86A2	Känker India
85D4	Kanniyākumari India
97C3	Kano Nig
74C4	Kanoya Japan
86A1	Kānpur India
9D3	Kansas State, USA
18A2	Kansas R USA
10A3	Kansas City USA
73D5	Kanshi China
63B2	Kansk Russian Fed
97C3	Kantchari Burkina
86B2	Kanthi India
12D2	Kantishna USA
12D2	Kantishna R USA
68D4	Kanye Botswana
68D4	Kao-hsiung Taiwan
100A2	Kaoka Veld Plain Namibia
97A3	Kaolack Sen
100B2	Kaoma Zambia
21C4	Kapaa Hawaiian Is
98C3	Kapanga Zaïre
6F3	Kap Cort Adelaer C Greenland
6H3	Kap Dalton C Greenland
39H7	Kapellskär Sweden
6F3	Kap Farvel C Greenland
6G3	Kap Gustav Holm C Greenland
100B2	Kapiri Zambia
78C2	Kapit Malay
19B3	Kaplan USA
57C3	Kaplice Czech Republic
76B3	Kapoe Thai
99C3	Kapona Zaïre
52C1	Kaposvár Hung
6C2	Kap Parry C Can
6H3	Kap Ravn C Greenland
78B3	Kapuas R Indon
108A2	Kapunda Aust
84D2	Kapurthala India
7B5	Kapuskasing Can
109D2	Kaputar Mt Aust
93E2	Kapydzhik Mt Armenia
6D2	Kap York C Greenland
92B1	Karabük Turk
55C2	Karacabey Turk
61F5	Karachevo-Cherkesiya Division, Russian Fed
85B4	Karachi Pak
87A1	Kāräd India
60E5	Kara Daglari Mt Turk
54C5	Karadeniz Boğazi Sd Turk
68D1	Karaftit Russian Fed
65J5	Karaganda Kazakhstan
65J5	Karagayly Kazakhstan
87B2	Karaikal India
90B2	Karaj Iran
84B3	Karak Jordan
65G5	Kara Kalpakskaya Respublika, Uzbekistan
84B4	Karakax He R China
71D3	Karakelong I Indon
84D1	Karakoram Mts India
84D1	Karakoram P India/China
97A3	Karakoro R Maur/Sen
65G6	Karakumy Desert Russian Fed
94B3	Karama Jordan
92B2	Karaman Turk
111B2	Karamea NZ
111B2	Karamea Bight B NZ
85D4	Karanja India
92B2	Karapinar Turk
64J2	Kara S Russian Fed
100A3	Karasburg Namibia
38K5	Karasjok Nor
65J4	Karasuk Russian Fed
92C2	Karataş Turk
65J5	Kara Tau Mts Kazakhstan
76B3	Karathuri Myan
74B4	Karatsu Japan
91B4	Karāz Iran
93D3	Karbalā' Iraq
59C3	Karcag Hung
55B3	Kardhitsa Greece
38J5	Karesvando Sweden
96B2	Karet Desert Region Maur
97D3	Kari Nig
100B2	Kariba Zim
100B2	Kariba L Zim/Zambia
100B2	Kariba Dam Zim/Zambia
95C3	Karima Sudan
78B3	Karimata I Indon
86C2	Karimganj Bang
87B1	Karimnagar India
99E1	Karin Somalia
39J6	Karis Fin
99C3	Karishimbe Mt Zaïre
55B3	Káristos Greece
87A2	Kārkal India
71F4	Karkar I PNG
90A3	Karkheh R Iran
60D4	Karkinitskiy Zaliv B Ukraine
63B3	Karlik Shan Mt China
58B2	Karlino Pol
52C2	Karlobag Croatia
52C1	Karlovac Croatia
54B2	Karlovo Bulg
57C2	Karlovy Vary Czech Republic
39G7	Karlshamn Sweden
39G7	Karlskoga Sweden
39H7	Karlskrona Sweden
57B3	Karlsruhe Germany
39G7	Karlstad Sweden
12D3	Karluk USA
86C2	Karnafuli Res Bang
84D3	Karnal India
87A1	Karnataka State, India
54C2	Karnobat Bulg
100B2	Karoi Zim
99D3	Karonga Malawi
95C3	Karora Sudan
78D3	Karossa Indon
55C3	Kárpathos I Greece
6E2	Karrats Fjord Greenland
93D1	Kars Turk
65H4	Karsakpay Kazakhstan
58D1	Kārsava Latvia
80E2	Karshi Uzbekistan
38J6	Karstula Fin
94B1	Kartaba Leb
54C2	Kartal Turk
61K3	Kartaly Russian Fed
90A3	Kārūn R Iran
86A1	Karwa India
87A2	Kārwār India
68D1	Karymskoye Russian Fed
98B3	Kasai R Zaïre
100B2	Kasaji Zaïre
101C2	Kasama Zambia
99D3	Kasanga Tanz
87A2	Kāsaragod India
5H3	Kasba L Can
100B2	Kasempa Zambia
100B2	Kasenga Zaïre
99D3	Kasese Uganda
90B3	Kashan Iran
12C2	Kashegelok USA
82B2	Kashi China
84D3	Kāshipur India
74D3	Kashiwazaki Japan
90C2	Kashmar Iran
66D3	Kashmir State, India
61F3	Kasimov Russian Fed
52C4	Kaskaskia R USA
38J6	Kaskinen Fin
61K2	Kasli Russian Fed
5G5	Kaslo Can
98C3	Kasonga Zaïre
99B3	Kasongo-Lunda Zaïre
55C3	Kásos I Greece
	Kaspiyskiy = Lagan'
95C3	Kassala Sudan
56B2	Kassel Germany

Kulata

Le Buet

78C4 Madiun Indon
99D2 Madoka Kenya
47D1 Madonna Di
  Campiglio Italy
87C2 Madras India
20B2 Madras USA
29A6 Madre de Dios I
  Chile
32D6 Madre de Dios R Bol
50B1 Madrid Spain
50B2 Madridejos Spain
78C4 Madura I
87B3 Madurai India
75B1 Maebashi Japan
76B3 Mae Khlong R Thai
77B4 Mae Nam Lunang R
  Thai
76C2 Mae Nam Mun R
  Thai
76B2 Mae Nam Ping R
  Thai
101D2 Maevatanana Madag
51C2 Mafeteng Lesotho
109C3 Maffra Aust
99D3 Mafia I Tanz
101G1 Mafikeng S Africa
30G4 Mafra Brazil
92C3 Mafraq Jordan
32C2 Magangué Colombia
34D3 Magdalena Arg
24A1 Magdalena Mexico
26C4 Magdalena R
  Colombia
78D1 Magdalena,Mt Malay
56C2 Magdeburg Germany
31C6 Magé Brazil
87C4 Magelang Indon
47C1 Magga R Switz
92B4 Maghâgha Egypt
45C1 Magherafelt N Ire
55A2 Maglie Italy
61J3 Magnitogorsk
  Russian Fed
19B3 Magnolia USA
101C2 Magoé Mozam
15D1 Magog Can
23B1 Magosal Mexico
13E2 Magrath Can
7A3 Maguse River Can
76B1 Magwe Myan
90A2 Mahabad Iran
86B1 Mahabharat Range
  Mts Nepal
87A1 Mahad India
101D2 Mahajanga Madag
100B3 Mahalapye Botswana
86A2 Mahānadi R India
101D2 Mahanoro Madag
16A2 Mahanoy City USA
87A1 Maharashtra State,
  India
86A2 Mahāsamund India
76C2 Maha Sarakham Thai
101D2 Mahavavy R Madag
87B1 Mahbubnagar India
96D1 Mahdia Tunisia
87B2 Mahé India
99D3 Mahenge Tanz
13D2 Mahesāna India
11D1 Mahia Pen NZ
85D3 Mahoba India
51C2 Mahón Spain
12J1 Mahony L Can
85C4 Mahuva India
32C1 Maicao Colombia
41D1 Maiche France
43E4 Maidstone Eng
99B1 Maiduguri Nig
86A2 Maihar India
86C2 Maijdi Bang
76D3 Mali Kyun I Myan
84A1 Maimana Afghan
14B1 Main Chan Can
98B3 Mai-Ndombe L Zaire
10D2 Maine State,USA
48B2 Maine Region
  France
44C2 Mainland I Scot
85D3 Mainpuri India

46A2 Maintenon France
101D2 Maintirano Madag
57B2 Mainz Germany
97A4 Maio I Cape Verde
29C2 Maipo Mt Arg/Chile
34D3 Maipú Arg
32D1 Maiquetia Ven
47B2 Maira R Italy
86B1 Maiskhal I India
86C2 Maiskhal I India
107E4 Maitland New South
  Wales, Aust
108A2 Maitland S Australia,
  Aust
112C12 Maitri Base Ant
74D3 Maizuru Japan
70C4 Majene Indon
85A3 Maji R Peru
99D2 Maji Eth
72D2 Majia He R China
  Majunga =
  Mahajanga
70C4 Makale Indon
86B1 Makalu Mt China/
  Nepal
98B2 Makanza Zaire
52C2 Makarska Croatia
61F2 Makaryev
  Russian Fed
  Makassar = Ujung
  Pandang
78D3 Makassar Str Indon
61H4 Makat Kazakhstan
97A4 Makeni Sierra Leone
60E4 Makeyevka Ukraine
100B3 Makgadikgadi Salt
  Pan Botswana
61G5 Makhachkala
  Russian Fed
99D3 Makindu Kenya
89B5 Makkah S Arabia
7E4 Makkovik Can
59C3 Makó Hung
98B2 Makokou Gabon
110C1 Makorako,Mt NZ
98B2 Makoua Congo
85C3 Makrāna India
85A3 Makran Coast Range
  Mts Pak
96C1 Makthar Tunisia
93D2 Mākū Iran
98C3 Makumbi Zaïre
74C4 Makurazaki Japan
97C4 Makurdi Nig
79B4 Malabang Phil
87A2 Malabar Coast India
98E7 Malabo Bioko
77C5 Malacca,Str of
  S E Asia
32C2 Málaga Colombia
50B2 Málaga Spain
101D3 Malaimbandy Madag
107F1 Malaita I Solomon Is
99D2 Malakal Sudan
84C2 Malakand Pak
70C4 Malang Indon
98B3 Malange Angola
97C3 Malanville Benin
39H7 Mälaren L Sweden
34B3 Malargüe Arg
12F3 Malaspina Gl USA
93C2 Malatya Turk
101C2 Malawi Republic,
  Africa
  Malawi,L = Nyasa,L
79C4 Malaybalay Phil
90A3 Malāyer Iran
70B3 Malaysia Federation,
  S E Asia
93D2 Malazgirt Turk
58B2 Malbork Pol
56C2 Malchin Germany
18C2 Malden USA
83B5 Maldives Is Indian O
104B4 Maldives Ridge
  Indian O
29F2 Maldonado Urug
47D1 Male Italy
85C4 Malegaon India
59B3 Malé Karpaty Upland
  Slovakia
101C2 Malema Mozam
84B2 Mālestan Afghan
38H5 Malgomaj L Sweden

95B3 Malha Well Sudan
20C2 Malheur L USA
97B3 Mali Republic, Africa
78D1 Malinau Indon
99E3 Malindi Kenya
  Malines = Mechelen
40B2 Malin Head Pt
  Irish Rep
86A2 Malkāla Range Mts
  India
85D4 Malkāpur India
55C2 Malkara Turk
54C2 Malko Tŭrnovo Bulg
44B3 Mallaig Scot
95C2 Mallawi Egypt
47D1 Malles Venosta Italy
51C2 Mallorca I Spain
45B2 Mallow Irish Rep
38G6 Malm Nor
38J5 Malmberget Sweden
46D1 Malmédy Germany
43C4 Malmesbury Eng
100A4 Malmesbury S Africa
39G7 Malmö Sweden
61G2 Malmyzh
  Russian Fed
79B3 Maloelap Phil
15D2 Malone USA
101G1 Maloti Mts Lesotho
38F6 Måløy Nor
82C1 Malpelo I Colombia
34A2 Malpo R Chile
85D3 Mālpura India
8C2 Malta Montana, USA
53B3 Malta Chan Malta/
  Italy
53B3 Malta I Medit S
100A3 Maltahöhe Namibia
42D2 Malton Eng
39G6 Malung Sweden
87A1 Mälvan India
19B3 Malvern USA
85D4 Malwa Plat India
61G4 Malyy Uzen' R
  Kazakhstan
63D2 Mama Russian Fed
61H2 Mamadysh
  Russian Fed
99C2 Mambasa Zaire
71E4 Mamberamo R
  Indon
98B2 Mambéré R CAR
97A4 Mamfé Cam
33D6 Mamoré R Bol
97A3 Mamou Guinea
101D2 Mampikony Madag
97B4 Mampong Ghana
94B3 Mamshit Hist Site
  Israel
100B3 Mamuno Botswana
97B4 Man Côte d'Ivoire
21C4 Mana Hawaiian Is
101D3 Manabo Madag
33E4 Manacapuru Brazil
51C2 Manacor Spain
71D3 Manado Indon
25D3 Managua Nic
101D3 Manakara Madag
101D2 Mananara Madag
101D3 Mananjary Madag
111A3 Manapouri NZ
111A3 Manapouri,L NZ
86C1 Manas Bhutan
82C1 Manas China
65K5 Manas Hu L China
86B1 Manaslu Mt Nepal
16B2 Manasquan USA
33F4 Manaus Brazil
92B2 Manavgat Turk
92C2 Manbij Syria
42B2 Man,Calf of I Eng
87B1 Mancheral India
15D2 Manchester
  Connecticut, USA
16C2 Manchester Eng
10C2 Manchester New
  Hampshire, USA
16A2 Manchester
  Pennsylvania, USA
69E2 Manchuria Hist
  Region, China
91B4 Mand R Iran
101C2 Manda Tanz
35A2 Mandaguari Brazil

39F7 Mandal Nor
76B1 Mandalay Myan
68C2 Mandalgovi
  Mongolia
8C2 Mandan USA
14A2 Mandelona USA
99E2 Mandera Eth
26B3 Mandeville Jamaica
101C2 Mandimba Mozam
86A2 Mandla India
101D2 Mandritsara Madag
85D4 Mandsaur India
53C2 Manduria Italy
85B4 Mandvi India
87B2 Mandya India
58D2 Manevichi Ukraine
42D3 Manfield Eng
53C2 Manfredonia Italy
99B1 Manga Desert
  Region Niger
110C1 Mangakino NZ
54C2 Mangalia Rom
99B1 Mangalmé Chad
87A2 Mangalore India
78B3 Manggar Indon
88B3 Mangnia China
101C2 Mangoche Malawi
101D3 Mangoky R Madag
71D4 Mangole I Indon
85B4 Māngral India
8D3 Manhattan USA
31C6 Manhuaçu Brazil
101D2 Mania R Madag
7D5 Manicouagan R Can
91A4 Manifah S Arabia
79B3 Manila Phil
109D2 Manilla Aust
97B3 Maninian Côte
  d'Ivoire
86C2 Manipur State, India
86C2 Manipur R Myan
92A2 Manisa Turk
41C3 Man,Isle of Irish S
14A2 Manistee USA
14A2 Manistee R USA
14A1 Manistique USA
5H4 Manitoba Province,
  Can
5J4 Manitoba,L Can
13F2 Manito L Can
14A1 Manitou Is USA
7B5 Manitoulin I Can
14A2 Manitowoc USA
15C1 Maniwaki Can
32B2 Manizales Colombia
101D3 Manja Madag
106A4 Manjimup Aust
87B1 Mānjra R India
10A2 Mankato USA
97B4 Mankono Côte
  d'Ivoire
12D2 Manley Hot Springs
  USA
111B1 Manly NZ
85C4 Manmād India
78A3 Mann Indon
87B3 Mannar Sri Lanka
87B3 Mannar,G of India
83B2 Mannārgudi India
57B3 Mannheim Germany
13D1 Manning Can
17B1 Manning USA
108A2 Mannum Aust
97A4 Mano Sierra Leone
71E4 Manokwari Indon
98C3 Manono Zaire
76B3 Manoron Myan
75B1 Mano-wan B Japan
74B2 Manp'o N Korea
84D3 Mānsa India
100B2 Mansa Zambia
6B3 Mansel I Can
19B2 Mansfield Arkansas,
  USA
108C3 Mansfield Aust
19B3 Mansfield Louisiana,
  USA
16D1 Mansfield
  Massachusetts, USA
10B2 Mansfield Ohio,
  USA

15C2	Mansfield Pennsylvania, USA
71E2	Mansyu Deep Pacific O
32A4	Manta Ecuador
79A4	Mantalingajan,Mt Phil
32B6	Mantaro R Peru
22B2	Manteca USA
48C2	Mantes France
52B1	Mantova Italy
38J6	Mantta Fin
61F2	Manturovo Russian Fed
35A2	Manuel Ribas Brazil
79B4	Manukan Phil
110B1	Manukau NZ
71F4	Manus I Pacific O
50B2	Manzanares Spain
25E2	Manzanillo Cuba
24B3	Manzanillo Mexico
63D3	Manzhouli China
94C3	Manzil Jordan
101C3	Manzini Swaziland
98B1	Mao Chad
72A2	Maomao Shan Mt China
73C5	Maoming China
101C3	Mapai Mozam
71E3	Mapia Is Pacific O
79A4	Mapin I Phil
5H5	Maple Creek Can
101H1	Maputo Mozam
101H1	Maputo R Mozam
	Ma Qu = Huange He
72A3	Maqu China
86B1	Maquan He R China
98B3	Maquela do Zombo Angola
29C4	Maquinchao Arg
31B3	Marabá Brazil
32C1	Maracaibo Ven
32D1	Maracay Ven
95A2	Marādah Libya
97C3	Maradi Niger
90A2	Marāgheh Iran
99D2	Maralal Kenya
107F1	Maramasike I Solomon Is
100B2	Maramba Zambia
90A2	Marand Iran
31B2	Maranhãoa State, Brazil
109C1	Maranoa R Aust
32B4	Marañón R Peru
7B5	Marathon Can
17B2	Marathon Florida, USA
78D2	Maratua I Indon
23A2	Maravatío Mexico
79B4	Marawi Phil
34B2	Marayes Arg
50B2	Marbella Spain
106A3	Marble Bar Aust
60B3	Marblehall S Africa
16D1	Marblehead USA
57B2	Marburg Germany
57B2	Marche Belg
50A2	Marchean Spain
46C1	Marche-en-Famenne Belg
32J7	Marchena I Ecuador
17B2	Marco USA
34C2	Marcos Juárez Arg
12E2	Marcus Baker,Mt USA
15D2	Marcy,Mt USA
84C2	Mardan Pak
29E3	Mar del Plata Arg
93D2	Mardin Turk
99D1	Mareb R Eritrea/Eth
16B1	Margaretville USA
43E4	Margate Eng
54B1	Marghita Rom
109C4	Maria I Aust
13E1	Mariana Lake Can
104F3	Marianas Trench Pacific O
86C1	Mariāni India
19B3	Marianna Arkansas, USA
17A1	Marianna Florida, USA

7G4	Maria Van Diemen,C NZ
59B3	Mariazell Austria
52C1	Maribor Slovenia
99C2	Maridi Sudan
112B5	Marie Byrd Land Region, Ant
27E3	Marie Galante I Caribbean S
39H6	Mariehamn Fin
46C1	Mariembourg Belg
33G2	Marienburg Surinam
100A3	Mariental Namibia
39G7	Mariestad Sweden
17B1	Marietta Georgia, USA
14B3	Marietta Ohio, USA
19A3	Marietta Oklahoma, USA
27Q2	Marigot Dominica
60B3	Marijampole Lithuania
31B6	Marilia Brazil
98B3	Marimba Angola
10B2	Marinette USA
30P3	Maringá Brazil
98C2	Maringa R Zaire
18B2	Marion Arkansas, USA
18C2	Marion Illinois, USA
10B2	Marion Indiana, USA
10B2	Marion Ohio, USA
17C1	Marion S Carolina, USA
11B3	Marion,L USA
107E2	Marion Reef Aust
21B2	Mariposa USA
22B2	Mariposa R USA
22B2	Mariposa Res USA
60C5	Marista R Bulg
60E4	Mariupol' Ukraine
61G2	Mari El Division, Russian Fed
94B2	Marjayoun Leb
58D2	Marjina Gorki Belarus
94B3	Marka Jordan
99E2	Marka Somalia
56C1	Markaryd Sweden
43C3	Market Drayton Eng
43D3	Market Harborough Eng
112A	Markham,Mt Ant
22C1	Markleeville USA
16D1	Marlboro Massachusetts, USA
107D3	Marlborough Aust
46B2	Marle France
19A3	Marlin USA
48C3	Marmande France
55C2	Marmara Adası I Turk
92A1	Marmara,S of Turk
55C3	Marmaris Turk
14B3	Marmet USA
52B1	Marmolada Mt Italy
12D3	Marmot B USA
47A1	Marnay France
46B2	Marne Department, France
46B2	Marne R France
98B2	Maro Chad
101D2	Maroantsetra Madag
101C2	Marondera Zim
33G3	Maroni R French Guiana
109D1	Maroochydore Aust
98B1	Maroua Cam
101D2	Marovoay Madag
11B4	Marquesas Keys USA
10B2	Marquette USA
46A1	Marquise France
109C2	Marra R Aust
101H1	Marracuene Mozam
96B1	Marrakech Mor
106C3	Marree Aust
19B4	Marrero USA
101C2	Marromeu Mozam
101C2	Marrupa Mozam
95C2	Marsa Alam Egypt
99D2	Marsabit Kenya

53B3	Marsala Italy
49D3	Marseille France
12B2	Marshall Alaska, USA
14A3	Marshall Illinois, USA
14B2	Marshall Michigan, USA
18B2	Marshall Missouri, USA
11A3	Marshall Texas, USA
105G3	Marshall Is Pacific O
18B2	Marshfield Missouri, USA
26B1	Marsh Harbour The Bahamas
19B4	Marsh I USA
12H2	March L Can
76B2	Martaban,G of Myan
78A3	Martapura Indon
78C3	Martapura Indon
15D2	Martha's Vineyard I USA
49D2	Martigny Switz
59B3	Martin Slovakia
111C2	Martinborough NZ
34B3	Martin de Loyola Arg
23B1	Martinez de la Torre Mexico
27E4	Martinique I Caribbean S
17A1	Martin,L USA
15C3	Martinsburg USA
14B2	Martins Ferry USA
103G6	Martin Vaz I Atlantic O
49D3	Martigues France
110C2	Marton NZ
50B2	Martos Spain
84B2	Maruf Afghan
75A2	Marugame Japan
85C3	Mārwār India
65H6	Mary Turkmenistan
107E3	Maryborough Queensland, Aust
108B3	Maryborough Victoria, Aust
5F4	Mary Henry,Mt Can
10C3	Maryland State, USA
42C2	Maryport Eng
21A2	Marysville California, USA
18A2	Marysville Kansas, USA
20B1	Marysville Washington, USA
10A2	Maryville Iowa, USA
18B1	Maryville Missouri, USA
95A2	Marzuq Libya
94B2	Masada = Mezada
94B2	Mas'adah Syria
99D3	Masai Steppe Upland Tanz
99D3	Masaka Uganda
93E2	Masally Azerbaijan
74B3	Masan S Korea
101C2	Masasi Tanz
25D3	Masaya Nic
79B3	Masbate Phil
79B3	Masbate I Phil
96C1	Mascara Alg
23A1	Mascota Mexico
35D1	Mascote Brazil
101G1	Maseru Lesotho
66C3	Mashad Iran
84B2	Mashaki Afghan
90C2	Mashhad Iran
98B3	Masi-Manimba Zaire
99D2	Masindi Uganda
99C3	Masisi Zaire
90A3	Masjed Soleyman Iran
101E2	Masoala C Madag
10A2	Mason City USA
91C5	Masqat Oman
52B2	Massa Italy
10C2	Massachusetts State, USA
15D2	Massachusetts B USA
98B1	Massakori Chad
101C3	Massangena Mozam

	Massawa = Mits'iwa
15D2	Massena USA
98B1	Massénya Chad
14B1	Massey Can
49C2	Massif Central Mts France
98B2	Massif de l'Adamaoua Mts Cam
26C3	Massif de la Hotte Mts Haiti
101D3	Massif de l'Isalo Upland Madag
98B2	Massif des Bongo Upland CAR
49D2	Massif du Pelvoux Mts France
101D2	Massif du Tsaratanana Mt Madag
14B2	Massillon USA
97B3	Massina Region, Mali
101C3	Massinga Mozam
101C3	Massingir Mozam
	Massoukou = Franceville
61H4	Masteksay Kazakhstan
111C2	Masterton NZ
74C4	Masuda Japan
100C3	Masvingo Zim
92C2	Masyaf Syria
98B3	Matadi Zaire
25D3	Matagalpa Nic
7C4	Matagami Can
9D4	Matagorda B USA
110A1	Matakana I NZ
100A2	Matala Angola
87C3	Matale Sri Lanka
97A3	Matam Sen
97C3	Matameye Niger
24C2	Matamoros Mexico
95B2	Ma'tan as Sarra Well Libya
7D5	Matane Can
25D2	Matanzas Cuba
34A2	Mataquito R Chile
87C3	Matara Sri Lanka
106A1	Mataram Indon
30B2	Matarani Peru
51C1	Mataró Spain
111A3	Mataura NZ
24C2	Matehuala Mexico
27L1	Matelot Trinidad
59C3	Mátészalka Hung
85D3	Mathura India
79C4	Mati Phil
78D3	Matisiri I Indon
43D3	Matlock Eng
33F6	Mato Grosso Brazil
33F6	Mato Grosso State, Brazil
30E2	Mato Grosso do Sul State, Brazil
101C3	Matola Mozam
91C5	Matrah Oman
92A3	Matrûh Egypt
74C3	Matsue Japan
74E2	Matsumae Japan
74C3	Matsumoto Japan
74C4	Matsusaka Japan
74C4	Matsuyama Japan
7B5	Mattagami R Can
15C1	Mattawa Can
52A1	Matterhorn Mt Italy/ Switz
26C2	Matthew Town The Bahamas
16C2	Mattituck USA
18C2	Mattoon USA
84B2	Matun Afghan
27L1	Matura B Trinidad
33E2	Maturín Ven
86A1	Mau India
101C2	Maúa Mozam
49C1	Maubeuge France
108B2	Maude Aust
103J8	Maud Seamount Atlantic O
21C4	Maui I Hawaiian Is
14B2	Maumee USA
14B2	Maumee R USA
100B2	Maun Botswana

21C4 Mauna Kea Mt Hawaiian Is
21C4 Mauna Loa Mt Hawaiian Is
4F3 Maunoir L Can
4F3 Maunoir,L Can
48C2 Mauriac France
96A2 Mauritania Republic, Africa
100E3 Mauritius I Indian O
100B2 Mavinga Angola
86C2 Mawlaik Myan
Mawlamyine = Moulmein
112C10 Mawson Base Ant
78B3 Maya I Indon
63F2 Maya R Russian Fed
93D2 Mayadin Syria
11C4 Mayaguana I The Bahamas
27D3 Mayagüez Puerto Rico
97C3 Mayahi Niger
98B3 Mayama Congo
90C2 Mayamey Iran
45B2 Maybole Scot
10C3 May,C USA
109C4 Maydena Aust
46D1 Mayen Germany
48B2 Mayenne France
18C2 Mayfield USA
61E5 Maykop Russian Fed
65H6 Maymaneh Afghan
76B1 Maymyo Myan
4E3 Mayo Can
45B2 Mayo County, Irish Rep
16A3 Mayo, Mts of Irish Rep
79B3 Mayon Mt Phil
51C2 Mayor Mt Arg
34C3 Mayor Buratovich Arg
110C1 Mayor I NZ
30D2 Mayor P Lagerenza Par
101D2 Mayotte I Indian O
27H2 May Pen Jamaica
16B3 May Point,C USA
47D1 Mayrhofen Aust
18B3 Mays Landing USA
14B3 Maysville USA
98B3 Mayumba Gabon
100B2 Mazabuka Zambia
84D1 Mazar China
94B3 Mazār Israel
53B3 Mazara del Vallo Italy
84B1 Mazar-i-Sharif Afghan
24B2 Mazatlán Mexico
60B2 Mazeikiai Lithuania
94B3 Mazra Jordan
101C3 Mbabane Swaziland
98B2 Mbaiki CAR
99D3 Mbala Zambia
100B3 Mbalabala Zim
99D2 Mbale Uganda
98B2 Mbalmayo Cam
101C2 Mbamba Bay Tanz
98B2 Mbandaka Zaïre
98B3 Mbanza Congo Angola
98B3 Mbanza-Ngungu Zaïre
99D3 Mbarara Uganda
98B2 Mbénza Congo
98B2 Mbère R Cam
99D3 Mbeya Tanz
98B3 Mbinda Congo
97A3 Mbout Maur
98C3 Mbuji-Mayi Zaïre
99D3 Mbulu Tanz
96B2 Mcherrah Region, Alg
101C2 Mchinji Malawi
76D3 Mdrak Viet
9B3 Mead,L USA
5H4 Meadow Lake Can
14B2 Meadville USA
7E4 Mealy Mts Can
109C1 Meandarra Aust
5G4 Meander River Can

45C2 Meath County, Irish Rep
49C2 Meaux France
16C1 Mechanicville USA
56A2 Mechelen Belg
96B1 Mecheria Alg
56C2 Mecklenburg-Vorpommern State Germany
56C2 Mecklenburger Bucht B Germany
101C2 Meconta Mozam
101C2 Mecubori Mozam
101D2 Mecufi Mozam
101C2 Mecula Mozam
70A3 Medan Indon
34C3 Medanos Arg
34D2 Médanos Arg
13E2 Medecine Hat Can
32B2 Medellin Colombia
13E2 Medenine Tunisia
8A2 Medford USA
54C2 Medgidia Rom
34B2 Media Agua Arg
54B1 Mediaş Rom
5G5 Medical Lake USA
35C1 Medina Brazil
80B3 Medina S Arabia
50B1 Medinaceli Spain
50B1 Medina del Campo Spain
50A1 Medina de Rio Seco Spain
86B2 Medinipur India
88E4 Mediterranean S Europe
13F2 Medley Can
61J3 Mednogorsk Russian Fed
86D1 Mêdog China
98B2 Medouneu Gabon
61F3 Medvedista R Russian Fed
64E3 Medvezh'yegorsk Russian Fed
106A3 Meekatharra Aust
84D3 Meerut India
99D2 Méga Eth
55B3 Megalópolis Greece
55B3 Mégara Greece
86C1 Meghálaya State, India
86C2 Meghna R India
94B2 Megiddo Hist Site Israel
91B4 Mehrān Iran
90B3 Mehriz Iran
35B1 Meia Ponte R Brazil
98B2 Meiganga Cam
76B1 Meiktila Myan
111B3 Meiringen Switz
57C2 Meissen Germany
73D5 Mei Xian China
73D5 Meizhou China
30B3 Mejillones Chile
98B2 Mékambo Gabon
99D1 Mek'elé Eth
76B3 Meknès Mor
76D3 Mekong R Camb
97C3 Mekrou R Benin
77C5 Melaka Malay
104F4 Melanesia Region Pacific O
78C3 Melawi R Indon
107D4 Melbourne Aust
11B4 Melbourne Aust
9C4 Melchor Múzquiz Mexico
61J3 Meleuz Russian Fed
98B1 Melfi Chad
5H4 Melfort Can
76B1 Melilla N W Africa
29B4 Melimoyu Mt Chile
34C2 Melincué Arg
34A2 Melipilla Chile
60E4 Melitopol' Ukraine
6D2 Melville B Greenland
99D2 Melka Guba Eth
101H1 Melmoth S Africa
34C2 Melo Arg
29F2 Melo Urug

22B2 Melones Res USA
12D1 Melozitna R USA
47C1 Mels Switz
43D3 Melton Mowbry Eng
49C2 Melun France
5H4 Melville Can
27D2 Melville I Dominica
4F3 Melville Hills Mts Can
106C2 Melville I Can
4G2 Melville I Can
7E4 Melville L Can
6B3 Melville Pen Can
45B1 Melvin,L Irish Rep
101D2 Memba Mozam
106A1 Memboro Indon
57C3 Memmingen Germany
78B2 Mempawan Indon
11B3 Memphis Tennessee, USA
19B3 Mena USA
43B3 Menai Str Wales
97C3 Ménaka Mali
14A2 Menasha USA
74C4 Mendawai R Indon
49C3 Mende France
99D2 Mendebo Mts Eth
43C4 Mendip Hills Upland Eng
20B2 Mendocino,C USA
105J2 Mendocino Seascarp Pacific O
22B2 Mendota California, USA
29C2 Mendoza Arg
29C3 Mendoza State, Arg
55C3 Menemen Turk
46B1 Menen Belg
72D3 Mengcheng China
78B3 Menggala Indon
76B1 Menghai China
73A5 Mengla China
76B1 Menglian China
73A5 Mengzi China
107D4 Menindee Aust
108B2 Menindee L Aust
14A1 Meningie Aust
14A2 Menomonee Falls USA
100A2 Menongue Angola
51C1 Menorca I Spain
12F2 Mentasta Mts USA
78B3 Mentok Indon
14B2 Mentor USA
72A2 Menyuan China
61H2 Menzelinsk Russian Fed
56B2 Meppen Germany
78D2 Merah Indon
18B2 Meramec R USA
52B1 Merano Italy
71F4 Merauke Indon
8B3 Merced USA
22B2 Merced R USA
29B2 Mercedario Mt Chile
29C2 Mercedes Arg
29E2 Mercedes Buenos Aires, Arg
30E4 Mercedes Corrientes, Arg
29C2 Mercedes Urug
110C1 Mercury B NZ
110C1 Mercury Is NZ
4F2 Mercy,C Can
96B3 Meregh Somalia
76B3 Mergui Myan
76B3 Mergui Arch Myan
25D2 Mérida Mexico
50A2 Mérida Spain
32B2 Mérida Ven
11B3 Meridian USA
109C3 Merimbula Aust
108B2 Meringur Aust
95C3 Merowe Sudan
106A4 Merredin Aust
42B2 Merrick Mt Scot
14A2 Merrillville USA
13C2 Merritt Can
17B2 Merritt Island USA
109D2 Merriwa Aust

99E1 Mersa Fatma Eritrea
51B2 Mers el Kebir Alg
42C3 Mersey R Eng
42C3 Merseyside Metropolitan County, Eng
92B2 Mersin Turk
77C5 Mersing Malay
85C3 Merta India
43C4 Merthyr Tydfil Wales
43C4 Merthyr Tydfil County Wales
50A2 Mertola Port
99D3 Meru Mt Tanz
60E5 Merzifon Turk
46D2 Merzig Germany
98B3 Mésa USA
46E1 Meschede Germany
93D1 Mescit Dağ Mt Turk
12C3 Meshik USA
99C2 Meshra Er Req Sudan
47C1 Mesocco Switz
55B3 Mesolóngion Greece
19A3 Mesquite Texas, USA
101C2 Messalo R Mozam
53C2 Messina Italy
100B3 Messina S Africa
55B3 Messini Greece
55B3 Messiniakós Kólpos G Greece
54B2 Mesta R Bulg
52B1 Mestre Italy
32C3 Meta R Colombia
60D2 Meta R Russian Fed
32D2 Meta R Ven
6C3 Meta Incognito Pen Can
19B4 Metairie USA
20C1 Metaline Falls USA
30D4 Metán Arg
101C2 Metangula Mozam
53C2 Metaponto Italy
44C3 Methil Scot
16D1 Methuen USA
111B2 Methven NZ
12H3 Metlakatla USA
18C2 Metropolis USA
87B2 Mettür India
49D2 Metz France
70A3 Meulaboh Indon
46A2 Meulan France
46C2 Meuse Department, France
49D2 Meuse R France
19A3 Mexia USA
24A1 Mexicali Mexico
24B2 Mexico Federal Republic, Cent America
23A2 México State, Mexico
18B2 Mexico USA
24C2 Mexico,G of Cent America
94B3 Mezada Hist Site Israel
23B2 Mezcala Mexico
64F3 Mezen' Russian Fed
64G2 Mezhdusharskiy, Ostrov I Russian Fed
85D4 Mhow India
23B2 Miahuatlán Mexico
11B4 Miami Florida, USA
18B2 Miami Oklahoma, USA
11B4 Miami Beach USA
90A2 Miandowāb Iran
101D2 Miandrivazo Madag
90A2 Miäneh Iran
84C2 Mianwali Pak
73C3 Mianyang China
73C3 Mianyang China
73A3 Mianzhu China
72E2 Miaodao Qundao Arch China
73B4 Miao Ling Upland China
61K3 Miass Russian Fed
57C3 Michalovce Slovakia
27D3 Miches Dom Rep
10B2 Michigan State, USA
14A2 Michigan City USA

21C4 Molokai / Hawaiian Is
61G2 Moloma *R* Russian Fed
109C2 Molong Aust
100B3 Molopo *R* Botswana
98B2 Moloundlou Cam
8D1 Molson L Can
71D4 Molucca *S* Indon
71D4 Moluccas *Is* Indon
101C2 Moma Mozam
31C3 Mombaca Brazil
99D3 Mombasa Kenya
98C2 Mompono Zaïre
56C2 Mon / Den
44A3 Monach *Is* Scot
49D3 Monaco Principality, Europe
44B3 Monadhliath *Mts* Scot
45C1 Monaghan County, Irish Rep
45C1 Monaghan Irish Rep
27D3 Mona Pass Caribbean S
13B2 Monarch Mt Can
5G4 Monashee Mts Can
41B3 Monasterevin Irish Rep
48B2 Moncalieri Italy
31B2 Monção Brazil
38L5 Monchegorsk Russian Fed
56B2 Mönchen-gladbach Germany
24B2 Monclova Mexico
7D5 Moncton Can
9C4 Mondovia Mexico
50A1 Mondego *R* Port
52A2 Mondovi Italy
27H1 Moneague Jamaica
14C2 Monessen USA
18B2 Monett USA
52B1 Monfalcone Italy
50A1 Monforte de Lemos Spain
98C2 Monga Zaïre
98C2 Mongala *R* Zaïre
99D2 Mongalla Sudan
76D1 Mong Cai Viet
98B1 Mongo Chad
68B2 Mongolia Republic, Asia
100B2 Mongu Zambia
21B2 Monitor Range *Mts* USA
98C3 Monkoto Zaïre
43C4 Monmouth Wales
18B1 Monmouth USA
13C2 Monmouth, Mt Can
43C4 Monmouthshire County Wales
97C4 Mono *R* Togo
21B2 Mono L USA
53C2 Monopoli Italy
51B1 Monreal del Campo Spain
19B3 Monroe Louisiana, USA
14B2 Monroe Michigan, USA
20B1 Monroe Washington, USA
18B2 Monroe City USA
97A4 Monrovia Lib
20D3 Monrovia USA
56A2 Mons Belg
47D2 Monselice Italy
16C1 Monson USA
58B1 Mönsterås Sweden
101D2 Montagne d'Ambre Mt Madag
96C1 Montagnes des Ouled Nail *Mts* Alg
12E3 Montague I USA
49C3 Mont Aigoual *Mt* France
48B2 Montaigu France
53C3 Montalto *Mt* Italy
8B2 Montana State, USA
50A1 Montañas de León Spain
49C2 Montargis France
48C3 Montauban France

15D2 Montauk USA
15D2 Montauk Pt USA
49D2 Montbéliard France
52A1 Mont Blanc *Mt* France
49C2 Montceau les Mines France
51C1 Montceny *Mt* Spain
49D3 Mont Cinto *Mt* Corse
46C2 Montcornet France
48B3 Mont-de-Marsan France
48C2 Montdidier France
30D2 Monteagudo Bol
33G4 Monte Alegre Brazil
52B2 Monte Amiata *Mt* Italy
47D2 Monte Baldo Italy
15C1 Montebello Can
106A3 Monte Bello Is Aust
47E2 Montebelluna Italy
49D3 Monte Carlo Monaco
35B1 Monte Carmelo Brazil
34D2 Monte Caseros Arg
52B2 Monte Cimone *Mt* Italy
52A2 Monte Cinto *Mt* Corse
34B2 Monte Coman Arg
52B2 Monte Corno *Mt* Italy
27C3 Montecristi Dom Rep
52B2 Montecristo *I* Italy
23A1 Monte Escobedo Mexico
53C2 Monte Gargano *Mt* Italy
26B3 Montego Bay Jamaica
47D2 Monte Grappa *Mt* Italy
47C2 Monte Lesima *Mt* Italy
49C3 Montélimar France
53B2 Monte Miletto *Mt* Italy
50A2 Montemo-o-Novo Port
24C2 Montemorelos Mexico
26B5 Montená Colombia
54A2 Montenegro Republic, Yugos
35D1 Monte Pascoal *Mt* Brazil
34A2 Monte Patria Chile
53C3 Monte Pollino *Mt* Italy
101C2 Montepuez Mozam
8A3 Monterey California, USA
15C3 Monterey Virginia, USA
8A3 Monterey B USA
32B2 Montería Colombia
30D2 Montero Bol
47B2 Monte Rosa *Mt* Italy/ Switz
24B2 Monterrey Mexico
31C5 Montes Claros Brazil
50B2 Montes de Toledo *Mts* Spain
29E2 Montevideo Urug
52A2 Monte Viso *Mt* Italy
27P2 Mont Gimie *Mt* St Lucia
11B3 Montgomery Alabama, USA
96C2 Mont Gréboun Niger
47B1 Montherme France
47B1 Monthey Switz
19B3 Monticello Arkansas, USA
16B2 Monticello New York, USA
9C3 Monticello Utah, USA
53A2 Monti del Gennargentu *Mt* Sardegna
47D2 Monti Lessini *Mts* Italy

53B3 Monti Nebrodi *Mts* Italy
7C5 Mont-Laurier Can
48C2 Montluçon France
7C5 Montmagny Can
46C2 Montmédy France
49C3 Mont Mézenc *Mt* France
46B2 Montmirail France
50B2 Montoro Spain
49D3 Mont Pelat *Mt* France
14B2 Montpelier Ohio, USA
10C2 Montpelier Vermont, USA
49C3 Montpellier France
7C5 Montréal Can
48C1 Montreuil France
52A1 Montreux Switz
47B1 Mont Risoux *Mt* France
8C3 Montrose Colorado, USA
40C2 Montrose Scot
48B2 Mont-St-Michel France
96B1 Monts des Ksour *Mts* Alg
51C3 Monts des Ouled Neil *Mts* Alg
51C2 Monts du Hodna *Mts* Alg
27E3 Montserrat *I* Caribbean S
10C1 Monts Otish *Mts* Can
12B1 Monument Mt USA
9B3 Monument V USA
98C2 Monveda Zaïre
76B1 Monywa Myan
52A1 Monza Italy
100B2 Monze Zambia
101H1 Mooi *R* S Africa
101G1 Mooi River S Africa
108B1 Moomba Aust
109D2 Moonbi Range *Mts* Aust
108B1 Moonda L Aust
109D1 Moonie Aust
109C1 Moonie *R* Aust
108A2 Moonta Aust
108A4 Moora Aust
109B1 Moore,L Aust
108A4 Moorfoot Hills USA
8D2 Moorhead USA
22C3 Moorpark USA
7B4 Moose *R* Can
5H4 Moose Jaw Can
5H4 Moosomin Can
7B4 Moosonee Can
16D2 Moosup USA
101C2 Mopeia Mozam
97B3 Mopti Mali
32C6 Moquegua Peru
39G6 Mora Sweden
31D3 Morada Brazil
84D3 Morādābād India
35B1 Morada Nova de Minas *L* Brazil
101D2 Morafenobe Madag
101D2 Moramanga Madag
27J2 Morant Bay Jamaica
27J2 Morant Pt Jamaica
87B3 Moratuwa Sri Lanka
59B3 Morava *R* Austria/ Slovakia
54B2 Morava *R* Serbia, Yugos
90C2 Moräveh Tappeh Iran
44C3 Moray Division, Scot
40C2 Moray Firth Estuary Scot
47C1 Morbegno Italy
85C4 Morbi India
93D2 Mor Dağ *Mt* Turk
5J5 Morden Can
61F3 Mordoviya Division, Russian Fed
42C2 Morecambe Eng
42C2 Morecambe B Eng
107D3 Moree Aust
14B3 Morehead USA
47C1 Mörel Switz

24B3 Morelia Mexico
23B2 Morelos State, Mexico
85D3 Morena India
5E4 Moresby I Can
109D1 Moreton I Aust
48B2 Moreuil France
47B1 Morez France
19B4 Morgan City USA
22B2 Morgan Hill USA
14C3 Morgantown USA
101G1 Morgenzon S Africa
47B1 Morges Switz
46D2 Morhange France
74E2 Mori Japan
27C1 Moriatio Tobago
13B2 Morice L Can
13E2 Morinville Can
74E3 Morioka Japan
109D2 Morisset Aust
63D1 Morkoka *R* Russian Fed
48B2 Morlaix France
27Q2 Morne Diablotin *Mt* Dominica
106C2 Mornington *I* Aust
85B3 Moro Pak
96B2 Morocco Kingdom, Africa
79B4 Moro G Phil
99D3 Morogoro Tanz
23A1 Moroleon Mexico
101D3 Morombe Madag
26B2 Morón Cuba
101D3 Morondava Madag
50A2 Morón de la Frontera Spain
101D1 Moroni Comoros
71D3 Morotai *I* Indon
99D2 Moroto Uganda
61F4 Morozovsk Russian Fed
42D2 Morpeth Eng
19B2 Morrilton USA
35B1 Morrinhos Brazil
110C1 Morrinsville NZ
16B2 Morristown New Jersey, USA
15C2 Morristown New York, USA
16B2 Morrisville Pennsylvania, USA
21A2 Morro Bay USA
23A2 Morro de Papanoa Mexico
23A2 Morro de Petatlán Mexico
101C2 Morrumbala Mozam
101C3 Morrumbene Mozam
61F3 Morshansk Russian Fed
78B3 Morss *Is* Myan Moscow = Moskva
20C1 Moscow Idaho, USA
56B2 Mosel *R* Germany
46D2 Moselle Department, France
46D2 Moselle *R* France
20C1 Moses Lake USA
111B3 Mosgiel NZ
38G5 Moshi Tanz
38G5 Mosjøen Nor
63G2 Moskal'vo Russian Fed
60E2 Moskva Russian Fed
60E2 Moskva Division, Russian Fed
35C1 Mosquito *R* Brazil
39G7 Moss Nor
98B3 Mossaka Congo
100B4 Mossel Bay S Africa
98B3 Mossendjo Congo

Mossgiel

86D2 Myingyan Myan	90B3 Najafábád Iran	84C1 Nanga Parbat Mt Pak	19B3 Nashville Arkansas, USA
76B1 Myingyao Myan	74C2 Najin N Korea	78C3 Nangapinoh Indon	11B3 Nashville Tennessee, USA
76B3 Myinmoletkat Mt Myan	75A2 Nakama Japan	78C3 Nangatayap Indon	54A1 Našice Croatia
82D3 Myitkyina Myan	74E3 Nakaminato Japan	74B2 Nangnim Sanmaek Mts N Korea	85D4 Näsik India
76B3 Myitta Myan	75A2 Nakamura Japan	86C1 Nang Xian China	97D3 Nasir Sudan
86C2 Mymensingh Bang	75B1 Nakano Japan	73F3 Nangzhou China	13B1 Nass R Can
69F3 Myojin I Japan	75A1 Nakano-shima I Japan	87B2 Nanjangúd India	26B1 Nassau The Bahamas
39F6 Myrdal Nor	74C4 Nakatsu Japan	72D3 Nanjing China	16C1 Nassau USA
38B2 Myrdalsjökur Ice Cap Iceland	75B1 Nakatsu-gawa Japan	Nanking = Nanjing	95C2 Nasser,L Egypt
17C1 Myrtle Beach USA	95C3 Nak' fa Eritrea	74C4 Nankoku Japan	39G7 Nässjö Sweden
20B2 Myrtle Creek USA	93E2 Nakhichevan Azerbaijan	73C4 Nan Ling Region, China	7C4 Nastapoka Is Can
39G7 Mysen Nor	93E2 Nakhichevan Division, Azerbaijan	76D1 Nanliu R China	100B3 Nata Botswana
56C2 Mysiloborz Pol	92B4 Nakhl Egypt	73B5 Nanning China	31D3 Natal Brazil
64F3 Mys Kanin Nos C Russian Fed	74C2 Nakhodka Russian Fed	6F3 Nanortalik Greenland	70A3 Natal Indon
59B3 Myslenice Pol	76C3 Nakhon Pathom Thai	73A5 Nanpan Jiang R China	90B3 Natanz Iran
69H1 Mys Lopatka C Russian Fed	76C3 Nakhon Ratchasima Thai	86A1 Nánpára India	7D4 Natashquan Can
87B2 Mysore India	77C4 Nakhon Si Thammarat Thai	73D4 Nanping China	7D4 Natashquan R Can
60D5 Mys Sarych C Ukraine	12H3 Nakina Can	6A1 Nansen Sd Can	19B3 Natchez USA
16D2 Mystic USA	7B4 Nakina Ontario, Can	99D3 Nansio Tanz	19B3 Natchitoches USA
61H5 Mys Tyub-Karagan C Kazakhstan	12C3 Naknek USA	48B2 Nantes France	108C3 Nathalia Aust
63G2 Mys Yelizavety C Russian Fed	12C3 Naknek L USA	13E2 Nanton Can	6H2 Nathorsts Land Region Greenland
64H2 Mys Zhelaniya C Russian Fed	4C4 Nakrek USA	72C3 Nantong China	13C1 Nation R Can
77D3 My Tho Viet	39G8 Nakskov Den	10C2 Nantucket I USA	21B3 National City USA
20B2 Mytle Point USA	99D3 Nakuru Kenya	72C3 Nanyang China	75C1 Natori Japan
101C2 Mzimba Malawi	13D2 Nakusp Can	72D2 Nanyang Hu L China	99D3 Natron L Tanz
101C2 Mzuzú Malawi	61F5 Nal'chik Russian Fed	99D2 Nanyuki Kenya	106A4 Naturaliste,C Aust
	87B1 Nalgonda India	74D3 Naoetsu Japan	47D1 Nauders Austria
N	87B1 Nallamala Range Mts India	85B4 Naokot Pak	56C4 Nauen Germany
21C4 Naalehu Hawaiian Is	95A1 Nálút Libya	22A1 Napa USA	16C2 Naugatuck USA
39J6 Naantali Fin	101H1 Namaacha Mozam	12B2 Napaiskak USA	57C2 Naumburg Germany
45C2 Naas Irish Rep	65G6 Namak L Iran	15C2 Napanee Can	94B3 Naur Jordan
75B2 Nabari Japan	90C3 Namakzar-e Shadad Salt Flat Iran	64K2 Napas Russian Fed	105G4 Nauru I Pacific O
61H2 Naberezhnye Chelny Russian Fed	65J5 Namangan Uzbekistan	6E3 Napassoq Greenland	63C2 Naushki Russian Fed
12F2 Nabesna R USA	101C2 Nampa Mozam	76D2 Nape Laos	23B1 Nautla Mexico
96D1 Nabeul Tunisia	100A4 Namapualand Region, S Africa	110C1 Napier NZ	50A2 Navahermosa Spain
94B2 Nablus Israel	109D1 Nambour Aust	Naples = Napoli	50A2 Navalmoral de la Mata Spain
101D2 Nacala Mozam	109D2 Nambucca Heads Aust	17B2 Naples Florida, USA	29C7 Navarino I Chile
20D1 Naches USA	77D4 Nam Can Viet	19B3 Naples Texas, USA	51B1 Navarra Province, Spain
101C2 Nachingwea Tanz	82D2 Nam Co L China	73B5 Napo China	34D3 Navarro Arg
19B3 Nacogdoches USA	72D1 Nam Dinh Viet	32C4 Napo R Peru/Ecuador	19A3 Navasota USA
76A3 Nacondam I Indian O	101C2 Nametil Mozam	53B2 Napoli Italy	19A3 Navasota R USA
24B1 Nacozari Mexico	74B4 Namhae-do I S Korea	90A2 Naqadeh Iran	50A1 Navia R Spain
85C4 Nadiad India	100A2 Namib Desert Namibia	92C4 Naqb Ishtar Jordan	34A2 Navidad Chile
50B2 Nador Mor	100A2 Namibe Angola	75B2 Nara Japan	85C4 Navlakhi India
90B3 Nadushan Iran	100A3 Namibia Republic, Africa	97B3 Nara Mali	60D3 Navlya Russian Fed
55C3 Nadvornaya Ukraine	82D3 Namjagbarwa Feng Mt China	107D4 Naracoorte Aust	24B2 Navojoa Mexico
56C1 Naestved Den	71D4 Namlea Indon	23B1 Naranjos Mexico	55B3 Návpaktos Greece
95B2 Nafúrah Libya	109C2 Namoi R Aust	87C1 Narasaráopet India	55B3 Návplion Greece
75A2 Nagahama Japan	13D1 Nampa Can	77C4 Narathiwat Thai	85C4 Navsári India
82D3 Naga Hills Myan	20C2 Nampa USA	86C2 Narayanganj Bang	94C2 Nawá Syria
75B1 Nagai Japan	97B3 Nampala Mali	87B1 Náráyenpet India	86B2 Nawada India
86C1 Nágáland State, India	76C2 Nam Phong Thai	49C3 Narbonne France	84B2 Nawah Afghan
74D3 Nagano Japan	74B3 Namp'o N Korea	84D2 Narendranagar India	85B3 Nawrabshah Pak
74D3 Nagaoka Japan	101C2 Nampula Mozam	56C2 Narew R Pol	73B4 Naxi China
86C1 Nagaon India	38G6 Namsos Nor	75C1 Narita Japan	55C3 Náxos I Greece
87B2 Nágappattinam India	76B1 Namton Myan	85C4 Narmada R India	23A1 Nayar Mexico
85C4 Nagar Parkar Pak	86D2 Namtu Myan	84D3 Narnaul India	90C3 Nay Band Iran
74B4 Nagasaki Japan	13B2 Namu Can	60E2 Naro Fominsk Russian Fed	91B4 Nay Band Iran
75B2 Nagashima Japan	101C2 Namuno Mozam	99D3 Narok Kenya	74E2 Nayoro Japan
75A2 Nagato Japan	46C1 Namur Belg	84C2 Narowal Pak	94B2 Nazareth Israel
85C3 Nágaur India	100A2 Namutoni Namibia	107D4 Narrabri Aust	48B2 Nazay France
87B3 Nágercoil India	74B3 Namwŏn S Korea	109C1 Narran R Aust	32C6 Nazca Peru
85B3 Nagha Kalat Pak	74B2 Nanam N Korea	109C2 Narrandera Aust	92A2 Nazilli Turk
84D3 Nagina India	109D1 Nanango Aust	106A4 Narrogin Aust	63B2 Nazimovo Russian Fed
74D3 Nagoya Japan	74D3 Nanao Japan	109C2 Narromine Aust	13C2 Nazko R Can
85D4 Nágpur India	75B1 Nanatsu-jima I Japan	85D4 Narsimhapur India	99D2 Nazret Eth
82D2 Nagqu China	73B3 Nanbu China	87C1 Narsipatnam India	91C5 Nazwa Oman
59G2 Nagykanizsa Hung	73D4 Nanchang China	6F3 Narssalik Greenland	65J4 Nazyvayevsk Russian Fed
59B3 Nagykörös Hung	73B3 Nanchong China	6F3 Narssaq Greenland	98B3 Ndalatando Angola
69E4 Naha Japan	97D2 Nancy France	6F3 Narssarssuaq Greenland	98C2 Ndélé CAR
8A2 Nahaimo Can	87B1 Nânded India	75C1 Narugo Japan	98B2 Ndende Gabon
84D3 Náhan India	109D2 Nandewar Range Mts Aust	74D3 Naruto Japan	98B1 Ndjamena Chad
4F3 Nahanni Butte Can	85C4 Nandurbar India	60C2 Narva Russian Fed	98B3 Ndjolé Gabon
94B2 Nahariya Israel	87B1 Nandyál India	38H5 Narvik Nor	100B2 Ndola Zambia
90A3 Nahávand Iran	98B2 Nanga Eboko Cam	84D3 Narwána India	109C1 Nebal Aust
46D2 Nahe R Germany		64G3 Nar'yan Mar Russian Fed	108A1 Neales R Aust
72E1 Naimen Qi China		108B1 Narylico Aust	55B3 Neápolis Greece
7D4 Nain Can		65J5 Naryn Kyrgyzstan	43C4 Neath Wales
90B3 Nā'in Iran		97C4 Nasarawa Nigeria	43C4 Neath and Port Talbot County Wales
86D1 Naini Tal India		103D5 Nasca Ridge Pacific O	109C1 Nebine R Aust
44C3 Nairn Scot		16D1 Nashua USA	65G6 Nebit Dag Turkmenistan
99D3 Nairobi Kenya			8C2 Nebraska State, USA
			18A1 Nebraska City USA
			13C2 Nechako R Can

Nowa Sól

58B2	Nowa Sól Pol
18A2	Nowata USA
	Nowgong = Nagaon
12D2	Nowra *R* Aust
109D2	Nowra Aust
90B2	Now Shahr Iran
84C2	Nowshera Pak
59C3	Nowy Sącz Pol
12H3	Noyes I USA
46B2	Noyon France
97B4	Nsawam Ghana
99D1	Nuba *Mts* Sudan
81B3	Nubian Desert Sudan
34A3	Nuble *R* Chile
9D4	Nueces *R* USA
SJ3	Nueltin *L* Can
26A2	Nueva Gerona Cuba
34A3	Nueva Imperial Chile
	Nueva Laredo
34D2	Nueva Palmira Urug
24B2	Nueva Rosita Mexico
26B2	Nuevitas Cuba
24B1	Nuevo Casas Grandes Mexico
24C2	Nuevo Laredo Mexico
99E2	Nugaal Region, Somalia
6E2	Nugâtsiaq Greenland
6E2	Nugssuaq *Pen* Greenland
6E2	Nûgussaq *I* Greenland
108A2	Nukey Bluff *Mt* Aust
93D3	Nukhayb Iraq
65G5	Nukus Uzbekistan
12C2	Nulato USA
106B4	Nullarbor Plain Aust
97D4	Numan Nig
71A4	Numata Japan
98C2	Numatinna *R* Sudan
74D3	Numazu Japan
71E4	Numfoor *I* Indon
108C3	Numurkah Aust
12B2	Nunapitchuk USA
84D2	Nunkun *Mt* India
53A2	Nuoro Sardegna
91B3	Nūrābād Iran
47C2	Nure *R* Italy
108A2	Nuriootpa Aust
84C1	Nuristan *Upland* Afghan
61H3	Nurlat Russian Fed
38K6	Nurmes Fin
57C3	Nürnberg Germany
108C2	Nurri,Mt Aust
93D2	Nusaybin Turk
12C3	Nushagak *R* USA
12C3	Nushagak *B* USA
12C3	Nushagak *Pen* USA
84B3	Nushki Pak
7D4	Nutak Can
12F2	Nutzotin *Mts* USA
	Nuuk = Godthåb
86A1	Nuwakot Nepal
87C3	Nuwara-Eliya Sri Lanka
6C3	Nuyukjuak Can
16C2	Nyack USA
99D2	Nyahururu Kenya
108B3	Nyah West Aust
46B3	Nyah WB
68B3	Nyainentanglha Shan *Mts* China
99D3	Nyakabindi Tanz
98C1	Nyala Sudan
68B1	Nyalam China
98C2	Nyamlell Sudan
64F3	Nyandoma
100C2	Nyanga Zim
98B3	Nyanga *R* Gabon
101C2	Nyasa *L* Malawi/Mozam
76B2	Nyaunglebin Myan
61J2	Nyazepetrovsk Russian Fed
39G7	Nyborg Den
39H7	Nybro Sweden
64J3	Nyda Russian Fed
6D1	Nyeboes Land *Region* Can
99D3	Nyeri Kenya

101C2	Nyimba Zambia
82D3	Nyingchi China
59C3	Nyíregyháza Hung
99D2	Nyiru,Mt Kenya
38J6	Nykarleby Fin
39F7	Nykøbing Den
39G8	Nykøbing Den
39H7	Nyköping Sweden
100B3	Nylstroom S Africa
109C2	Nymagee Aust
39H7	Nynäshamn Sweden
109C2	Nyngan Aust
47B1	Nyon Switz
98B2	Nyong *R* Cam
49D3	Nyons France
59B2	Nysa Pol
20C2	Nyssa USA
63D1	Nyurba Russian Fed
99D3	Nzega Tanz
97B4	Nzérékore Guinea
98B3	N'zeto Angola

O

6F3	Oaggsimiut Greenland
8C2	Oahe Res USA
21C4	Oahu *I* Hawaiian Is
22B2	Oakdale USA
109D1	Oakey Aust
21A2	Oakland California, USA
20B2	Oakland Oregon, USA
14A3	Oak Lake Can
14A2	Oak Lawn USA
22B2	Oakley California, USA
20B2	Oakridge USA
14C2	Oakville Can
111B3	Oamaru NZ
112B7	Oates Land *Region*, Ant
109C4	Oatlands Aust
23B2	Oaxaca Mexico
23B2	Oaxaca State, Mexico
65J3	Ob' *R* Russian Fed
75B1	Obama Japan
111A3	Oban NZ
44B3	Oban Scot
75C1	Obanazawa Japan
47D1	Oberammergau Germany
46D1	Oberhausen Germany
47D1	Oberstdorf Germany
71D4	Obi *I* Indon
33F4	Óbidos Brazil
74E2	Obihiro Japan
98C2	Obo CAR
99E1	Obock Djibouti
58B2	Oborniki Pol
63D2	Oboyan Russian Fed
20B2	O'Brien USA
61H3	Obshchiy Syrt *Mts* Russian Fed
64J3	Obskaya Guba *B* Russian Fed
97B4	Obuasi Ghana
17B2	Ocala USA
32C2	Ocana Colombia
50B2	Ocaña Spain
12G3	Ocean *C* USA
15C3	Ocean City Maryland, USA
16B3	Ocean City New Jersey, USA
5F4	Ocean Falls Can
22D4	Oceanside USA
19C3	Ocean Springs USA
44C3	Ochil Hills Scot
17B1	Ochlockonee *R* USA
27H1	Ocho Rios Jamaica
17B1	Ocmulgee *R* USA
17B1	Oconee *R* USA
14A2	Oconto USA
23A1	Ocotlán Jalisco, Mexico
23B2	Ocotlán Oaxaca, Mexico
97B4	Oda Ghana
75A1	Oda Japan

38B2	Óðáðahraun *Region*, Iceland
74E2	Odate Japan
74D3	Odawara Japan
39F6	Odda Nor
50A2	Odemira Port
55C3	Ödemiş Turk
101G1	Odendaalsrus S Africa
39G7	Odense Den
56C2	Oder *R* Pol/Germany
9C3	Odessa Texas, USA
60D4	Odessa Ukraine
20C1	Odessa Washington, USA
97B4	Odienné Côte d'Ivoire
59B2	Odra *R* Pol
53C2	Ofanto *R* Italy
94B3	Ofaqim Israel
45C2	Offaly County, Irish Rep
49D1	Offenbach Germany
49D2	Offenburg Germany
74D3	Oga Japan
99E2	Ogaden Region, Eth
74D3	Ogaki Japan
8C2	Ogallala USA
69G4	Ogasawara Gunto *Is* Japan
97C4	Ogbomosho Nig
8B2	Ogden Utah, USA
15C2	Ogdensburg USA
17B1	Ogeechee *R* USA
12G1	Ogilvie Can
17B1	Oglethorpe,Mt USA
47D2	Oglio *R* Italy
47B1	Ognon *R* France
97C4	Ogoja Nig
98A3	Ogooué *R* Gabon
58C1	Ogre Latvia
96B2	Oguilet Khenachich *Well* Mali
52C1	Ogulin Croatia
111A3	Ohai NZ
110C1	Ohakune NZ
96C2	Ohanet Alg
110B2	Ohau,L NZ
14A3	Ohio State, USA
10A2	Ohio *R* USA
100A2	Ohopoho Namibia
57C2	Ohre *R* Czech Republic
55B2	Ohrid Macedonia
55B2	Ohridsko Jezero *L* Macedonia/Alb
110B1	Ohura NZ
14C2	Oil City USA
21B2	Oildale USA
46B2	Oise Department, France
49C2	Oise *R* France
74C4	Oita Japan
22C3	Ojai USA
24B2	Ojinaga Mexico
23B2	Ojitlán Mexico
30C4	Ojos del Salado *Mt* Arg
23A1	Ojueloz Mexico
60E3	Oka *R* Russian Fed
100A3	Okahandja Namibia
20C1	Okanagan Falls Can
13D2	Okanagan *L* Can
20C1	Okanogan USA
20B1	Okanogan *R* USA
20B1	Okanogan Range *Mts* Can/USA
84C2	Okara Pak
100A2	Okavango *R* Angola/Namibia
100B2	Okavango Delta *Marsh* Botswana
74D3	Okaya Japan
74C4	Okayama Japan
75B2	Okazaki Japan
17B2	Okeechobee USA
17B2	Okeechobee,L USA

17B1	Okefenokee Swamp USA
97C4	Okene Nig
85B4	Okha India
69G1	Okha Russian Fed
86B1	Okhaldunga Nepal
62J3	Okhotsk,S of Russian Fed
69E4	Okinawa *I* Japan
69E4	Okinawa gunto *Arcfl* Japan
74C3	Oki-shoto *Is* Japan
9D3	Oklahoma State, USA
18A2	Oklahoma City USA
18A2	Okmulgee USA
98B3	Okondja Gabon
98B3	Okoyo Congo
97C4	Okpara *R* Nig
61J4	Oktyabr'sk Kazakhstan
61H3	Oktyabr'skiy Russian Fed
74D2	Okushiri-tō *I* Japan
38A2	Ólafsvík Iceland
39H7	Øland *I* Sweden
108B2	Olary Aust
18B2	Olathe USA
29D3	Olavarría Arg
53A2	Olbia Sardegna
12G1	Old Crow Can
56B2	Oldenburg Niedersachsen, Germany
56C2	Oldenburg Schleswig-Holstein, Germany
15C2	Old Forge USA
42C3	Oldham Eng
12D3	Old Harbor USA
41B3	Old Head of Kinsale *C* Scot
16C2	Old Lyme USA
13E2	Olds Can
72B1	Óldziyt Mongolia
15C2	Olean USA
63E2	Olekma *R* Russian Fed
63D1	Olekminsk Russian Fed
38L5	Olenegorsk Russian Fed
58D2	Olevsk Ukraine
69F2	Ol'ga Russian Fed
100A3	Olifants *R* Namibia
55B2	Olimbos *Mt* Greece
35B2	Olimpia Brazil
23B2	Olinala Mexico
31E3	Olinda Brazil
34C2	Oliva Arg
29C2	Olivares *Mt* Arg
35C2	Oliveira Brazil
13D3	Oliver Can
30D3	Ollagüe Chile
30D3	Ollagüe *Mt* Bol
18C2	Olney USA
68E1	Olochi Russian Fed
39G7	Olofström Sweden
99B3	Olombo Congo
99B3	Olomouc Czech Republic
60D1	Olonets Russian Fed
79B3	Olongapo Phil
48B3	Oloron Ste Marie France
68D1	Olovyannaya Russian Fed
56B2	Olpe Germany
58C2	Olsztyn Pol
54B2	Olt *R* Rom
47B1	Olten Switz
20B1	Olympia USA
20B1	Olympic Nat Pk USA
	Olympus = Olimbos
20B1	Olympus,Mt USA
65J4	Om' *R* Russian Fed
75B1	Omachi Japan
75B2	Omae-zaki *C* Japan
45C1	Omagh N Ire
18A1	Omaha USA
20C1	Omak USA
91C4	Oman Sultanate, Arabian Pen
91C4	Oman,G of UAE
98A3	Omboué Gabon

99D1 Omdurman Sudan
23B2 Ometepec Mexico
99D1 Om Hâjer Eritrea
13B1 Omineca R Can
13B1 Omineca Mts Can
75B1 Omiya Japan
12H3 Ommanney B Can
4H2 Ommanney C Can
99C2 Omo R Eth
65J4 Omsk Russian Fed
74B4 Omura Japan
74C4 Omuta Japan
61H2 Omutninsk Russian Fed
78D3 Onang Indon
14B1 Onaping L Can
100A2 Oncócua Angola
100A2 Ondangua Namibia
59C3 Ondava R Slovakia
68D2 Ondörhaan Molgolia
83B5 One and Half Degree Chan Indian O
64E3 Onega Russian Fed
64E3 Onega R Russian Fed
15C2 Oneida L USA
8D2 O'Neill USA
69H2 Onekotan I Russian Fed
98C3 Onema Zaire
15C2 Oneonta USA
54C1 Oneşti Rom
64E3 Onezhskoye Ozero L Russian Fed
100A2 Ongiva Angola
74B3 Ongjin N Korea
72D1 Ongniud Qi China
87C1 Ongole India
15C2 Onieda L USA
101D3 Onilahy R Madag
97C4 Onitsha Nig
68C2 Onjüül Mongolia
75B1 Ono Japan
75B2 Onohara-jima I Japan
74C4 Onomichi Japan
106A3 Onslow Aust
17C1 Onslow B USA
75B1 Ontake-san Mt Japan
22D3 Ontario California, USA
20C2 Ontario Oregon, USA
7A4 Ontario Province, Can
15C2 Ontario L Can/USA
51B2 Onteniente Spain
106C3 Oodnadatta Aust
106C4 Ooldea Aust
18A2 Oologah L USA
46B1 Oostende Belg
46B1 Oosterschelde Estuary Neth
87B2 Ootacamund India
13B2 Ootsa L Can
69H1 Opala Russian Fed
98C3 Opala Zaire
87C3 Opanake Sri Lanka
61G2 Oparino Russian Fed
59B3 Opava Czech Republic
17A1 Opelika USA
19B3 Opelousas USA
12C2 Ophir USA
58D1 Opochka Russian Fed
59B2 Opole Pol
Oporto = Porto
110C1 Opotiki NZ
17A1 Opp USA
38F6 Oppdal Nor
110B1 Opunake NZ
54B1 Oradea Rom
38B2 Oraefajökull Mts Iceland
85D3 Orai India
96B1 Oran Alg
30D3 Orán Arg
109C2 Orange Aust
22D4 Orange California, USA
49C3 Orange France
19B3 Orange Texas, USA
100A3 Orange R S Africa

17B1 Orangeburg USA
17B1 Orange Park USA
14B2 Orangeville Can
56C2 Oranienburg Germany
79C3 Oras Phil
54B1 Orăştie Rom
54B1 Oravita Rom
52B2 Orbetello Italy
109C3 Orbost Aust
46B1 Orchies France
47B2 Orco R Italy
10B2 Ord R Aust
108B2 Ord,Mt Aust
93C1 Orda Kaz
39H7 Örebro Sweden
8A2 Oregon State, USA
20B1 Oregon City USA
39H6 Öregrund Sweden
60E2 Orekhovo Zuyevo Russian Fed
60E3 Orel Russian Fed
60E3 Orel Division Russian Fed
61H3 Orenburg Russian Fed
61H3 Orenburg Division Russian Fed
34D3 Orense Arg
50A1 Orense Spain
56C1 Oresund Str Den/Sweden
111A3 Oreti R NZ
55C3 Orhaneli R Turk
68C2 Orhon Gol R Mongolia
23B2 Oriental Mexico
108B1 Orientos Aust
51B2 Orihuela Spain
15C2 Orillia Can
33E2 Orinoco R Ven
86A2 Orissa State, India
53A3 Oristano Sardegna
38K6 Orivesi L Fin
33F4 Oriximina Brazil
23B2 Orizaba Mexico
35B1 Orizona Brazil
38F6 Örkelljunga Sweden
32A2 Orkney I Scot
35B2 Orlândia Brazil
17B2 Orlando USA
48C2 Orléanais Region France
48C2 Orléans France
63B2 Orlik Russian Fed
82A3 Ormara Pak
79B3 Ormoc Phil
17B2 Ormond Beach USA
46C2 Ornain R France
47B1 Ornans France
48B2 Orne R France
38H6 Örnsköldsvik Sweden
32C3 Orocue Colombia
94B3 Oron Israel
Orontes = 'Asi
79B4 Oroquieta Phil
59C3 Oroshaza Hung
21A2 Oroville California, USA
20C1 Oroville Washington, USA
47B1 Orsières Switz
65G4 Orsk Russian Fed
38F6 Ørsta Nor
38F7 Orthez France
50A1 Ortigueira Spain
47D1 Ortles Mts Italy
27L1 Ortoire R Trinidad
30C2 Oruro Bol
61J2 Osa Russian Fed
18B2 Osage R USA
75B1 Osaka Japan
25D4 Osa,Pen de Costa Rica
18C2 Osceola Arkansas, USA
18B1 Osceola Iowa, USA
20C2 Osgood Mts USA
15C2 Oshawa Can
75B2 O-shima I Japan
10B2 Oshkosh USA
97C4 Oshogbo Nig

7B5 Oshosh USA
98B3 Oshwe Zaire
54A1 Osijek Croatia
65K4 Osinniki Russian Fed
58D2 Osipovichi Belarus
18B1 Oskaloosa USA
60A2 Oskarshamn Sweden
39G7 Oslo Nor
92C2 Osmaniye Turk
56B2 Osnabrück Germany
30F4 Osório Brazil
29B4 Osorno Chile
50B1 Osorno Spain
20C1 Osoyoos Can
13C1 Ospika R Can
107D5 Ossa,Mt Aust
16C2 Ossining USA
60D2 Ostashkov Russian Fed
Ostend = Oostende
38G6 Østerdalen V Nor
38G6 Östersund Sweden
56B2 Ostfriesische Inseln Is Germany
39H6 Östhammar Sweden
53B2 Ostia Italy
47D2 Ostiglia Italy
59B3 Ostrava Czech Republic
59B2 Ostróda Pol
58B2 Ostrołeka Pol
60C2 Ostrov Russian Fed
64J2 Ostrov Belyy I Russian Fed
64H1 Ostrov Greem Bell I Barents S
64F3 Ostrov Kolguyev I Russian Fed
74F2 Ostrov Kunashir I Russian Fed
64F2 Ostrov Mechdusharskiy I Barents S
90B2 Ostrov Ogurchinskiy I Turkmenistan
64G1 Ostrov Rudol'fa I Barents S
64G2 Ostrov Vaygach I Russian Fed
1B7 Ostrov Vrangelya I Russian Fed
58C2 Ostrów Wlkp. Pol
59C2 Ostrowiec Pol
58C2 Ostrów Mazowiecka Pol
50A2 Osuna Spain
15C2 Oswego USA
43C3 Oswestry Eng
59B2 Oświęcim Pol
75B1 Ota Japan
111B3 Otago Pen NZ
110C2 Otaki NZ
74E2 Otaru Japan
32B3 Otavalo Ecuador
100A2 Otavi Namibia
75C1 Otawara Japan
20C1 Othello USA
55B3 Othris Mt Greece
16C1 Otis Massachusetts, USA
16B2 Otisville USA
100A3 Otjiwarongo Namibia
72B2 Otog Qi China
110C1 Otorohanga NZ
55A2 Otranto Italy
55A2 Otranto,Str of Chan Italy/Alb
14A2 Otsego USA
75B1 Otsu Japan
39F6 Otta Nor
39F7 Otta R Nor
15C1 Ottawa Can
18A2 Ottawa Kansas, USA
15C1 Ottawa R Can
7B4 Ottawa Is Can
6B1 Otto Fjord Can
101G1 Ottosdal S Africa
18B1 Ottumwa USA
46D2 Ottweiler Germany
97C4 Oturkpo Nig

32B5 Otusco Peru
108B3 Otway,C Aust
58C2 Otwock Pol
47D1 Ötztal Mts Austria
76C1 Ou R Laos
19B3 Ouachita R USA
19B3 Ouachita,L USA
19B3 Ouachita Mts USA
96A2 Ouadane Maur
98C2 Ouadda CAR
98C1 Ouaddaï Desert Region Chad
97B3 Ouagadougou Burkina
97B3 Ouahigouya Burkina
96A2 Ouaka CAR
97C3 Oualam Niger
96C2 Ouallen Alg
98C2 Ouanda Djallé CAR
96A2 Ouarane Region, Maur
96C1 Ouargla Alg
96A2 Ouarra R CAR
96B1 Ouarzazate Mor
51C2 Ouassel R Alg
98B2 Oubangui R Congo
46B1 Oudenaarde Belg
100B4 Oudtshoorn S Africa
51B2 Oued Tlélat Alg
96A2 Oued Zem Mor
98B2 Ouesso Congo
96B1 Ouezzane Mor
98B2 Ouham R Chad
96A4 Ouidah Benin
96B1 Oujda Mor
38J6 Oulainen Fin
38K5 Oulu Fin
38K6 Oulu R Fin
38K6 Oulujärvi L Fin
95B3 Oum Chalouba Chad
98B1 Oum Hadjer Chad
95B3 Oum Haouach Watercourse Chad
38K5 Ounas R Fin
95B3 Ounianga Kébir Chad
46D1 Our R Germany
46B2 Ourcq R France
31C3 Ouricuri Brazil
35B2 Ourinhos Brazil
35C2 Ouro Prêto Brazil
47F2 Ourthe R Belg
42D2 Ouse R Eng
43E3 Ouse R Eng
40B2 Outer Hebrides Is Scot
22C4 Outer Santa Barbara Chan USA
100A3 Outjo Namibia
38K6 Outokumpu Fin
108B3 Ouyen Aust
47C2 Ovada Italy
34A2 Ovalle Chile
100A2 Ovamboland Region, Namibia
61H5 Ova Tyuleni Is Kazakhstan
38J5 Övertorneå Sweden
50A1 Oviedo Spain
60E3 Ovruch Ukraine
63E2 Ovsyanka Russian Fed
111A3 Owaka NZ
75B2 Owase Japan
11B3 Owensboro USA
21B2 Owens L USA
14B2 Owen Sound Can
107D1 Owen Stanley Range Mts PNG
97C4 Owerri Nig
97C4 Owo Nig
14B2 Owosso USA
20C2 Owyhee Mts USA
32B6 Oxapampa Peru
39H7 Oxelösund Sweden
43D4 Oxford County, Eng
16D1 Oxford Massachusetts, USA
19C3 Oxford Mississippi, USA
45B1 Ox Mts Irish Rep

Oxnard

22C3	Oxnard USA	14B2	Painesville USA
74D3	Oyama Japan	9B3	Painted Desert USA
13E2	Oyen Can	42B2	Paisley Scot
98B2	Oyem Gabon	32A5	Paita Peru
44B3	Oykel R Scot	38J5	Pajala Sweden
39E6	Øyre Nor	80E3	Pakistan Republic, Asia
109C4	Oyster B Aust		
79B4	Ozamiz Phil	76C2	Pak Lay Laos
17A1	Ozark USA	86D2	Pakokku Myan
22C3	Ozark Plat USA	12E3	Pakowki L Can
18B2	Ozarks,L of the USA	52C1	Pakrac Croatia
59C3	Ózd Hung	54A1	Paks Hung
65K5	Ozero Alakol L Kazakhstan/	76C2	Pak Sane Laos
	Russian Fed	76D2	Pakse Laos
65J5	Ozero Balkhash L	99D2	Pakwach Uganda
	Kazakhstan	98B2	Pala Chad
63C2	Ozero Baykal L	52C2	Palagruža I Croatia
	Russian Fed	46B2	Palaiseau France
65J4	Ozero Chany L		Palakhat = Palghat
	Russian Fed	78C3	Palangkaraya Indon
69F1	Ozero Chukchagirskoye	87B2	Palani India
	Russian Fed	85C4	Palanpur India
69F1	Ozero Evoron	100B3	Palapye Botswana
	Russian Fed	17B2	Palatka USA
	Ozero Chudskoye = Peipus,L	17E3	Palau Is Pacific O
60D2	Ozero Il'men L	76B3	Palaw Myan
	Russian Fed	79A4	Palawan I Phil
38L5	Ozero Imandra L	79A4	Palawan Pass Phil
	Russian Fed	87B3	Palayankottai India
82B1	Ozero Issyk Kul' L	39J7	Paldiski Estonia
	Kyrgyzstan	78A3	Palembang Indon
69F2	Ozero Khanka L	50B1	Palencia Spain
	China/Russian Fed	94B1	Paleokhorio Cyprus
38L5	Ozero Kovdozero L	53B3	Palermo Italy
	Russian Fed	19A3	Palestine USA
38L5	Ozero Kuyto L	86C2	Paletwa Myan
	Russian Fed	87B2	Pālghāt India
38L5	Ozero Pyaozero L	85C3	Pāli India
	Russian Fed	85C4	Pālitana India
65H4	Ozero Tengiz L	87B3	Palk Str India/ Sri Lanka
	Kazakhstan	61G3	Pallasovka Russian Fed
38L5	Ozero Topozero L		
	Russian Fed	38J5	Pallastunturi Mt Fin
65K5	Ozero Zaysan L	111B2	Palliser B NZ
	Kazakhstan	111B2	Palliser,C NZ
23B1	Ozuluama Mexico	101D2	Palma Mozam
		51C2	Palma de Mallorca Spain

	P	31D3	Palmares Brazil
		26A5	Palmar Sur Costa Rica
100A4	Paarl S Africa		
44A3	Pabbay I Scot	31B4	Palmas Brazil
58B2	Pabianice Pol	97B4	Palmas,C Lib
86B2	Pabna Bang	26B2	Palma Soriano Cuba
58D2	Pabrade Lithuania	17B2	Palm Bay USA
32B5	Pacasmayo Peru	17B2	Palm Beach USA
20K6	Pachuca Mexico	22C3	Palmdale USA
105K6	Pacific-Antarctic Ridge Pacific O	31D3	Palmeira dos Indos Brazil
22B2	Pacific Grove USA	12E2	Palmer USA
78C4	Pacitan Indon	112C3	Palmer Base Ant
35C1	Pacui R Brazil	112C3	Palmer Arch Ant
70D4	Padang Indon	112B3	Palmer Land Region Ant
56B2	Paderborn Germany		
5J3	Padlei Can	111B3	Palmerston NZ
86C2	Padma R Bang	110C2	Palmerston North NZ
47D2	Padova Italy	16B2	Palmerton USA
9D4	Padre I USA	17B2	Palmetto USA
43B4	Padstow Eng	53C3	Palmi Italy
108B3	Padthaway Aust	32B3	Palmira Colombia
	Padua = Padova	107D2	Palm Is Aust
14A3	Paducah Kentucky, USA	21B3	Palm Springs USA
		18B2	Palmyra Missouri, USA
11B3	Paducah USA		
38L5	Padunskoye More L Russian Fed	16A2	Palmyra Pennsylvania, USA
74A3	Paegyong-do I S Korea	86B2	Palmyras Pt India
		22A2	Palo Alto USA
110C1	Paeroa NZ	78B2	Paloh Indon
100C3	Pafuri Mozam	99D1	Paloich Sudan
52B2	Pag I Croatia	23B1	Palomar Mt USA
78B4	Pagai Selatan I Indon	70D4	Palopo Indon
78B4	Pagai Utara I Indon	70C4	Palu Indon
71F2	Pagan I Pacific O	93C2	Palu Turk
78D3	Pagatan Indon	84D3	Palwal India
55C3	Pagonohdas Greece	97C3	Pama Burkina
110C2	Pahiatua NZ	78C4	Pamekasan Indon
		78B4	Pameungpeuk Indon
21C4	Pahoa Hawaiian Is	48C3	Pamiers France
17B2	Pahokee USA	82B2	Pamir Mts China
39K6	Päijänne L Fin	65J6	Pamir R Russian Fed
21C4	Pailola Chan Hawaiian Is	11C3	Pamlico Sd USA
		9C3	Pampa USA

34B2	Pampa de la Salinas Salt pan Arg	34C2	Paraná Urug
		29E2	Paraná R Arg
34B3	Pampa de la Varita Plain Arg	31B4	Paraná R Brazil
		35A2	Paraná R Brazil
32C2	Pamplona Colombia	30G4	Paranaguá Brazil
50B1	Pamplona Spain	35A2	Paranaíba Brazil
18C2	Pana USA	35A1	Paranaíba R Brazil
54B2	Panagyurishte Bulg	35A2	Paranapanema R Brazil
87A1	Panaji India		
32B2	Panamá Panama	35A2	Paranavai Brazil
32A2	Panama Republic, Cent America	79B4	Parang Phil
		35C1	Paraope R Brazil
26B5	Panama Canal	110B2	Paraparaumu NZ
		87B1	Parbhani India
17A1	Panama City USA	14B2	Pardes Hanna Israel
21B2	Panamint Range Mts USA	34D3	Pardo Arg
		35D1	Pardo R Bahia, Brazil
21B2	Panamint V USA	35A2	Pardo R Mato Grosso do Sul, Brazil
47D2	Panaro R Italy		
79B3	Panay I Phil	35B1	Pardo R Minas Gerais, Brazil
54B2	Pancevo Serbia, Yugos	35B2	Pardo R Sao Paulo, Brazil
79B3	Pandan Phil		
87B1	Pandharpur India	59B2	Pardubice Czech Republic
108A1	Pandie Pandie Aust	69F4	Parece Vela Reef Pacific O
58C1	Panevėžys Lithuania		
65K5	Panfilov Kazakhstan	10C2	Parent Can
76B1	Pang R Myan	70C4	Parepare Indon
99D3	Pangani Tanz	34C3	Parera Arg
99D3	Pangani R Tanz	70B4	Pariaman Indon
98C3	Pangi Zaïre	33E2	Paria,Pen de Ven
78B3	Pangkalpinang Indon	48C1	Paris France
6D3	Pangnirtung Can	14B3	Paris Kentucky, USA
76B1	Pangtara Myan	19A3	Paris Texas, USA
79B4	Pangutaran Group Is Phil	14B3	Parkersburg USA
		109C2	Parkes Aust
84D3	Panipat India	16B3	Parkesburg USA
84B2	Panjao Afghan	14A2	Park Forest USA
74B3	P'anmunjŏm N Korea	20B1	Parksville Can
86A2	Panna India	87B1	Parli India
35A2	Panorama Brazil	47D2	Parma Italy
53B3	Pantelleria I Medit S	14B2	Parma USA
23B1	Pantepec Mexico	31C2	Parnaíba Brazil
23B1	Panuco Mexico	31C2	Parnaíba R Brazil
23B1	Panuco R Mexico	55B3	Párnon Oros Mts Greece
73A4	Pan Xian China		
53C3	Paola Italy	60B2	Pärnu Estonia
18B2	Paola USA	86B1	Paro Bhutan
14A3	Paoli USA	108B1	Paroo R Aust
59B3	Pápa Hung	108B2	Paroo Channel R Aust
108B1	Papakura NZ		
23B2	Papaloapan R Mexico	55C3	Páros I Greece
		47B2	Parpaillon Mts France
23B1	Papantla Mexico		
76B2	Papa Stour I Scot	34A3	Parral Chile
72A1	Papatoetoe NZ	109D2	Parramatta Aust
44C2	Papa Westray I Scot	9C4	Parras Mexico
107D1	Papua,G of PNG	6B3	Parry B Can
107D1	Papua New Guinea Republic, S E Asia	4G2	Parry Is Can
		7C5	Parry Sd Can
34A2	Papudo Chile	14B1	Parry Sound Can
76B2	Papun Myan	57C3	Parsberg Germany
33G4	Para State, Brazil	5C4	Parsnip R Can
31B2	Pará R Brazil	18A2	Parsons Kansas, USA
106A3	Paraburdoo Aust	14C3	Parsons West Virginia, USA
32B6	Paracas,Pen de Peru		
35B1	Paracatu Brazil	48B2	Parthenay France
35B1	Paracatu R Brazil	53B3	Partinico Italy
108A2	Parachilna Aust	74C2	Partizansk Russian Fed
84C2	Parachinar Pak		
54B2	Paracin Serbia, Yugos	33G4	Paru R Brazil
		101G1	Parys S Africa
35C1	Pará de Minas Brazil	19A4	Pasadena Texas, USA
21A2	Paradise California, USA		
		22C3	Pasadena California, USA
18B2	Paragould USA		
33E6	Paraguá R Bol	78D3	Pasangkayu Indon
30E2	Paraguá R Ven	76B2	Pasawing Myan
30E2	Paraguaí R Brazil	19C3	Pascagoula USA
30E4	Paraguari Par	54C1	Pascani Rom
30E3	Paraguay Republic, S America	20C1	Pasco USA
		46B1	Pas-de-Calais Department, France
30E3	Paraguay R Par		
31D3	Paraíba State, Brazil	39G8	Pasewalk Germany
35B2	Paraíba R Brazil	35C1	Pashūi'yeh Iran
35C2	Paraíba do Sul R Brazil	108B4	Pasley,C Aust
		29E2	Paso de los Toros Urug
97C4	Parakou Benin		
108A2	Parakylia Aust	29B4	Paso Limay Arg
87B3	Paramakkudi India	21A2	Paso Robles USA
33F2	Paramaribo Surinam	45B3	Passage West Irish Rep
69H1	Paramushir I Russian Fed		
		16B2	Passaic USA
30F3	Paraná State, Brazil		

16B2 Philadelphia Pennsylvania, USA
Philippeville = Skikda
46C1 Philippeville Belg
71D2 Philippine S Pacific O
71D2 Philippines Republic, S E Asia
104E3 Philippine Trench Pacific O
15C2 Philipsburg Pennsylvania, USA
12E1 Philip Smith Mts USA
79B2 Philippine S Phil
6B1 Phillips B Can
16B2 Phillipsburg New Jersey, USA
6B2 Philpots Pen Can
76C3 Phnom Penh Camb
9B3 Phoenix Arizona, USA
16B2 Phoenixville USA
76C1 Phong Saly Laos
Phra Nakhon = Bangkok
76C2 Phu Bia Mt Laos
76D3 Phu Cuong Viet
77B4 Phuket Thai
86A2 Phulbani India
76C2 Phu Miang Mt Thai
76D2 Phu Set Mt Laos
76D1 Phu Tho Viet
77D4 Phu Vinh Viet
47C2 Piacenza Italy
109C2 Pian R Aust
52B2 Pianosa I Italy
52C2 Pianosa I Italy
58C2 Piaseczno Pol
54C1 Piatra-Neamţ Rom
31C3 Piauí State, Brazil
47E2 Piave R Italy
99D2 Pibor R Sudan
99D2 Pibor Post Sudan
46B1 Picardie Region, France
19C3 Picayune USA
47B2 Pic de Rochebrune Mt France
34A2 Pichilemu Chile
34C3 Pichi Mahuida Arg
42D2 Pickering Eng
7A4 Pickle Lake Can
96A1 Pico I Açores
47C1 Pico Bernina Mt Switz
51C1 Pico de Anito Mt Spain
24B3 Pico del Infiernillo Mt Mexico
27C3 Pico Duarte Mt Dom Rep
31C3 Picos Brazil
50B1 Picos de Europa Mt Spain
109D2 Picton Aust
111B2 Picton NZ
95A2 Pic Toussidé Mt Chad
35B2 Piedade Brazil
22C2 Piedra USA
24B2 Piedras Negras Mexico
38K6 Pieksämäki Fin
38K6 Pielinen L Fin
47B2 Piemonte Region, Italy
8C2 Pierre USA
59B3 Piešťany Slovakia
101H1 Pietermaritzburg S Africa
100B3 Pietersburg S Africa
101H1 Piet Retief S Africa
60B4 Pietrosu Mt Rom
47E1 Pieve di Cadore Italy
13E2 Pigeon L Can
18B2 Piggott USA
34C3 Pigüé Arg
7A4 Pikangikum L Can
8C3 Pikes Peak USA
100A4 Piketberg S Africa
6F3 Pikintaleg Greenland
82B2 Pik Kommunizma Mt Tajikistan
98B2 Pikounda Congo

82C1 Pik Pobedy Mt China/Kyrgyzstan
34D3 Pila Arg
58B2 Piła Pol
30E4 Pilar Par
30D3 Pilcomayo R Arg/Par
84D3 Pilibhit India
59B2 Pilica R Pol
109C4 Pillar,C Aust
55B3 Pilos Greece
12C3 Pilot Point USA
12B2 Pilot Station USA
19C3 Pilottown USA
33F4 Pimenta Brazil
77C4 Pinang I Malay
26A2 Pinar del Rio Cuba
34B2 Pinas Arg
46C1 Pinche Belg
13E2 Pincher Creek Can
31B2 Pindaré R Brazil
55B3 Pindhos Mts Greece
10C2 Pine Bluff USA
106C2 Pine Creek Aust
22C1 Pinecrest USA
22C2 Pinedale California, USA
22C2 Pine Flat Res USA
64F3 Pinega R Russian Fed
16A2 Pine Grove USA
17B2 Pine Hills USA
17B2 Pine I USA
19B3 Pineland USA
17B2 Pinellas Park USA
5G3 Pine Point Can
47C2 Pinerolo Italy
19B3 Pines,Lo'the USA
19B3 Pineville USA
72C3 Pingdingshan China
73B5 Pingguo China
72B2 Pingliang China
72B2 Pinglu China
73D4 Pingtan Dao I China
73E5 P'ing tung Taiwan
72A3 Pingwu China
73B5 Pingxiang Guangxi, China
73C4 Pingxiang Jiangxi, China
31B2 Pinheiro Brazil
70A3 Pini I Indon
55B3 Piniós R Greece
106A4 Pinjarra Aust
13C1 Pink Mountain Can
108B3 Pinnaroo Aust
Pinos,I de, I = Isla de la Juventud
21A2 Pinos,Pt USA
23B2 Pinotepa Nacional Mexico
70C4 Pinrang Indon
60C3 Pinsk Belarus
32J7 Pinta I Ecuador
61G1 Pinyug Russian Fed
8B3 Pioche USA
52B2 Piombino Italy
6H3 Piórsá Iceland
59B2 Piotrkow Trybunalski Pol
44E2 Piper Oilfield N Sea
21B2 Piper Peak Mt USA
10C2 Pipmuacan Res Can
14B2 Piqua USA
35B1 Piracanjuba Brazil
35B2 Piracicaba Brazil
35B2 Piraçununga Brazil
31C2 Piraí do Sul Brazil
55B3 Piraiévs Greece
35B2 Pirajuí Brazil
35A1 Piranhas Brazil
35C1 Pirapora Brazil
35B1 Pirenópolis Brazil
35B1 Pires do Rio Brazil
55B3 Pírgos Greece
Pirineos = Pyrénées
31C2 Piripiri Brazil
46D2 Pirmasens Germany
54B2 Pirot Serbia, Yugos
84C2 Pir Panjal Range Mts Pak
71D4 Piru Indon
22C3 Piru Creek R USA
49E3 Pisa Italy
32B6 Pisco Peru

57C3 Pisek Czech Republic
84B2 Pishin Pak
30C4 Pissis Mt Arg
49E3 Pistoia Italy
50B1 Pisuerga R Spain
20B2 Pit R USA
32B3 Pitalito Colombia
105K5 Pitcairn I Pacific O
38H5 Pite R Sweden
38J5 Piteå Sweden
54B2 Piteşti Rom
63B2 Pit Gorodok Russian Fed
38L6 Pitkyaranta Russian Fed
44C3 Pitlochry Scot
34A3 Pitrutquén Chile
13B2 Pitt I Can
22B1 Pittsburg California, USA
18B2 Pittsburg Kansas, USA
14C2 Pittsburgh USA
18B2 Pittsfield Illinois, USA
16C1 Pittsfield Massachusetts, USA
109D1 Pittsworth Aust
86A1 Piuthan Nepal
47D1 Pizzo Redorta Mt Italy
38B2 Pjórsá Iceland
32A5 Pjura Peru
7E5 Placentia B Can
22B1 Placerville USA
46B1 Plaine des Flandres Plain Belg/France
96C2 Plaine du Tidikelt Desert Region
9C3 Plainview Texas, USA
22B2 Planada USA
30F2 Planalto de Mato Grosso Plat Brazil
31D3 Planalto do Borborema Plat Brazil
32A1 Planalto do Mato Grosso Mts Brazil
19A3 Plano USA
17B2 Plantation USA
17B2 Plant City USA
50A1 Plasencia Spain
61K3 Plast Russian Fed
69F2 Plastun Russian Fed
96C2 Plateau du Tademait Alg
46D2 Plateau Lorrain Plat France
48C2 Plateaux de Limousin Plat France
51C2 Plateaux du Sersou Plat Alg
26C5 Plato Colombia
8C2 Platte R USA
15D2 Plattsburgh USA
18A1 Plattsmouth USA
57C2 Plauen Germany
60E3 Plavsk Russian Fed
23A2 Playa Azul Mexico
32A4 Playas Ecuador
23B2 Playa Vicente Mexico
22B2 Pleasanton California, USA
18B3 Pleasantville USA
14A3 Pleasure Ridge Park USA
76D3 Pleiku Viet
110C1 Plenty,B of NZ
8C2 Plentywood USA
7C4 Pletipi,L Can
54B2 Pleven Bulg
54A2 Pljevlja Montenegro, Yugos
52C2 Ploče Croatia
58B2 Płock Pol
48B2 Ploërmel France
54C2 Ploieşti Rom
58B2 Płońsk Pol
54B2 Plovdiv Bulg
20C1 Plummer USA
12C2 Plummer,Mt USA

100B3 Plumtree Zim
22B1 Plymouth California, USA
43B4 Plymouth Eng
14A2 Plymouth Indiana, USA
16D2 Plymouth Massachusetts, USA
15C2 Plymouth Pennsylvania, USA
43B4 Plymouth Sd Eng
43C3 Plynlimon Mt Wales
57C3 Plzeň Czech Republic
58B2 Pniewy Pol
38K6 Pnyäselkä L Fin
97B3 Pô Burkina
47E2 Po R Italy
97C4 Pobé Benin
69G2 Pobedino Russian Fed
8B2 Pocatello USA
15C3 Pocomoke City USA
35B2 Pocos de Caldas Brazil
54A2 Podgorica Montenegro, Yugos
47D2 Po di Volano R Italy
63B1 Podkamennaya R
60E2 Podol'sk Russian Fed
59D3 Podol'skaya Vozvyshennost' Upland Ukraine
60D1 Podporozh'ye Russian Fed
61F1 Podyuga Russian Fed
100A3 Pofadder S Africa
74B3 P'ohang S Korea
112C9 Poinsett,C Ant
108C2 Point Aust
27E3 Pointe-a-Pitre Guadeloupe
48B2 Pointe de Barfleur Pt France
98B3 Pointe Noire Congo
98A2 Pointe Pongara Pt Gabon
108B3 Point Fairy Aust
27L1 Point Fortin Trinidad
4B3 Point Hope USA
4G3 Point L Can
12B1 Point Lay USA
16B2 Point Pleasant USA
14B3 Point Pleasant W Virginia, USA
47B2 Point St Bernard Mt France
48C2 Poitiers France
48B2 Poitou Region, France
46A2 Poix France
85C3 Pokaran India
109C1 Pokataroo Aust
61G3 Pokrovsk Yugos
63E1 Pokrovsk Russian Fed
58B2 Poland Republic, Europe
92B2 Polatlı Turk
78D3 Polewali Indon
47A1 Poligny France
55B2 Políviros Greece
87B2 Polláchi India
79B3 Polillo Is Phil
59D2 Polonnye Ukraine
58D1 Połotsk Russian Fed
60B4 Poltava Russian Fed
52C1 Pölten Austria
64F3 Poluostrov Kanin Pen Russian Fed
61H5 Poluostrov Mangyshlak Pen Kazakhstan
38L5 Poluostrov Rybachiy Pen Russian Fed
64H2 Poluostrov Yamal Pen Russian Fed
38L5 Polyarnyy Murmansk, Russian Fed

1B8 Polyarnyy Yakutskaya, Russian Fed
105H3 Polynesia *Region* Pacific O
32B5 Pomabamba Peru
35C2 Pomba *R* Brazil
22D3 Pomona USA
18A2 Pomona Res USA
17B2 Pompano Beach USA
16B2 Pompton Lakes USA
18A2 Pona City USA
27D3 Ponce Puerto Rico
17B2 Ponce de Leon *B* USA
87B2 Pondicherry India
6C2 Pond Inlet Can
50A1 Ponferrada Spain
98C2 Pongo *R* Sudan
10H1 Pongola *R* S Africa
87B2 Ponnani India
86C2 Ponnyadoung Range *Mts* Myan
13E2 Ponoka Can
64F3 Ponoy Russian Fed
48B2 Pons France
35D1 Ponta da Baleia *Pt* Brazil
96A1 Ponta Delgada Açores
98B3 Ponta do Padrão *R* Angola
35C2 Ponta dos Búzios *Pt* Brazil
30F4 Ponta Grossa Brazil
35B2 Pontal Brazil
46D2 Pont-à-Mousson France
30E3 Ponta Porã Brazil
49D2 Pontarlier France
19B3 Pontchartrain,L USA
52A2 Pontedera Italy
52A2 Ponte Leccia Corse
50A1 Pontevedra Spain
18C1 Pontiac Illinois, USA
14B2 Pontiac Michigan, USA
78B3 Pontianak Indon
48B2 Pontivy France
19C3 Pontoise France
43C4 Pontypool Wales
43C4 Pontypridd Wales
43D4 Poole Eng
Poona = Pune
108B2 Pooncarie Aust
108B2 Popelloe,L *L* Aust
12C2 Poorman USA
32B3 Popayán Colombia
46B1 Poperinge Belg
108B2 Popilta *L* Aust
18B2 Poplar Bluff USA
19C3 Poplarville USA
107D1 Popndetta PNG
23B2 Popocatepetl *Mt* Mexico
98B3 Popokabaka Zaire
71F4 Popondetta PNG
54C2 Popovo Bulg
85B4 Porbandar India
13A2 Porcher I Can
12F1 Porcupine *R* Can/ USA
52B1 Poreč Croatia
35A2 Porecatu Brazil
39J6 Pori Fin
17B2 Porirua NZ
38H5 Porjus Sweden
69G2 Poronaysk Russian Fed
47B1 Porrentruy Switz
39F7 Porsgrunn Nor
45C1 Portadown N Ire
8D2 Portage la Prairie Can
13C3 Port Alberni Can
50A2 Portalegre Port
9C3 Portales USA
100B4 Port Alfred S Africa
13B2 Port Alice Can

19B3 Port Allen USA
20B1 Port Angeles USA
26B3 Port Antonio Jamaica
45C2 Portarlington Irish Rep
19B4 Port Arthur USA
108A2 Port Augusta Aust
26C3 Port-au-Prince Haiti
14B2 Port Austin USA
108B3 Port Campbell Aust
86B2 Port Canning India
7D5 Port Cartier Can
111B3 Port Chalmers NZ
17B2 Port Charlotte USA
16C2 Port Chester USA
16C2 Port Colborne Can
15C2 Port Credit Can
109C4 Port Davey Aust
26C3 Port-de-Paix Haiti
77C5 Port Dickson Malay
100C4 Port Edward S Africa
35C1 Porteirinha Brazil
14B2 Port Elgin Can
100B4 Port Elizabeth S Africa
57N2 Porter Pt St Vincent and the Grenadines
21B2 Porterville USA
107D4 Port Fairy Aust
98A3 Port Gentil Gabon
19B3 Port Gibson USA
12D3 Port Graham USA
20B1 Port Hammond Can
89E7 Port Harcourt Nig
13B2 Port Hardy Can
7D5 Port Hawkesbury Can
106A3 Port Hedland Aust
Port Heiden = Meshik
43B3 Porthmadog Wales
7E4 Port Hope Simpson Can
22C3 Port Hueneme USA
14B2 Port Huron USA
50A2 Portimão Port
109D2 Port Jackson *B* Aust
16C2 Port Jefferson USA
16B2 Port Jervis USA
109D2 Port Kembla Aust
14B2 Portland Indiana, USA
10C2 Portland Maine, USA
109C2 Portland New South Wales, Aust
20B1 Portland Oregon, USA
108B3 Portland Victoria, Aust
27H2 Portland Bight *B* Jamaica
43C4 Portland Bill *Pt* Eng
109C4 Portland,C Aust
13A1 Portland Canal Can/ USA
110C1 Portland I NZ
27H2 Portland Pt Jamaica
45C2 Port Laoise Irish Rep
108A2 Port Lincoln Aust
97A4 Port Loko Sierra Leone
101E3 Port Louis Mauritius
108B3 Port MacDonnell Aust
13B2 Port McNeill Can
109D2 Port Macquarie Aust
12B3 Port Moller USA
107D1 Port Moresby PNG
100A3 Port Nolloth S Africa
16B3 Port Norris USA
89E7 Porto Novo Benin
50A1 Porto Port
30F5 Pôrto Alegre Brazil
33E6 Pôrto Artur Brazil
30F3 Pôrto E Cunha Brazil
52B2 Portoferraio Italy
27E4 Port of Spain Trinidad
47D2 Portomaggiore Italy
97C4 Porto Novo Benin
20B1 Port Orchard USA
20B2 Port Orford USA
96A1 Porto Santo I Medeira

31D5 Pôrto Seguro Brazil
53A2 Porto Torres Sardegna
53A2 Porto Vecchio Corse
33E5 Pôrto Velho Brazil
111A3 Port Pegasus *B* NZ
108B3 Port Phillip *B* Aust
108A2 Port Pirie Aust
44A3 Portree Scot
20B1 Port Renfrew Can
27J2 Port Royal Jamaica
17B1 Port Royal Sd USA
45C1 Portrush N Ire
92B3 Port Said Egypt
17A2 Port St Joe USA
100B4 Port St Johns S Africa
7E4 Port Saunders Can
100C4 Port Shepstone S Africa
13A2 Port Simpson Can
27Q2 Portsmouth Dominica
43D4 Portsmouth Eng
14B3 Portsmouth Ohio, USA
11C3 Portsmouth Virginia, USA
109D2 Port Stephens *B* Aust
95C3 Port Sudan Sudan
19C3 Port Sulphur USA
38K5 Porttipahdan Tekojärvi *Res* Fin
50A2 Portugal Republic, Europe
14A2 Port Washington USA
77C5 Port Weld Malay
32D6 Porvenir Chile
39K6 Porvoo Fin
30E4 Posadas Arg
50A2 Posadas Spain
47D1 Poschiavo Switz
6B2 Posheim Pen Can
90C3 Posht-e Badam Iran
71D4 Poso Indon
52B1 Postojna Slovenia
65C2 Pos'yet Russian Fed
101G1 Potchefstroom S Africa
19B2 Poteau USA
53C2 Potenza Italy
100B3 Potgietersrus S Africa
97D3 Potiskum Nig
20C1 Potlatch USA
15C3 Potomac *R* USA
30C4 Potosí Bol
30C4 Potrerillos Chile
56C2 Potsdam Germany
16C2 Potsdam USA
16C2 Pottstown USA
16C2 Pottsville USA
16C2 Poughkeepsie USA
35B2 Pouso Alegre Brazil
110C1 Poverty *B* NZ
61F3 Povorino Russian Fed
7C4 Povungnituk Can
16C2 Powder *R* USA
106C2 Powell Creek Aust
9B3 Powell,L USA
13C3 Powell River Can
8C2 Power *R* USA
43C3 Powys County, Wales
73D4 Poyang Hu *L* China
92B2 Pozanti Turk
23B1 Poza Rica Mexico
58B2 Poznań Pol
30E3 Pozo Colorado Par
53B2 Pozzuoli Italy
97B4 Pra *R* Ghana
76C3 Prachin Buri Thai
76B3 Prachuap Khiri Khan Thai
59B2 Praděd *Mt* Czech Republic
49C3 Pradelles France
35D1 Prado Brazil

Prague = Praha
57C2 Praha Czech Republic
96A4 Praia Cape Verde
33E5 Prainha Brazil
18B2 Prairie Village USA
76C3 Prakhon Chai Thai
35B1 Prata Brazil
35B1 Prata *R* Brazil
Prates = Dongsha Qundao
49E3 Prato Italy
16B1 Prattsville USA
17A1 Prattville USA
48B1 Prawle Pt Eng
78D4 Praya Indon
47D1 Predazzo Italy
63B2 Predivinsk Russian Fed
58C2 Pregolyu *R* Russian Fed
76D3 Prek Kak Camb
56C2 Prenzlau Germany
76A3 Preparis I Myan
76A2 Preparis North Chan Myan
59B3 Přerov Czech Republic
23A2 Presa del Infiernillo Mexico
9B3 Prescott Arizona, USA
19B3 Prescott Arkansas, USA
15C2 Prescott Can
30D4 Presidencia Roque Sáenz Peña Arg
35A2 Presidente Epitácio Brazil
112C2 Presidente Frei *Base* Ant
23B2 Presidente Miguél Aleman *L* Mexico
35A2 Presidente Prudente Brazil
35A2 Presidente Venceslau Brazil
59C3 Prešov Slovakia
55B2 Prespansko Jezero *L* Macedonia, Yugos
10D2 Presque Isle USA
8B2 Preston Idaho, USA
42B2 Preston Eng
18B2 Preston Missouri, USA
42B2 Prestwick Scot
31B6 Prêto Brazil
35B1 Prêto *R* Brazil
101G1 Pretoria S Africa
55B3 Préveza Greece
76D3 Prey Veng Camb
8B3 Price USA
13B2 Price I Can
61D4 Prichernomorskaya Nizmennost' *Lowland* Ukraine
77M2 Prickly Pt Grenada
58C1 Priekule Lithuania
108B3 Prieska S Africa
20C1 Priest L USA
20C1 Priest River USA
55B2 Prilep Macedonia, Yugos
60D3 Priluki Ukraine
34C2 Primero *R* Arg
39K6 Primorsk Russian Fed
60E4 Primorsko-Akhtarsk Russian Fed
13F2 Primrose L Can
5H4 Prince Albert Can
4F2 Prince Albert,C Can
4G2 Prince Albert Pen Can
4G2 Prince Albert Sd Can
6C3 Prince Charles I Can
112B10 Prince Charles Mts Ant
7D5 Prince Edward I Can
13C2 Prince George Can
4H2 Prince Gustaf Adolf *S* Can
5E4 Prince of Wales I USA

Razim

10B2 Rockford USA
11B3 Rock Hill USA
10A2 Rock Island USA
10B3 Rocklands Res Aust
17B2 Rockledge USA
8C4 Rock Springs Wyoming, USA
110B2 Rocks Pt NZ
109C3 Rock,The Aust
16C2 Rockville Connecticut, USA
14A3 Rockville Indiana, USA
16A3 Rockville Maryland, USA
14B1 Rocky Island L Can
13E2 Rocky Mountain House Can
8B1 Rocky Mts Can/USA
12B2 Rocky Pt USA
56C2 Rødbyhavn Den
34B2 Rodeo Arg
49C3 Rodez France
55C3 Ródhos Greece
55C3 Ródhos I Greece
52C2 Rodi Garganico Italy
54B2 Rodopi Planina Mts Bulg
106A3 Roebourne Aust
46C1 Roermond Neth
46B1 Roeselare Belg
6B3 Roes Welcome Sd Can
18B2 Rogers USA
14B1 Rogers City USA
20B2 Rogue R USA
85B3 Rohn Pak
84D3 Rohtak India
58C1 Roja Latvia
91A4 Rolândia Brazil
18B2 Rolla USA
109C1 Roma Aust
52B2 Roma Italy
47C2 Romagnano Italy
17C1 Roman,C USA
54C1 Roman Rom
103H5 Romanche Gap Atlantic O
71D4 Romang I Indon
60B4 Romania Republic, E Europe
17B2 Romano,C USA
49D2 Romans sur Isère France
79B3 Romblon Phil
Rome = Roma
17A1 Rome Georgia, USA
15C2 Rome New York, USA
49C2 Romilly-sur-Seine France
15C3 Romney USA
60D3 Romny Ukraine
56B1 Rømø I Den
47B1 Romont Switz
48C2 Romorantin France
50A2 Ronda Spain
33E6 Rondônia Brazil
24F6 Rondônia State, Brazil
30F2 Rondonópolis Brazil
73B4 Rong'an China
73B4 Rongcheng China
72E2 Rongcheng China
73B4 Rongjiang China
73B4 Rong Jiang R China
76A1 Rongklang Range Mts Myan
39G7 Ronne Den
39H7 Ronneby Sweden
112B2 Ronne Ice Shelf Ant
46B1 Ronse Belg
46A1 Ronthieu Region, France
9C3 Roof Butte Mt USA
84D3 Roorkee India
46C1 Roosendaal Neth
112B6 Roosevelt I Ant
106C2 Roper R Aust
33E3 Roraima State, Brazil
33E2 Roraima Mt Ven
38G6 Røros Nor
47C1 Rorschach Switz
38G6 Rørvik Nor

27Q2 Rosalie Dominica
22C3 Rosamond L USA
34C2 Rosario Arg
34C2 Rosario Brazil
31C2 Rosario del Tala Arg
48B2 Roscoff France
45B2 Roscommon County, Irish Rep
41B3 Roscommon Irish Rep
45C2 Roscrea Irish Rep
27E3 Roseau Dominica
109C4 Rosebery Aust
20B2 Roseburg USA
19A4 Rosenberg USA
57C3 Rosenheim Germany
13F2 Rosetown Can
54B2 Rosiori de Vede Rom
39G7 Roskilde Den
60D3 Roslavl' Russian Fed
61E2 Roslyatino Russian Fed
111B2 Ross NZ
12H2 Ross R Can
40B3 Rossan Pt Irish Rep
53C3 Rossano Italy
19C3 Ross Barnett Res USA
6C1 Rosseau L Can
107E2 Rossel I Solomon Is
112A Ross Ice Shelf Ant
20B1 Ross L USA
13D3 Rossland Can
45C2 Rosslare Irish Rep
111C2 Ross,Mt NZ
97A3 Rosso Maur
43C4 Ross-on-Wye Eng
60E4 Rossosh' Russian Fed
4E3 Ross River Can
112B6 Ross S Ant
91B4 Rossoú Arg
56C2 Rostock Germany
Rostov = Rostov-na-Donu
61E4 Rostov-na-Donu Russian Fed
17B1 Roswell Georgia, USA
9C3 Roswell New Mexico, USA
71F2 Rota Pacific O
56B2 Rotenburg Niedersachsen, Germany
46E1 Rothaar-Geb Region Germany
112C3 Rothera Base Ant
42D3 Rotherham Eng
42B2 Rothesay Scot
71D5 Roti I Indon
108C2 Roto Aust
111B2 Rotoiti,L NZ
111B2 Rotorua,L NZ
111C1 Rotorua NZ
56A2 Rotterdam Neth
46B1 Roubaix France
48C2 Rouen France
42E3 Rough Oilfield N Sea
Roulers = Roeselare
101E3 Round I Mauritius
109D2 Round Mt Aust
8C2 Roundup USA
44C2 Rousay I Scot
48C3 Roussillon Region, France
10C2 Rouyn Can
38K5 Rovaniemi Fin
47D2 Rovereto Italy
47D2 Rovigo Italy
52B1 Rovinj Croatia
59D2 Rovno Ukraine
90A2 Row'ān Iran
109C1 Rowena Aust
6C3 Rowley I Can
106A2 Rowley Shoals Aust
79A3 Roxas Palawan, Phil
79B3 Roxas Panay, Phil
111A3 Roxburgh NZ
45C2 Royal Canal Irish Rep
43D3 Royal Leamington Spa Eng
14B2 Royal Oak USA
43E4 Royal Tunbridge Wells Eng

48B2 Royan France
46B2 Roye France
43D3 Royston Eng
59C3 Rožňava Slovakia
48B2 Rozoy France
61F3 Rtishchevo Russian Fed
99D3 Ruaha Nat Pk Tanz
110C1 Ruahine Range Mts NZ
110C1 Ruapehu,Mt NZ
65D3 Rub al Khali Desert S Arabia
44A3 Rubha Hunish Scot
35A2 Rubinéia Brazil
65K4 Rubtsovsk Russian Fed
12C2 Ruby USA
91C4 Rudan Iran
90A2 Rūdbār Iran
69F2 Rudnaya Pristan' Russian Fed
54B2 Rudoka Planina Mt Macedonia
72E3 Rudong China
14B1 Rudyard USA
46A1 Rue France
47C2 Ruffec France
99D3 Rufiji R Tanz
34C2 Rufino Arg
97A3 Rufisque Sen
100B2 Rufunsa Zambia
43D3 Rugby Eng
93D3 Rugby USA
39G8 Rügen I Germany
73D4 Ruijin China
54B2 Rujen Mt Bulg/Macedonia
99D3 Rukwa L Tanz
44A3 Rum I Scot
54A1 Ruma Serbia, Yugos
91A4 Rumāh S Arabia
98C2 Rumbek Sudan
26C2 Rum Cay / Caribbean S
47C2 Rumilly France
106C2 Rum Jungle Aust
101C2 Rumphi Malawi
111B2 Runanga NZ
100A2 Rundu Namibia
99D3 Rungwa Tanz
99D3 Rungwa R Tanz
99D3 Rungwe Mt Tanz
82C2 Ruoqiang China
68C2 Ruo Shui R China
7C4 Rupert R Can
46D1 Rur R Germany
32D6 Rurrenabaque Bol
101C2 Rusape Zim
54C2 Ruse Bulg
11B1 Rushville Illinois, USA
108B3 Rushworth Aust
19A3 Rusk USA
17B2 Ruskin USA
11D1 Russell USA
18B2 Russellville Arkansas, USA
18C2 Russellville Kentucky, USA
21A2 Russian R USA
62C3 Russian Fed Asia/Europe
93E1 Rustavi Georgia
101G1 Rustenburg S Africa
19B3 Ruston USA
99C3 Rutana Burundi
23B2 Rüthen Germany
76C3 Rutland USA
15D2 Rutland USA
87B2 Rutog China
Ruvu = Pangani
101D2 Ruvuma R Tanz/Mozam
99D2 Ruwenzori Range Mts Uganda/Zaire
101C2 Ruya R Zim
59B3 Rużomberok Slovakia
99C3 Rwanda Republic, Africa

60E3 Ryazan' Russian Fed
60E3 Ryazan' Division, Russian Fed
61F3 Ryazhsk Russian Fed
60E2 Rybinsk Russian Fed
60E2 Rybinskoye Vodokhranilishche Res Russian Fed
13D1 Rycroft Can
43E4 Ryde Eng
43E4 Rye Eng
20C2 Rye Patch Res USA
60D3 Ryl'sk Russian Fed
61G4 Ryn Peski Desert Kazakhstan
74D3 Ryōtsu Japan
59D3 Ryskany Moldova
69E4 Ryūkyū Retto Arch Japan
61G3 Rzeszów Pol
60D2 Rzhev Russian Fed

S

91B3 Sa'ādatābād Iran
56C2 Saale R Germany
47B1 Saanen Switz
46D2 Saar R Germany
46D2 Saarbrücken Germany
46D2 Saarburg Germany
39J7 Saaremaa I Estonia
46D2 Saarland State, Germany
46D2 Saarlouis Germany
54A2 Šabac Serbia, Yugos
51C1 Sabadell Spain
75B1 Sabae Japan
78D1 Sabah State, Malay
26A3 Sabanalarga Colombia
76C4 Sabang Indon
87C1 Sabari R India
94B2 Sabastiya Israel
52B2 Sabaya Bol
95A2 Sabhā Libya
24B2 Sabinas Mexico
24B2 Sabinas Hidalgo Mexico
19A3 Sabine R USA
19B4 Sabine L USA
91B5 Sabkhat Matti Salt Marsh UAE
94A3 Sabkhet El Bardawil Lg Egypt
79B3 Sablayan Phil
7D5 Sable,C Can
7D5 Sable,C USA
7D5 Sable I Can
90C2 Sabzevar Iran
20C1 Sacajawea Peak USA
10A1 Sachigo R Can
56C2 Sachsen State, Germany
56C2 Sachsen-Anhalt State, Germany
4F2 Sachs Harbour Can
47B1 Säckingen Germany
22B1 Sacramento R USA
22B1 Sacramento USA
22A1 Sacramento V USA
9C3 Sacramento Mts USA
81C4 Sa'dah Yemen
54B2 Sadanski Bulg
50A2 Sado R Port
74D3 Sado-shima I Japan
85C3 Sādri India
Safad = Zefat
84A2 Safed Koh Mts Afghan
39G7 Säffle Sweden
92C3 Safi Jordan
96B1 Safi Mor
90D3 Safīdabeh Iran
94B1 Safītā Syria
93E3 Safwān Iraq
75A2 Saga Japan
76B1 Sagaing Myan
75B2 Sagami-nada B Japan

29B6 Santa Inés *I* Chile
34B3 Santa Isabel La Pampa, Arg
34C2 Santa Isabel Sante Fe, Arg
107E1 Santa Isabel *I* Solomon Is
21A2 Santa Lucia *R* USA
21A2 Santa Lucia Range *Mts* USA
97A4 Santa Luzia *I* Cape Verde
9B4 Santa Margarita *I* Mexico
22D4 Santa Margarita *R* USA
30F4 Santa Maria Brazil
26C4 Santa Maria Colombia
21A3 Santa Maria *I* Açores
96A1 Santa Maria *I* Açores
23B1 Santa Maria *R* Queretaro, Mexico
23A1 Santa Maria del Rio Mexico
32C1 Santa Marta Colombia
22C3 Santa Monica USA
22C4 Santa Monica *B* USA
29E2 Santana do Livramento Brazil
32B3 Santander Colombia
50B1 Santander Spain
51C2 Santañy Spain
22C3 Santa Paula USA
31A3 Santa Quitéria Brazil
33G4 Santarém Brazil
50A2 Santarém Port
22A1 Santa Rosa California, USA
25D3 Santa Rosa Honduras
34C3 Santa Rosa La Pampa, Arg
34B2 Santa Rosa Mendoza, Arg
34B2 Santa Rosa San Luis, Arg
22B3 Santa Rosa *I* USA
24A2 Santa Rosalia Mexico
20C2 Santa Rosa Range *Mts* USA
31D3 Santa Talhada Brazil
35C1 Santa Teresa Brazil
53A2 Santa Teresa di Gallura Sardegna
22B3 Santa Ynez *R* USA
22B3 Santa Ynez Mts USA
17C1 Santee *R* USA
47C2 Santhia Italy
29B6 Santiago Chile
27C3 Santiago Dom Rep
32A2 Santiago Panama
79B2 Santiago Phil
32B4 Santiago *R* Peru
50A1 Santiago de Compostela Spain
26B2 Santiago de Cuba Cuba
30A4 Santiago del Estero Arg
30D4 Santiago del Estero State, Arg
22D4 Santiago Peak *Mt* USA
31C5 Santo State, Brazil
35A2 Santo Anastácio Brazil
30F4 Santo Angelo Brazil
97A4 Santo Antão *I* Cape Verde
35A2 Santo Antonio da Platina Brazil
27D3 Santo Domingo Dom Rep
35B2 Santos Brazil
35C2 Santos Dumont Brazil
30E4 Santo Tomé Arg
29B5 San Valentín *Mt* Chile
34A2 San Vicente Chile
98B3 Sanza Pomba Angola

30E4 São Borja Brazil
35B2 São Carlos Brazil
33G5 São Félix Mato Grosso, Brazil
35C2 São Fidélis Brazil
35C1 São Francisco Brazil
31D3 São Francisco *R* Brazil
30G4 São Francisco do Sul Brazil
35B2 São Gotardo Brazil
99D3 São Hill Tanz
35C2 São João da Barra Brazil
35B2 São João da Boa Vista Brazil
35C1 São João da Ponte Brazil
35B2 São João del Rei Brazil
35B2 São Joaquim da Barra Brazil
96A1 São Jorge *I* Açores
35B2 São José do Rio Prêto Brazil
35B2 São José dos Campos Brazil
31C2 São Luís Brazil
35B1 São Marcos *R* Brazil
35C1 São Maria do Suaçui Brazil
35D1 São Mateus Brazil
35C1 São Mateus *R* Brazil
96A1 São Miguel *I* Açores
49C2 Saône *R* France
35A2 São Nicolau *I* Cape Verde
35B2 São Paulo Brazil
35B2 São Paulo State, Brazil
31C3 São Raimundo Nonato Brazil
35B1 São Romão Brazil
35B2 São Sebastiao do Paraiso Brazil
35A1 São Simão Goias, Brazil
35B2 São Simão Sao Paulo, Brazil
35A2 São Tiago *I* Cape Verde
97C4 São Tomé *I* W Africa
97C4 São Tomé and Principe Republic, W Africa
96B2 Saoura *Watercourse* Alg
35B2 São Vicente Brazil
97A4 São Vincente *I* Cape Verde
55C2 Sápai Greece
78C2 Sape Indon
79A3 Sapele Nig
74E2 Sapporo Japan
53C2 Sapri Italy
18A2 Sapulpa USA
90A4 Saqqez Iran
10C2 Saquenay *R* Can
90A2 Sarab Iran
54A2 Sarajevo Bosnia-Herzegovina
90D2 Sarakhs Iran
61J3 Saraktash Russian Fed
63A2 Sarala Russian Fed
15D2 Saranac L USA
15D2 Saranac Lake USA
55B3 Sarandë Alb
79C4 Sarangani Is Phil
61G3 Saransk Russian Fed
61H2 Sarapul Russian Fed
17B2 Sarasota USA
54C1 Sarata Ukraine
15D2 Saratoga Springs USA
78C2 Saratok Malay
61G3 Saratov Russian Fed
61G3 Saratov Division, Russian Fed
61G3 Saratovskoye Vodokhranilishche *Res* Russian Fed
67F4 Sarawak State, Malay

92A2 Saraykoy Turk
90C3 Sarbisheh Iran
47D1 Sarca *R* Italy
95A2 Sardalas Libya
78A4 Sar Dasht Iran
52A2 Sardegna *I* Medit S
Sardinia = Sardegna
38H5 Sarektjåkkå *Mt* Sweden
84C2 Sargodha Pak
98B2 Sarh Chad
90B2 Sārī Iran
94B2 Sarida *R* Isreal
93D1 Sarikamiş Turk
107D3 Sarina Aust
47B1 Sarine *R* Switz
84B1 Sar-i-Pul Afghan
95B2 Sarir Libya
95A2 Sarir Tibesti *Desert* Libya
74B3 Sariwŏn N Korea
48B2 Sark *I* UK
92C2 Sarkişla Turk
71E4 Sarmi Indon
29C5 Sarmiento Arg
39G6 Särna Sweden
47C1 Sarnen Switz
14B2 Sarnia Can
58D2 Sarny Ukraine
6E2 Saroaq Greenland
84B2 Sarobi Afghan
78A3 Saroilagun Indon
55B3 Saronikós Kólpos *G* Greece
47C2 Saronno Italy
55C2 Saros Körfezi *B* Turk
39G7 Sarpsborg Nor
46D2 Sarralbe France
46D2 Sarrebourg France
46C2 Sarreguemines France
46D2 Sarre-Union France
51B1 Sarrion Spain
85B3 Sartanala Pak
52A2 Sartène Corse
48B2 Sarthe *R* France
61H4 Sarykamys Kazakhstan
65H5 Sarysu *R* Kazakhstan
86B2 Sasaram India
74B4 Sasebo Japan
5H4 Saskatchewan Province, Can
5H4 Saskatchewan *R* Can
13F2 Saskatoon Can
101G1 Sasolburg S Africa
61F3 Sasovo Russian Fed
97B4 Sassandra Côte d'Ivoire
97B4 Sassandra *R* Côte d'Ivoire
53A2 Sassari Sardegna
56C2 Sassnitz Germany
47D2 Sassuolo Italy
34C2 Sastre Arg
87A1 Sātāra India
4G2 Satellite B Can
78D4 Satengar Indon
39H6 Säter Sweden
17B1 Satilla *R* USA
61J2 Satka Russian Fed
84D2 Satluj *R* India
86A2 Satna India
85C4 Sātpura Range *Mts* India
54B1 Satu Mare Rom
34D2 Sauce Arg
39F7 Sauda Nor
80C3 Saudi Arabia Kingdom, Arabian Pen
46D2 Sauer *R* Germany/Lux
46D1 Sauerland Region, Germany
38B1 Sauðárkrókur Iceland
14A2 Saugatuck USA
16C1 Saugerties USA
13B2 Saugstad,Mt Can
7B5 Sault Sainte Marie Can
14B1 Sault Ste Marie Can
14B1 Sault Ste Marie USA

71E4 Saumlaki Indon
48B2 Saumur France
98C3 Saurimo Angola
27M2 Sauteurs Grenada
7A4 Sava *R* Serbia, Yugos
97C4 Savalou Benin
17B1 Savannah Georgia, USA
17B1 Savannah *R* USA
76C2 Savannakhet Laos
26B3 Savanna la Mar Jamaica
7A4 Savant Lake Can
76D2 Savaré Laos
97C4 Savé Benin
101C3 Save *R* Mozam
90B3 Sāveh Iran
46D2 Saverne France
47B2 Savigliano Italy
46B2 Savigny France
49D2 Savoie *Region* France
49D3 Savona Italy
38K6 Savonlinna Fin
4A3 Savoonga USA
38K5 Savukoski Fin
71D4 Savu S Indon
76A1 Saw Myan
85D3 Sawai Mādhopur India
78A2 Sawang Indon
76B2 Sawankhalok Thai
75C1 Sawara Japan
12E1 Sawtooth Mt USA
106B2 Sawu *I* Indon
43E3 Saxmundham Eng
44C2 Scalloway Scot
44C2 Scapa Flow *Sd* Scot
15C2 Scarborough Can
42D2 Scarborough Eng
27E4 Scarborough Tobago
44A2 Scarp *I* Scot
45B2 Scarriff Irish Rep
52A1 Schaffhausen Switz
57C3 Scharding Austria
46D1 Scharteberg *Mt* Germany
7D4 Schefferville Can
46B1 Schelde *R* Belg
10C2 Schenectady USA
47D2 Schio Italy
46D1 Schleiden Germany
56B2 Schleswig Germany
56B2 Schleswig Holstein State, Germany
16B1 Schoharie USA
71F4 Schouten Is PNG
7B5 Schreiber Can
21B2 Schurz USA
16A2 Schuylkill Haven USA
16B2 Schuylkill *R* USA
57B3 Schwabische Alb Upland Germany
57B3 Schwarzwald Upland Germany
12C1 Schwatka Mts USA
47D1 Schwaz Austria
57C2 Schweinfurt Germany
101G1 Schweizer Reneke S Africa
56C2 Schwerin Germany
47C1 Schwyz Switz
53B3 Sciacca Italy
14B3 Scioto *R* USA
109D2 Scone Aust
6H2 Scoresby Sd Greenland
103F7 Scotia Ridge Atlantic O
103F7 Scotia S Atlantic O

Shaver L

Sorsatunturi

Sorsele

38H5 Sorsele Sweden
79B3 Sorsogon Phil
38L6 Sortavala Russian Fed
74B3 Sösan S Korea
59B2 Sosnowiec Pol
65H4 Sos'va Russian Fed
98B2 Souanké Congo
97B4 Soubré Côte d'Ivoire
16B2 Souderton USA
27F2 Soufrière St Lucia
27N2 Soufrière Mt St Vincent and the Grenadines
48C3 Souillac France
96C1 Souk Ahras Alg
74B3 Soul S Korea
51C2 Soummam R Alg
Sour = Tyr
101G1 Sources,Mt aux Lesotho
31D3 Sousa Brazil
96D1 Sousse Tunisia
100B2 South Africa Republic, Africa
16B2 South Amboy USA
14B2 Southampton Can
43D4 Southampton Eng
16C2 Southampton USA
6B3 Southampton I Can
28F6 South Atlantic O
7D4 South Aulatsivik I Can
106C3 South Australia State, Aust
104E5 South Australian Basin Indian O
42B2 South Ayrshire Division, Scot
19C3 Southaven USA
17B2 South Bay USA
14B1 South Baymouth Can
14A2 South Bend Indiana, USA
20B1 South Bend Washington, USA
16D1 Southbridge USA
South Cape = Ka Lae
11B3 South Carolina State, USA
70C2 South China S S E Asia
8C2 South Dakota State, USA
16C1 South Deerfield USA
43D4 South Downs Eng
109C4 South East C Aust
111A2 Southen Alps Mts NZ
5H4 Southend Can
43E4 Southend-on-Sea Eng
111A2 Southern Alps Mts NZ
106A4 Southern Cross Aust
5J4 Southern Indian L Can
27H2 Southfield Jamaica
105G5 South Fiji Basin Pacific O
12D2 South Fork R Alaska, USA
22B1 South Fork R California, USA
28F8 South Georgia I S Atlantic O
43C4 South Gloucestershire County Eng
14A2 South Haven USA
5J3 South Henik L Can
104F3 South Honshu Ridge Pacific O
111A2 South I NZ
16C2 Southington USA
74B3 South Korea Republic, S E Asia
21A2 South Lake Tahoe USA
42C2 South Lanarkshire Division, Scot
112C8 South Magnetic Pole Ant

17B2 South Miami USA
16A3 South Mt USA
4F3 South Nahanni R Can
26G1 South Negril Pt Jamaica
103F8 South Orkney Is Atlantic O
8C2 South Platte R USA
80E South Pole Ant
42C3 Southport Eng
27R3 South Pt Barbados
16B2 South River USA
44B2 South Ronaldsay I Scot
103G7 South Sandwich Trench Atlantic O
22A2 South San Francisco USA
5H4 South Saskatchewan R Can
42D2 South Shields Eng
110B1 South Taranaki Bight B NZ
44A3 South Uist I Scot
South West Africa = Namibia
107D5 South West C Aust
105J5 South West Pacific Basin Pacific O
103D5 South West Peru Ridge Pacific O
43D3 South Yorkshire County, Eng
58C1 Sovetsk Russian Fed
61G2 Sovetsk Russian Fed
101G1 Soweto S Africa
98B3 Soyo Congo Angola
60D3 Sozh R Belarus
46C1 Spa Belg
50A1 Spain Kingdom
Spalato = Split
43D3 Spalding Eng
14B1 Spanish R Can
26B3 Spanish Town Jamaica
21B2 Sparks USA
11B3 Spartanburg USA
55B3 Sparti Greece
69F2 Spassk Dal'niy Russian Fed
27R3 Speightstown Barbados
12E2 Spenard USA
14A3 Spencer Indiana, USA
8D2 Spencer Iowa, USA
6A3 Spencer Bay Can
108A3 Spencer,C Aust
108A2 Spencer G Aust
6C3 Spencer I Can
111B2 Spenser Mts NZ
45C1 Sperrin Mts N Ire
44C3 Spey R Scot
57B3 Speyer Germany
27K1 Speyside Tobago
47B1 Spiez Switz
12F1 Spike Mt USA
20C1 Spirit Lake USA
5G4 Spirit River Can
Spitsbergen = Svalbard
64C2 Spitsbergen I Barents S
57C3 Spittal Austria
38F6 Spjelkavik Nor
52C2 Split Croatia
47C1 Splügen Switz
20C1 Spokane USA
55C3 Sporádhes Is Greece
20C2 Spray USA
56C2 Spree R Germany
100A3 Springbok S Africa
18B2 Springdale USA
10B3 Springfield Illinois, USA
10C2 Springfield Massachusetts, USA
18B2 Springfield Missouri, USA
14B3 Springfield Ohio, USA
20B2 Springfield Oregon, USA

15D2 Springfield Vermont, USA
100B4 Springfontein S Africa
101G1 Springs S Africa
41D3 Spurn Head Pt Eng
13C3 Squamish Can
60E3 Sredne-Russkaya Vozvyshennost Upland Russian Fed
63B1 Sredne Sibirskoye Ploskogorve Tableland Russian Fed
61J2 Sredniy Ural Mts Russian Fed
76D3 Srepok R Camb
68D1 Sretensk Russian Fed
76C3 Sre Umbell Camb
83C5 Sri Lanka Republic, S Asia
84C2 Srinagar India
87A1 Srivardhan India
58B2 Środa Wlk. Pol
30H6 Sta Clara I Chile
32J7 Sta Cruz I Ecuador
56B2 Stade Germany
44A3 Staffa I Scot
43C3 Stafford County, Eng
16C2 Stafford Springs USA
Stalingrad = Volgograd
6A1 Stallworthy,C Can
59C2 Stalowa Wola Pol
32J7 Sta Maria I Ecuador
16C2 Stamford Connecticut, USA
16B1 Stamford New York, USA
100A3 Stampriet Namibia
101G1 Standerton S Africa
14B2 Standish USA
101H1 Stanger S Africa
22B2 Stanislaus R USA
54B2 Stanke Dimitrov Bulg
109C4 Stanley Aust
29E6 Stanley Falkland Is
87B2 Stanley Res India
Stanleyville = Kisangani
25D3 Stann Creek Belize
63E2 Stanovoy Khrebet Mts Russian Fed
47C1 Stans Switz
109D1 Stanthorpe Aust
59C2 Starachowice Pol
54B2 Stara Planiná Mts Bulg
60D2 Staraya Russa Russian Fed
54C2 Stara Zagora Bulg
58B2 Stargard Szczeciński Pol
59D3 Starokonstantinov Ukraine
43C4 Start Pt Eng
60E3 Staryy Oskol Russian Fed
15C2 State College USA
16B2 Staten I USA
17B1 Statesboro USA
15C3 Staunton USA
39F7 Stavanger Nor
46C1 Stavelot Belg
61F4 Stavropol' Russian Fed
61F4 Stavropol' Division, Russian Fed
108B3 Stawell Aust
58B2 Stawno Pol
13C2 Stayton USA
12B2 Stebbins USA
12F2 Steele,Mt USA
16A2 Steelton USA
20C2 Steens Mt USA

6E2 Steenstrups Gletscher Gl Greenland
4H2 Stefansson I Can
101H1 Stegi Swaziland
57C3 Steinach Austria
8D2 Steinbach Can
38G6 Steinkjer Nor
13C2 Stein Mt Can
23B2 Stenaco Mexico
46C2 Stenay France
56C2 Stendal Germany
110B2 Stephens,C NZ
108B2 Stephens Creek Aust
14B1 Stephenson Can
12H3 Stephens Pass USA
7E5 Stephenville Can
100B4 Sterkstroom S Africa
8C2 Sterling Colorado, USA
14B2 Sterling Heights USA
61J3 Sterlitamak Russian Fed
13E2 Stettler Can
14B2 Steubenville USA
4D3 Stevens Village USA
13B1 Stewart Can
21B2 Stewart I Can
12G2 Stewart R Can
12G2 Stewart Crossing Can
111A3 Stewart I NZ
107F1 Stewart Is Solomon Is
4E3 Stewart River Can
16A3 Stewartstown USA
10G1 Steyn S Africa
57C3 Steyr Austria
12G3 Stika USA
12H3 Stikine R Can
12H3 Stikine Ranges Mts Can
18A2 Stillwater Oklahoma, USA
21B2 Stillwater Range Mts USA
108A2 Stirling Aust
44C3 Stirling Scot
44B3 Stirling Division Scot
16C1 Stockbridge USA
59B3 Stockerau Austria
39H7 Stockholm Sweden
42C3 Stockport Eng
22B2 Stockton California, USA
18B2 Stockton L USA
42D2 Stockton-on-Tees County Eng
43C3 Stoke-on-Trent Eng
38A2 Stokksseyri Iceland
38G5 Stokmarknes Nor
39K8 Stolbtsy Belarus
58D2 Stolin Belarus
16B3 Stone Harbor USA
44C3 Stonehaven Scot
13A3 Stonewall USA
12D2 Stony R USA
38H5 Storavan L Sweden
38G6 Støren Nor
109C4 Storm B Aust
44A2 Stornoway Scot
59D3 Storozhinets Ukraine
16C2 Storrs USA
38G6 Storsjön L Sweden
39H5 Storuman Sweden
16D1 Stoughton USA
43E3 Stowmarket Eng
45C1 Strabane N Ire
109C4 Strahan Aust
56C2 Stralsund Germany
38F6 Stranda Nor
39H7 Strängnäs Sweden
42B2 Stranraer Scot
49D2 Strasbourg France
15C3 Strasburg USA
14B2 Stratford Can
110B1 Stratford NZ
43D3 Stratford-on-Avon Eng

108A3 Strathalbyn Aust
13E2 Strathmore Can
18C1 Streator USA
47C2 Stresa Italy
53C3 Stretto de Messina Str Italy/Sicily
38D3 Streymoy Føroyar
53C3 Stroboli I Italy
6E3 Strømfjord Greenland
44C2 Stromness Scot
18A1 Stromsburg USA
38H6 Stromsund Sweden
38G6 Ströms Vattudal L Sweden
44C2 Stronsay I Scot
43C4 Stroud Eng
16B2 Stroudsburg USA
54B2 Struma R Bulg
43B3 Strumble Head Pt Wales
55B2 Strumica Macedonia
59C3 Stryy Ukraine
59C3 Stryy R Ukraine
108B1 Strzelecki Creek R Aust
17B2 Stuart Florida, USA
13C2 Stuart R Can
12B2 Stuart I USA
13C2 Stuart L Can
47D1 Stubaier Alpen Mts Austria
76D3 Stung Sen Camb
76D3 Stung Treng Camb
52A2 Stura R Italy
52C3 Sturge I Ant
14A2 Sturgeon Bay USA
14C1 Sturgeon Falls Can
18C2 Sturgis Kentucky, USA
14A2 Sturgis Michigan, USA
106B2 Sturt Creek R Aust
108B1 Sturt Desert Aust
108A4 Stutterheim S Africa
19B3 Stuttgart USA
57B3 Stuttgart Germany
38A1 Stykkishólmur Iceland
59D2 Styr' R Ukraine
35C1 Suaçui Grande R Brazil
81B4 Suakin Sudan
73E5 Su-ao Taiwan
34C2 Suardi Arg
78B2 Subi I Indon
54A1 Subotica Serbia, Yugos
60C4 Suceava Rom
45B2 Suck R Irish Rep
30C2 Sucre Bol
35A1 Sucuriú R Brazil
98C1 Sudan Republic, Africa
14B1 Sudbury Can
43E3 Sudbury Eng
99C2 Sudd Swamp Sudan
33F2 Suddie Guyana
98C2 Sue R Sudan
4H2 Suerdrup Is Can
92B4 Suez Egypt
92B3 Suez Canal Egypt
92B4 Suez,G of Egypt
16B2 Suffern USA
43E3 Suffolk County, Eng
91C5 Suhar Oman
68C1 Sühbaatar Mongolia
84B3 Sui Pak
72C2 Suide China
69E2 Suihua China
73B3 Suining China
46C2 Suippes France
41B3 Suir R Irish Rep
73C3 Sui Xian China
72E1 Suizhong China
85C3 Sujängarth India
78B4 Sukabumi Indon
78C3 Sukadana Borneo, Indon
78B4 Sukadana Sumatra, Indon
74E3 Sukagawa Japan
78C3 Sukaraya Indon

60E3 Sukhinichi Russian Fed
61F2 Sukhona R Russian Fed
61F5 Sukhumi Georgia
6E3 Sukkertoppen Greenland
6E3 Sukkertoppen L Greenland
38L6 Sukkozero Russian Fed
85B3 Sukkur Pak
87C1 Sukma India
95A2 Süknah Libya
100A3 Sukses Namibia
75A2 Sukumo Japan
13C1 Sukunka R Can
60E3 Sula R Russian Fed
84B3 Sulaiman Range Mts Pak
70C4 Sulawesi I Indon
54C1 Sulina Rom
38H5 Sulitjelma Nor
32A4 Sullana Peru
18B2 Sullivan USA
13B2 Sullivan Bay Can
13E2 Sullivan L Can
52B2 Sulmona Italy
19B3 Sulphur Louisiana, USA
19A3 Sulphur Oklahoma, USA
19A3 Sulphur Springs USA
86A1 Sultánpur India
76C3 Sulu S Philip
30D4 Sumampa Arg
70B4 Sumatera I Indon
70C4 Sumba I Indon
78D4 Sumbawa I Indon
78D4 Sumbawa Besar Indon
99D3 Sumbawanga Tanz
100A2 Sumbe Angola
44E2 Sumburgh Head Pt Scot
78C4 Sumenep Indon
69G3 Sumisu I Japan
13D3 Summerland Can
5F4 Summit Lake Can
21B2 Summit Mt USA
111B2 Sumner,L NZ
75A2 Sumoto Japan
17B1 Sumter USA
60D3 Sumy Ukraine
16A2 Sunbury USA
34C2 Sunchales Arg
74B3 Sunch'ŏn N Korea
74B4 Sunch'ŏn S Korea
86A2 Sundargarh India
86B2 Sunderbans Swamp India
42D2 Sunderland Eng
13E2 Sundre Can
15C1 Sundridge Can
38H6 Sundsvall Sweden
38D3 Suduroy Føroyar
78D3 Sungaianyar Indon
78A3 Sungaipenuh Indon
78C3 Sunnyside USA
21A2 Sunnyvale USA
63D1 Suntar Russian Fed
97B4 Sunyani Ghana
75A2 Suó-nada B Japan
38K6 Suonenjoki Fin
18A1 Superior Nebraska, USA
10A2 Superior Wisconsin, USA
10B2 Superior,L Can/USA
76C2 Súphan Buri Thai
93D2 Süphan Dağ Turk
71E4 Supiori I Indon
93E3 Suq ash Suyukh Iraq
73D3 Suqian China
Suqutra = Socotra
91C5 Sür Oman
61G3 Sura R Russian Fed
78C4 Surabaya Indon
75B2 Suraga-wan B Japan
78C4 Surakarta Indon
109C1 Surat Aust
85C4 Süret India

84C2 Süratgarh India
77B4 Surat Thani Thai
85C4 Surendranagar India
16B3 Surf City USA
85A3 Surgut Russian Fed
87B1 Suriápet India
49D2 Sürich Switz
79C4 Surigao Phil
75C1 Surin Thai
33F3 Surinam Republic, S America
43D4 Surrey County, Eng
95A1 Surt Libya
38A2 Surtsey I Iceland
78A3 Surulangan Indon
75A2 Susaki Japan
21A1 Susanville USA
47D1 Süsch Switz
16D2 Susquehanna R USA
16B2 Sussex USA
43D4 Sussex West Eng
13B1 Sustut Peak Mt Can
100B4 Sutherland S Africa
84C2 Sutlej R Pak
21A2 Sutter Creek USA
14B3 Sutton USA
12C3 Sutwik I USA
74D3 Suwa Japan
58C2 Suwaki Pol
17B2 Suwannee R USA
94B2 Suweilih Jordan
74B3 Suwŏn S Korea
72D3 Su Xian China
73E3 Suzhou China
75B2 Suzuka Japan
75B1 Suzu-misaki C Japan
64C2 Svalbard Is Barents S
59C3 Svalyava Ukraine
38G5 Svartisen Mt Nor
76D3 Svay Rieng Camb
38G6 Sveg Sweden
39G7 Svendborg Den
63C2 Sverdlovsk = Yekaterinburg
6A1 Sverdrup Chan Can
69F2 Svetlaya Russian Fed
58C2 Svetlogorsk Russian Fed
39K6 Svetogorsk Russian Fed
54B2 Svetozarevo Serbia, Yugos
54C2 Svilengrad Bulg
58D2 Svir' Belarus
59B3 Svoboda Czech Republic
69E1 Svobodnyy Russian Fed
38G5 Svolvaer Nor
34K3 Swain Reefs Aust
17B1 Swainsboro USA
100A3 Swakopmund Namibia
42D2 Swale R Eng
70C3 Swallow Reef I S E Asia
87B2 Swämihalli India
25D3 Swan I Honduras
43D4 Swanage Eng
108B3 Swan Hill Aust
13D2 Swan Hills Can
13D2 Swan Hills Mts Can
26A3 Swan I Caribbean S
5H4 Swan River Can
43C4 Swansea Wales
43C4 Swansea County Wales
43C4 Swansea B Wales
101G1 Swartruggens S Africa
Swatow = Shantou
101H1 Swaziland Kingdom, S Africa

39G7 Sweden Kingdom, N Europe
20B2 Sweet Home USA
3C3 Sweetwater USA
100B4 Swellendam S Africa
59B2 Świdnica Pol
58B2 Świdwin Pol
58B2 Świebodzin Pol
58B2 Świecie Pol
5H4 Swift Current Can
43D4 Swindon Eng
45B2 Swinford Irish Rep
56C2 Świnoujście Pol
47C1 Switzerland Federal Republic, Europe
45C2 Swords Irish Rep
109D2 Sydney Aust
7D5 Sydney Can
64G3 Syktyvkar Russian Fed
17A1 Sylacauga USA
38G6 Sylarna Mt Sweden
86C2 Sylhet Bang
56B1 Sylt I Germany
14B2 Sylvania USA
112C11 Syowa Base Ant
Syracuse = Siracusa
57C3 Syracuse USA
65H5 Syr Darya R Kazakhstan
93C2 Syria Republic, S W Asia
61G2 Sysert' Russian Fed
61G3 Syzran' Russian Fed
58B2 Szczecin Pol
58C2 Szczecinek Pol
58C2 Szczytno Pol
59B3 Szeged Hung
59B3 Székesfehérvár Hung
59B3 Szekszard Hung
59B3 Szolnok Hung
59B2 Szombathely Hung
58B2 Szprotawa Pol

T

90C3 Tabas Iran
23A1 Tabasco Mexico
32D4 Tabatinga Brazil
96B2 Tabelbala Alg
76C3 Tabeng Camb
13E2 Taber Can
78B2 Tablas I Phil
100A4 Table Mt S Africa
12F1 Table Mt USA
18B2 Table Rock Res USA
78B3 Taboali Indon
57C3 Tábor Czech Republic
99B3 Tabora Tanz
97B4 Tabou Côte d'Ivoire
90A2 Tabriz Iran
92C4 Tabük S Arabia
23A2 Tacámbaro Mexico
82C1 Tacheng China
79B3 Tacloban Phil
30B2 Tacna Peru
8A2 Tacoma USA
99E1 Tadjoura Djibouti
87B2 Tädpatri India
74B3 Taebaek Sanmaek Mts S Korea
74B3 Taegu S Korea
74B3 Taehüksan I S Korea
74B3 Taejön S Korea
51B1 Tafalla Spain
96C2 Tafassaset Watercourse Alg
43C4 Taff R Wales
94B3 Tafila Jordan
60E4 Taganrog Ukraine
97A3 Tagant Region, Maur
79B4 Tagbilaran Phil
96B2 Taguenout Hagguerete Well Maur
107E2 Tagula I Solomon Is
79C4 Tagum Phil
Tagus = Tejo
96C2 Tahat Mt Alg
105J4 Tahiti I Pacific O
18A2 Tahlequah USA
21A2 Tahoe City USA
21A2 Tahoe,L USA
97C3 Tahoua Niger

Tahuna

71D3 Tahuna Indon
72D2 Tai'an China
72B3 Taibai Shan Mt China
72D1 Taibus Qi China
73E5 T'ai-chung Taiwan
111B3 Taieri R NZ
72C2 Taihang Shan China
110C1 Taihape NZ
72E3 Tai Hu L China
108A3 Tailem Bend Aust
44B3 Tain Scot
73E5 T'ai-nan Taiwan
35C1 Taiobeiras Brazil
73E5 T'ai pei Taiwan
77C5 Taiping Malay
75C1 Taira Japan
78A3 Tais Indon
75A1 Taisha Japan
29B5 Taitao,Pen de Chile
73E5 T'ai-tung Taiwan
38K5 Taivelkoski Fin
69E4 Taiwan Republic, China
Taiwan Haixia = Formosa Str
72C2 Taiyuan China
72D3 Taizhou China
81C4 Ta'izz Yemen
82A2 Tajikistan Republic, Asia
50B1 Tajo R Spain
76B2 Tak Thai
74D3 Takada Japan
75A2 Takahashi Japan
110B2 Takaka NZ
74C4 Takamatsu Japan
74D3 Takaoka Japan
110B1 Takapuna NZ
74D3 Takasaki Japan
75B1 Takayama Japan
74D3 Takefu Japan
70A3 Takengon Indon
76C3 Takeo Cam
75A2 Takeo Japan
Take-shima = Tok-do
90A2 Takestan Iran
75A2 Taketa Japan
4G3 Takjvik L Can
99D1 Takkaze R Eritrea/Eth
13B1 Takla L Can
13B1 Takla Landing Can
13B1 Taklesluk L USA
12H2 Taku Arm R Can
23A1 Tala Mexico
59B3 Talabanya Hung
84C2 Talagang Pak
83B3 Talaimannar Sri Lanka
97C3 Talak Desert Region, Niger
78A3 Talangbetutu Indon
32A4 Talara Peru
50B2 Talavera de la Reina Spain
34A3 Talca Chile
34A3 Talcahuano Chile
86B2 Tälcher India
52B1 Taldy Kurgan Kazakhstan
71D4 Taliabu Indon
84B1 Taligan Afghan
99D2 Tali Post Sudan
78D4 Taliwang Indon
12D2 Talkeetna USA
12E2 Talkeetna Mts USA
17A1 Talladega USA
93D2 Tall 'Afar Iraq
17A1 Tallahassee USA
94C1 Tall Bisah Syria
60B2 Tallinn Estonia
93C2 Tall Kalakh Syria
19B3 Tallulah USA
60D4 Tal'noye Ukraine
58C2 Talpaki Russian Fed
30B4 Taltal Chile
109C1 Talwood Aust
78D1 Tamabo Range Mts Malay
96C2 Tamale Ghana
96C2 Tamanrasset Alg
96C2 Tamanrasset Watercourse Alg

16B2 Tamaqua USA
Tamatave = Toamasina
23A2 Tamazula Jalisco, Mexico
23B2 Tamazulapán Mexico
23B1 Tamazunchale Mexico
97A3 Tambacounda Sen
61F3 Tambov Division, Russian Fed
61F3 Tambov Russian Fed
50A1 Tambre R Spain
98C2 Tambura Sudan
97A3 Tamchaket Maur
50A1 Tamega R Port
23B1 Tamiahua Mexico
87B2 Tamil Nadu State, India
76D2 Tam Ky Viet
17B2 Tampa USA
17B2 Tampa B USA
39J6 Tampere Fin
23B1 Tampico Mexico
68D2 Tamsagbulag Mongolia
86C2 Tamu Myan
23B2 Tamuís Mexico
109D2 Tamworth Aust
43D3 Tamworth Eng
38K4 Tana Nor
99D1 Tana L Eth
99E3 Tana R Kenya
38K5 Tana R Nor/Fin
75B2 Tanabe Japan
38K4 Tanafjord Inlet Nor
78D3 Tanahgrogot Indon
71E4 Tanahmerah Indon
12D1 Tanana USA
12E2 Tanana R USA
Tananarive = Antananarivo
47C2 Tanaro R Italy
74B2 Tanch'ŏn N Korea
34D3 Tandil Arg
71E4 Tandjong Datu Pt Indon
71E4 Tandjong d'Urville C Indon
78D3 Tandjung Layar C Indon
78D2 Tandjung Lumut C Indon
78D2 Tandjung Mangkalihat C Indon
78C3 Tandjung Sambar C Indon
78C2 Tandjung Sirik C Malay
71E4 Tandjung Vals C Indon
85B3 Tando Adam Pak
85B3 Tando Muhammad Khan Pak
108B2 Tandou L Aust
87B1 Tändür India
110C2 Taneatua NZ
76B2 Tanen Range Mts Myan/Thai
96B2 Tanezrouft Desert Region Alg
91C4 Tang Iran
99D3 Tanga Tanz
60E4 Tanganrog Russian Fed
99D3 Tanganyika,L Tanz/Zaïre
96B1 Tanger Mor
82C2 Tanggula Shan Mts China
Tangier = Tanger
78A2 Tangjungpinang Indon
82C2 Tangra Yumco L China
72D2 Tangshan China
78B3 Tangub Phil
63C2 Tanguy Russian Fed
79B4 Tanjay Phil
101D3 Tanjona Ankaboa C Madag

101D2 Tanjona Babaomby C Madag
101D2 Tanjona Vilanandro C Madag
101D3 Tanjona Vohimena C Madag
78C4 Tanjong Bugel C Indon
78B4 Tanjong Cangkuang C Indon
78C3 Tanjong Puting C Indon
78C3 Tanjong Selatan C Indon
78D3 Tanjung Indon
70A3 Tanjungbalai Indon
78A3 Tanjung Jabung Pt Indon
78B3 Tanjungpandan Indon
78B4 Tanjung Priok Indon
78D2 Tanjungredeb Indon
78D2 Tanjungselor Indon
84C2 Tank Pak
68B1 Tannu Ola Mts Russian Fed
97B4 Tano R Ghana
97C3 Tanout Niger
23B1 Tanquian Mexico
73E4 Tan-shui Taiwan
86A1 Tansing Nepal
95C1 Tanta Egypt
96A2 Tan-Tan Mor
4B3 Tanunak USA
99D3 Tanzania Republic, Africa
72A3 Tao He R China
72B2 Taole China
96B1 Taourirt Mor
60C2 Tapa Estonia
25C3 Tapachula Mexico
33F4 Tapajós R Brazil
34C3 Tapalquén Arg
70B4 Tapan Indon
111A3 Taparoa NZ
32D5 Tapauá R Brazil
85D4 Tapi R India
86B1 Taplejung Nepal
111B2 Tapuaenuku Mt NZ
35B2 Tapuaritinga Brazil
79B4 Tapul Group Is Phil
33E4 Tapurucuara Brazil
109D1 Tara Aust
65J4 Tara Russian Fed
65J4 Tara R Russian Fed
54A2 Tara R Bosnia-Herzegovina/Montenegro, Yugos
97D4 Taraba R Nig
30D2 Tarabuco Bol
Tarābulus = Tripoli
50B1 Taracón Spain
110C1 Taradale NZ
78D2 Tarakan Indon
110B1 Taranaki, Mt NZ
44A3 Taransay I Scot
53C2 Taranto Italy
32B5 Tarapoto Peru
49C2 Tarare France
110C2 Tararua Range Mts NZ
96C2 Tarat Alg
110C1 Tarawera NZ
51B1 Tarazona Spain
44C3 Tarbat Ness Pen Scot
84C2 Tarbela Res Pak
42B2 Tarbert Strathclyde, Scot
44A3 Tarbert Western Isles, Scot
48C3 Tarbes France
106C4 Tarcoola Aust
109C2 Tarcoon Aust
109D2 Taree Aust
96A2 Tarfaya Mor
95A1 Tarhūnah Libya
91B5 Tarif UAE
30D3 Tarija Bol
87B2 Tarikere India
81C4 Tarim Yemen
99D3 Tarime Tanz
82C1 Tarim He R China
82C2 Tarim Pendi Basin China

84B2 Tarin Kut Afghan
18A1 Tarkio USA
79B2 Tarlac Phil
32B6 Tarma Peru
49C3 Tarn R France
59C2 Tarnobrzeg Pol
59C3 Tarnów Pol
107D3 Taroom Aust
51C1 Tarragona Spain
109C4 Tarraleah Aust
51C1 Tarrasa Spain
16C2 Tarrytown USA
92B2 Tarsus Turk
47D2 Tartaro R Italy
60C2 Tartu Estonia
92C3 Tartūs Syria
35C1 Tarumirim Brazil
70A3 Tarutung Indon
52B1 Tarvisio Italy
80D1 Tashauz Turkmenistan
82A1 Tashigang Bhutan
82A1 Tashkent Uzbekistan
65K4 Tashtagol Russian Fed
63A2 Tashtyp Russian Fed
94B2 Tasil Syria
6H3 Tasiussaq Greenland
95A3 Tasker Niger
110B2 Tasman B NZ
107D5 Tasmania I Aust
111A2 Tasman Mts NZ
109C4 Tasman Pen Aust
107E4 Tasman S NZ/Aust
92C1 Taşova Turk
97C2 Tassili du Hoggar Desert Region, Alg
96C2 Tassili N'jjer Desert Region, Alg
96B2 Tata Mor
96D1 Tataouine Tunisia
65J4 Tatarsk Russian Fed
69G2 Tatarskiy Proliv Str Russian Fed
61G2 Tatarstan Russian Fed
75B1 Tateyama Japan
5G3 Tathlina L Can
12C2 Tatla Lake Can
58Y3 Tatry Mts Pol/Slovakia
75A2 Tatsuno Japan
85B4 Tatta Pak
93D2 Tatvan Turk
31C3 Tauá Brazil
35B2 Taubaté Brazil
110C1 Taumarunui NZ
101F1 Taung S Africa
76B2 Taungdwingyi Myan
76B1 Taung-gyi Myan
76A2 Taungup Myan
64C2 Taunsa Pak
43C4 Taunton Eng
16D2 Taunton USA
46E1 Taunus Region, Germany
110C1 Taupo NZ
110C1 Taupo,L NZ
52C1 Taurage Lithuania
110C1 Tauranga NZ
110C1 Tauranga Harbour B NZ
110B1 Tauroa Pt NZ
7A3 Tavani Can
7A3 Tavani Can
65H4 Tavda R Russian Fed
43B4 Tavistock Eng
76B3 Tavoy Myan
76B3 Tavoy Pt Myan
92A2 Tavsanli Turk
111B2 Tawa NZ
19A3 Tawakoni,L USA
14B2 Tawas City USA
70C3 Tawau Malay
98C1 Taweisha Sudan
79B4 Tawitawi I Phil
79B4 Tawitawi Group Is Phil
23B2 Taxco Mexico

23B2 Taxcoco Mexico
44C3 Tay R Scot
78C3 Tayan Indon
12B1 Taylor Alaska, USA
13C1 Taylor Can
14B2 Taylor Michigan, USA
19A3 Taylor Texas, USA
18C2 Taylorville USA
80B3 Taymā' S Arabia
63B1 Taymura R Russian Fed
76D3 Tay Ninh Viet
63B2 Tayshet Russian Fed
68B2 Tayshir Mongolia
79A3 Taytay Phil
90D3 Tayyebāt Iran
96B1 Taza Mor
95B2 Tazirbu Libya
12E2 Tazlina L USA
64J3 Tazovskiy Russian Fed
65F5 Tbilisi Georgia
98B3 Tchibanga Gabon
95A2 Tchigaï,Plat du Niger
97C3 Tchin Tabaradene Niger
98B2 Tcholliré Cam
58B2 Tczew Pol
111A3 Te Anau NZ
111A3 Te Anau,L NZ
110C1 Te Aroha NZ
110C1 Te Awamutu NZ
96C1 Tébessa Alg
23A2 Teboman Mexico
23A2 Tecailtlán Mexico
21B3 Tecate Mexico
61K2 Techa R Russian Fed
23A1 Tecolotlán Mexico
23A2 Tecpan Mexico
54C1 Tecuci Rom
18A1 Tecumseh USA
80E2 Tedzhen Turkmenistan
65H6 Tedzhen Turkmenistan
42D2 Tees R Eng
33E4 Tefé Brazil
78B4 Tegal Indon
78B4 Tegineneng Indon
25D3 Tegucigalpa Honduras
21B3 Tehachapi Mts USA
21B2 Tehachapi P USA
4J3 Tehek L Can
90B2 Tehrān Iran
23B2 Tehuacán Mexico
23B2 Tehuantepec Mexico
23B2 Tehuitzingo Mexico
43B3 Teifi R Wales
50A2 Tejo R Port
23A2 Tejupilco Mexico
111B2 Tekapo,L NZ
82B1 Tekeli Kazakhstan
92A1 Tekirdağ Turk
55C2 Tekir Dağlari Mts Turk
86C2 Teknaf Bang
110C1 Te Kuiti NZ
25D3 Tela Honduras
94B2 Tel Aviv Yafo Israel
34B3 Telén Arg
21B2 Telescope Peak Mt USA
33F5 Teles Pires R Brazil
47D1 Telfs Austria
63A2 Teli Russian Fed
78B4 Tell el Meise Mt Jordan
12A1 Teller USA
87B2 Tellicherry India
77C5 Telok Anson Malay
78D2 Télok Darvel Malay
71E4 Télok Flamingo B Indon
78C3 Télok Kumai B Indon
78B4 Télok Pelabuanratu B Indon
78C3 Télok Saleh B Indon
78C3 Télok Sampit B Indon
78B3 Télok Sukadona B Indon
23B2 Teloloapán Mexico

64G3 Tel'pos-iz Mt Russian Fed
58C1 Telšiai Lithuania
78C3 Telukbatang Indon
71E4 Teluk Berau B Indon
78B4 Telukbetung Indon
70D4 Teluk Bone B Indon
71E4 Teluk Cendrawasih B Indon
78D3 Teluk Mandar B Indon
70D3 Teluk Tolo B Indon
70D3 Teluk Tomini B Indon
71D3 Téluk Weda B Indon
14B1 Temagami,L Can
23B2 Temascal Mexico
78A3 Tembesi R Indon
78A3 Tembilahan Indon
27E5 Temblador Ven
77C5 Temerloh Malay
65G5 Temir Kazakhstan
65J4 Temirtau Kazakhstan
15C1 Temiscaming Can
109C2 Temora Aust
9B3 Tempe Aust
45C2 Templemore Irish Rep
23B1 Tempoal Mexico
34A3 Temuco Chile
111B2 Temuka NZ
32B4 Tena Ecuador
87C1 Tenāli India
23B2 Tenancingo Mexico
76B3 Tenasserim Myan
43B4 Tenby Wales
99E1 Tendaho Eth
83D5 Ten Degree Chan Indian O
98B1 Ténéré Desert Region Niger
96A2 Tenerife I Canary Is
76B1 Teng R Myan
72A2 Tengger Shamo Desert China
112C2 Teniente Jubany Base Ant
112C2 Teniente Rodolfo Marsh Martin Base Ant
87B3 Tenkäsi India
100B2 Tenke Zaïre
97B3 Tenkodogo Burkina
106C2 Tennant Creek Aust
11B3 Tennessee State, USA
18C2 Tennessee R USA
34A2 Teno Chile
78D1 Tenom Malay
25C3 Tenosique Mexico
109D1 Tenterfield Aust
17B2 Ten Thousand Is USA
23A1 Teocaltiche Mexico
35C1 Teófilo Otóni Brazil
23B2 Teotihuacan Hist Site, Mexico
23B2 Teotitlan Mexico
23A1 Tepatitlan Mexico
23A2 Tepehuanes Mexico
23B2 Tepeji Mexico
23A1 Tepic Mexico
57C2 Teplice Czech Republic
110C1 Te Puke NZ
23B2 Tequila Mexico
23B2 Tequistepec Mexico
51C1 Ter R Spain
97C3 Tera Niger
75B1 Teradomari Japan
52B2 Teramo Italy
38B3 Terceira I Açores
59D3 Terebovlya Ukraine
31C3 Teresina Brazil
35C2 Teresópolis Brazil
52B2 Terme Turk
80E2 Termez Uzbekistan
52B2 Termoli Italy
71D3 Ternate Indon
59D3 Ternopol Ukraine
13B2 Terrace Can

53B2 Terracina Italy
100B3 Terrafirma S Africa
112C8 Terre Adélie Region, Ant
19B4 Terre Bonne B USA
14A3 Terre Haute USA
19A3 Terrell USA
56B2 Terschelling I Neth
51B1 Teruel Spain
4C2 Teshekpuk USA
4C2 Teshekpuk L USA
74E2 Teshio R Japan
68B2 Tesiyn Gol Mts Mongolia
12H2 Teslin Can
12H2 Teslin R Can
12D2 Teslin L Can
63B3 Tesiyn Gol R Mongolia
96C2 Tessalit Mali
97C3 Tessaoua Niger
23A2 Tetela Mexico
96B1 Tetouan Mor
61G2 Tetyushi Russian Fed
30D3 Teuco R Arg
23A1 Teul de Gonzalez Ortega Mexico
71D4 Teun I Indon
52B2 Tevere R Italy
42C2 Teviot R Scot
65J4 Tevriz Russian Fed
111A3 Te Waewae B NZ
72C3 Tewah Indon
109D1 Tewantin Aust
72A3 Têwo China
19B3 Texarkana USA
19B3 Texarkana,L USA
109D1 Texas Aust
9C3 Texas State, USA
19A4 Texas City USA
56A2 Texel I Neth
19A3 Texoma,L USA
101G1 Teyateyaneng Lesotho
23B2 Teziutlán Mexico
86C1 Tezpur India
101G1 Tlabana Ntlenyana Mt Lesotho
101G1 Thaba Putsoa Mt Lesotho
76B3 Thagyettaw Myan
76D1 Thai Binh Viet
76C2 Thailand Kingdom, S E Asia
76D2 Thai Nguyen Viet
76C2 Thakhek Laos
84C2 Thal Pak
77C4 Thale Luang L Thai
109C1 Thallon Aust
110C1 Thames NZ
43E4 Thames R Eng
76D2 Thanh Hoah Viet
87B2 Thanjavur India
77E4 Thanlwin = Salween
85C3 Thar Desert India
108B1 Thargomindah Aust
55B2 Thásos I Greece
76B2 Thaton Myan
76B2 Thayetmyo Myan
5F5 The Dalles USA
91B4 The Gulf S W Asia
4H3 Thelon R Can
107E3 Theodore Aust
9B3 Theodore Roosevelt L USA
55B2 Thermaïkós Kólpos G Greece
8C2 Thermopolis USA
4F2 Thesiger B Can
55B2 Thessalon Can
55B2 Thessaloníki Greece
43E3 Thetford Eng
15D1 Thetford Mines Can
101G1 Theunissen S Africa
19B4 Thibodaux USA
5J4 Thicket Portage Can
8D2 Thief River Falls USA
20B2 Thielsen,Mt USA
49C2 Thiers France
98A3 Thiès Sen
99D3 Thika Kenya

86B1 Thimphu Bhutan
49D2 Thionville France
55C3 Thira I Greece
42D2 Thirsk Eng
Thiruvananthapuram = Trivandrum
39F7 Thisted Den
55B3 Thivai Greece
48C2 Thiviers France
17B1 Thomaston Georgia, USA
45C2 Thomastown Irish Rep
17B1 Thomasville Georgia, USA
6A2 Thom Bay Can
5J4 Thompson Can
18B1 Thompson R USA
43D3 Thompson Landing Can
13C2 Thompson R Can
16C2 Thompsonville USA
17B1 Thomson USA
107D3 Thomson R Aust
76C3 Thon Buri Thai
76B2 Thongwa Myan
48B3 Thonon-les-Bains France
42C2 Thornhill Scot
48B2 Thouars France
15C2 Thousand Is Can/USA
13E2 Three Hills Can
7G4 Three Kings Is NZ
76B2 Three Pagodas P Thai
14A2 Three Rivers Michigan, USA
20B2 Three Sisters Mt USA
Thrissur = Trichūr
6D2 Thule Greenland
47B1 Thun Switz
50B2 Thunder Bay Can
47B1 Thuner See L Switz
77B4 Thung Song Thai
47C1 Thur R Switz
57C2 Thüringen State, Germany
57C2 Thüringer Wald Upland Germany
45C2 Thurles Irish Rep
71F5 Thursday I Aust
44C2 Thurso Scot
112B4 Thurston I Ant
47C1 Thusis Switz
108B1 Thylungra Aust
73B5 Tiandong China
73B5 Tian'e China
72D2 Tianjin China
73B5 Tianlin China
82C1 Tian Shan Mts C Asia
72B3 Tianshui China
72D2 Tianzhu China
96C1 Tiaret Alg
93D2 Tiberias Israel
94B2 Tiberias,L Israel
Tiber,R = Tevere,R
95A2 Tibesti Mountain Region Chad
82C2 Tibet Autonomous Region, China
108B1 Tibooburra Aust
86A1 Tibrikot Nepal
24A2 Tiburón I Mexico
97B3 Tichitt Maur
96A2 Tichla Mor
47C1 Ticino R Italy/Switz
15D2 Ticonderoga USA
25D2 Ticul Mexico
47C1 Tiefencastel Switz
74A2 Tieling China
46B1 Tielt Belg
46C1 Tienen Belg
65J5 Tien Shan Mts China/Kyrgyzstan
72D2 Tientsin China
39H6 Tierp Sweden
23B2 Tierra Blanca Mexico
23B2 Tierra Colorada Mexico

29C6 Tierra del Fuego Territory, Arg
28C8 Tierra del Fuego / Arg/Chile
35B2 Tietê Brazil
35A2 Tietê R Brazil
14B2 Tiffin USA
17B1 Tifton USA
32A3 Tigre R Peru
33E2 Tigre R Ven
93E3 Tigris R Iraq
23B1 Tihuatlán Mexico
85D4 Tikamgarh India
60D2 Tikhin Russian Fed
61F4 Tikhoretsk Russian Fed
93D3 Tikrit Iraq
1B8 Tiksi Russian Fed
46C1 Tilburg Neth
43C4 Tilbury Eng
30C3 Tilcara Arg
108B1 Tilcha Aust
76A1 Tilin Myan
97C3 Tillabéri Niger
20B1 Tillamook USA
20B1 Tillia Niger
55C3 Tilos / Greece
54B2 Tilpa Aust
62A3 Tilva Colombia
64G3 Timanskiy Kryazh Mts Russian Fed
111B2 Timaru NZ
60E4 Timashevsk Russian Fed
55B3 Timbákion Greece
19B4 Timbalier B USA
97B3 Timbédra Maur
Timbuktu = Tombouctou
97B3 Timétrine Monts Mts Mali
97C3 Timia Niger
96C2 Timis R Rom
54B1 Timisoara Rom
10B1 Timmins Can
106B1 Timor / Indon
106B2 Timor S Aust/Indon
34C3 Timote Arg
79C4 Tinaca Pt Phil
27D5 Tinaco Ven
87B2 Tindivanam India
35B2 Tindouf Alg
56B2 Tinfouchy Alg
96C2 Tin Fouye Alg
6F3 Tingmiarmiut Greenland
32B5 Tingo Maria Peru
97B3 Tingréla Côte d'Ivoire
86B1 Tingri China
71F2 Tinian Pacific O
30C4 Tinogasta Arg
55C3 Tinos / Greece
43B4 Tintagel Head Pt Eng
96C2 Tin Tarabine Watercourse Alg
108B3 Tintinara Aust
96C2 Tin Zaouaten Alg
22C2 Tioga P USA
77C5 Tioman / Malay
47D1 Tione Italy
45C2 Tipperary County, Irish Rep
41B3 Tipperary Irish Rep
18B2 Tipton Missouri, USA
87B2 Tiptur India
23A2 Tiquicheo Mexico
55A2 Tiranë Alb
47D1 Tirano Italy
60C4 Tiraspol Moldova
87B2 Tirchchiráppalli India
55C3 Tire Turk
93C1 Tirebolu Turk
44A3 Tiree / Scot
54C2 Tirgoviste Rom
54B1 Tirgu Jiu Rom
54B1 Tirgu Mures Rom
84C1 Tirich Mir Mt Pak
96A2 Tiris Region, Mor
61J3 Tirlyanskiy Russian Fed
54B1 Tirnăveni Rom

55B3 Tírnavos Greece
85D3 Tirodi India
47D1 Tirol Province, Austria
53A2 Tirso R Sardegna
87B3 Tiruchchendür India
87B3 Tirunelveli India
87B3 Tirupati India
87B2 Tiruppattur India
87B2 Tiruppur India
87B2 Tiruvannamalai India
19A3 Tishomingo USA
94C2 Tisíyah Syria
59C3 Tisza R Hung
86A2 Titlagarh India
54B2 Titov Veles Macedonia
98C2 Titule Zaire
17B2 Titusville USA
43C4 Tiverton Eng
53B2 Tivoli Italy
23B2 Tixtla Mexico
99E2 Tiyeglow Somalia
23B2 Tizayuca Mexico
25D2 Tizimín Mexico
96C1 Tizi Ouzou Alg
96B2 Tiznit Mor
23A1 Tizpan el Alto Mexico
23B2 Tlacolula Mexico
23B2 Tlacotalpan Mexico
23A2 Tlalchapa Mexico
23B2 Tlalnepantla Mexico
23B2 Tlalpan Mexico
23A1 Tlaltenango Mexico
23B2 Tlancualpican Mexico
23B2 Tlapa Mexico
23B2 Tlapacoyan Mexico
23B1 Tlaquepaque Mexico
23B2 Tlaxcala Mexico
23B2 Tlaxcala State, Mexico
23B2 Tlaxiaco Mexico
96B1 Tlemcem Alg
101D2 Toamasina Madag
34C3 Toay Arg
75B2 Toba Japan
75B2 Toba and Kakar Ranges Mts Pak
27E4 Tobago / Caribbean S
13C2 Toba Inlet Sd Can
71D3 Tobelo Indon
14B1 Tobermory Can
44A3 Tobermory Scot
71E3 Tobi / Pacific O
21B1 Tobin,Mt USA
65H4 Tobol R Kazakhstan
70D4 Toboli Indon
65H4 Tobol'sk Russian Fed
Tobruk = Tubruq
31B2 Tocantins R Brazil
31B3 Tocantins State, Brazil
17B1 Toccoa USA
47C1 Toce R Italy
30B3 Tocopilla Chile
30C3 Tocorpuri Mt Chile
32C7 Tocuyo R Ven
85D3 Toda India
47C1 Tödi Mt Italy
74E2 Tokachi R Japan
75B1 Tokamachi Japan
95C3 Tokar Sudan
69E4 Tokara Retto Arch Japan
93C2 Tokat Turk
74B3 Tökchök-kundo Arch S Korea
82B1 Tokmak Kyrgyzstan
110C1 Tokomaru Bay NZ
12H3 Tok-to / S Korea
12H3 Toku R Can/USA

78C3 Tokung Indon
69E4 Tokuno / Japan
74C4 Tokushima Japan
75A2 Tokuyama Japan
75A2 Tökyö Japan
110C1 Tolaga Bay NZ
101D3 Tôlanaro Madag
30F3 Toledo Brazil
50B1 Toledo Spain
14B2 Toledo USA
19B3 Toledo Bend Res USA
101D3 Toliara Madag
23B1 Tolimán Mexico
32B3 Tolima Mt Colombia
51B1 Tolosa Spain
29B3 Toltén Chile
61G3 Tol'yatti Russian Fed
74E2 Tomakomai Japan
78D1 Tomani Malay
58C2 Tomaszów Mazowiecka Pol
11B3 Tombigbee R USA
98B3 Tomboco Angola
35C2 Tombos Brazil
97B3 Tombouctou Mali
100A2 Tombua Angola
34A3 Tomé Chile
50B2 Tomelloso Spain
50A2 Tomer Port
106B3 Tomkinson Range Mts Aust
63E2 Tommot Russian Fed
55B2 Tomorrit Mt Alb
65K4 Tomsk Russian Fed
16B3 Toms River USA
25C3 Tonalá Mexico
20C1 Tonasket USA
105H4 Tonga Is Pacific O
101H1 Tongat S Africa
73D3 Tongcheng China
72B2 Tongchuan China
72A3 Tongde China
46C1 Tongeren Belg
76E2 Tonggu Jiao / China
73A5 Tonghai China
74B2 Tonghua China
74B3 Tongjosön-man N Korea
76D1 Tongkin,G of China/Viet
72E1 Tongliao China
73D3 Tongling China
108B2 Tongo Aust
34A2 Tongoy Chile
73B4 Tongren Guizhou, China
72A3 Tongren Qinghai, China
86C1 Tongsa Bhutan
76B1 Tongta Myan
72A3 Tongtian He R China
44C2 Tongue Scot
72D2 Tong Xian China
72B2 Tongxin China
73B4 Tongzi China
9C4 Tonichi Mexico
99D2 Tonj Sudan
85D3 Tonk India
18A2 Tonkawa USA
76C3 Tonle Sap L Camb
21B2 Tonopah USA
12E2 Tonsina USA
8B2 Tooele USA
109D1 Toogoolawah Aust
108D1 Toompine Aust
109D1 Toowoomba Aust
22C2 Topaz L USA
18A2 Topeka USA
9C4 Topolobampo Mexico
20B1 Toppenish USA
99D2 Tor Eth
55C3 Torbali Turk
90C2 Torbat-e-Heydariyeh Iran
90D2 Torbat-e Jām Iran
12D2 Torbert,Mt USA
50A1 Tordesillas Spain
43C4 Torfaen County Wales

56C2 Torgau Germany
46B1 Torhout Belg
69G3 Tori / Japan
47B2 Torino Italy
99D2 Torit Sudan
35A1 Torixorea Brazil
50A1 Tormes R Spain
13E2 Tornado Mt Can
38J5 Torne L Sweden
38H5 Torneträsk Sweden
7D4 Torngat Mts Can
38J5 Tornio Fin
34J5 Tornquist Arg
15C2 Toronto Can
60D2 Toropets Russian Fed
99D2 Tororo Uganda
92B2 Toros Dağlari Mts Turk
43C4 Torquay Eng
22C4 Torrance USA
50A2 Torrão Port
51C1 Torreblanca Spain
53B2 Torre del Greco Italy
50B1 Torrelavega Spain
50B2 Torremolinos Spain
108A2 Torrens,L Aust
24B2 Torreón Mexico
47B2 Torre Pellice Italy
107D2 Torres Str Aust
50A2 Torres Vedras Port
16C2 Torrington Connecticut, USA
8C2 Torrington Wyoming, USA
9C4 Torrón Brits
38D3 Tórshavn Faroyar
47C2 Tortona Italy
51C1 Tortosa Spain
90C2 Torüd Iran
40B2 Tory / Irish Rep
60D2 Torzhok Russian Fed
75A2 Tosa Japan
75A2 Tosa-shimizu Japan
74C4 Tosa-wan B Japan
75B2 To-shima / Japan
Toshkent = Tashkent
60D2 Tosno Russian Fed
75A2 Tosu Japan
92B1 Tosya Turk
61F1 Tot'ma Russian Fed
43C4 Totnes Eng
33F2 Totness Surinam
23B2 Totolapan Mexico
51C2 Totota Spain
109C2 Tottenham Aust
74C3 Tottori Japan
97B4 Touba Côte d'Ivoire
97A3 Touba Sen
96B1 Toubkal Mt Mor
97B3 Tougan Burkina
96C1 Touggourt Alg
97A3 Tougué Guinea
46C2 Toul France
49D3 Toulon France
49C3 Toulouse France
97B4 Toumodi Côte d'Ivoire
76B2 Toungoo Myan
46B1 Tourcoing France
96A2 Tourine Maur
46B1 Tournai Belg
48C2 Tours France
74E2 Towada Japan
74E2 Towada-ko L Japan
15C2 Towanda USA
107D2 Townsville Aust
16A3 Towson USA
43C4 Towy R Wales
74D3 Toyama Japan
75B2 Toyama-wan B Japan
75B2 Toyohashi Japan
75B2 Toyonaka Japan
75A1 Toyooka Japan
96C1 Tozeur Tunisia
46D2 Traben-Trarbach Germany
93C1 Trabzon Turk
22B2 Tracy California, USA
34A3 Traiguén Chile

13D3 Trail Can
41B3 Tralee Irish Rep
45B2 Tralee B Irish Rep
45C2 Tramore Irish Rep
39G7 Tranås Sweden
77B4 Trang Thai
71E4 Trangan I Indon
109C2 Trangie Aust
12E2 Transalaskan Pipeline USA
Transylvanian Alps = Muntii Carpatii Meridionali
53B3 Trapani Italy
109C3 Traralgon Aust
97A3 Trarza Region, Maur
76C3 Trat Thai
108B2 Traveller's L Aust
56C2 Travemünde Germ
14A2 Traverse City USA
12C1 Traverse Peak Mt USA
111B2 Travers,Mt NZ
47C2 Trebbia R Italy
59B3 Třebíč Czech Republic
54A2 Trebinje Bosnia-Herzegovina
57C3 Trebon Czech Republic
29F2 Treinta y Tres Urug
29C4 Trelew Arg
39G7 Trelleborg Sweden
43B3 Tremadog B Wales
15D1 Tremblant,Mt Can
41B3 Trembleur L Can
16A2 Tremont USA
59B3 Trenčín Slovakia
34C3 Trenque Lauquén Arg
43D3 Trent R Eng
47D1 Trentino Region, Italy
47D1 Trento Italy
15C2 Trenton USA
18B1 Trenton Missouri, USA
16B2 Trenton New Jersey, USA
7E5 Trepassey Can
34C3 Tres Arroyos Arg
35B2 Três Corações Brazil
30F3 Três Lagoas Brazil
34C3 Tres Lomas Arg
22B2 Tres Pinos USA
35C2 Três Rios Brazil
47C2 Treviglio Italy
47C2 Treviso Italy
47C2 Trezzo Italy
87B2 Trichūr India
108C2 Trida Aust
46D2 Trier Germany
52B1 Trieste Italy
45C2 Trim Irish Rep
87C3 Trincomalee Sri Lanka
33E6 Trinidad Can
29E2 Trinidad Urug
9C3 Trinidad USA
34C3 Trinidad I Arg
27E4 Trinidad I Caribbean S
103G6 Trindade I Atlantic O
27E4 Trinidad & Tobago Republic Caribbean S
19A3 Trinity USA
9D3 Trinity R USA
9C3 Trinity B Can
12D3 Trinity Is USA
17A1 Trion USA
94B1 Tripoli Leb
95A1 Tripoli Libya
55B3 Tripolis Greece
86C2 Tripura State, India
103H6 Tristan da Cunha Is Atlantic O
87B3 Trivandrum India
59B3 Trnava Slovakia
107E1 Trobriand Is PNG
15D1 Trois-Rivières Can
65H4 Troitsk Russian Fed
39G7 Trollhättan Sweden
38F6 Trollheimen Mt Nor
89K9 Tromelin I Indian O

38H5 Tromsø Nor
38G6 Trondheim Nor
38G6 Trondheimfjord Inlet Nor
42B2 Troon Scot
102J3 Tropic of Cancer
103J6 Tropic of Capricorn
96B2 Troudenni Mali
7A4 Trout L Ontario, Can
17A1 Troy Alabama, USA
16C1 Troy New York, USA
14B2 Troy Ohio, USA
54B2 Troyan Bulg
49C2 Troyes France
91B5 Trucial Coast Region, UAE
21A2 Truckee R USA
25D3 Trujillo Honduras
32B5 Trujillo Peru
50A2 Trujillo Spain
32C2 Trujillo Ven
70S Trundle Aust
43B4 Truro Eng
68B2 Tsagaan Nuur L Mongolia
68B1 Tsagan-Tologoy Russian Fed
53xo Tsavo Kenya
99D3 Tsavo Nat Pk Kenya
65J4 Tselinograd Kazakhstan
35A5 Tses Namibia
68C2 Tsetserleg Mongolia
97C4 Tsévié Togo
100B3 Tshabong Botswana
100B3 Tshane Botswana
98B3 Tshela Zaire
98C3 Tshibala Zaire
98C3 Tshikapa Zaire
98C3 Tshuapa R Zaire
101D3 Tsihombe Madag
61F4 Tsimlyanskoye Vodokhranilishche Res Russian Fed
Tsinan = Jinan
Tsingtao = Qingdao
101D2 Tsiroanomandidy Madag
13B2 Tsitsutl Peak Mt Can
58D2 Tsna R Belarus
72B1 Tsogt Ovoo Mongolia
68C2 Tsomog Mongolia
75B2 Tsu Japan
75B1 Tsubata Japan
74E3 Tsuchiura Japan
74E2 Tsugaru-kaikyō Str Japan
100A2 Tsumeb Namibia
100A3 Tsumis Namibia
75B1 Tsuruga Japan
74D3 Tsuruoka Japan
74B4 Tsushima I Japan
74C3 Tsuyama Japan
50A1 Tua R Port
45B2 Tuam Irish Rep
60E5 Tuapse Russian Fed
111A3 Tuatapere NZ
30G4 Tubarão Brazil
94B2 Tubas Israel
79A4 Tubbataha Reefs Is Phil
57B3 Tübingen Germany
95B1 Tubruq Libya
16B3 Tuckerton USA
9B3 Tucson USA
30C4 Tucumán State, Arg
34B2 Tucunuco Arg
34B2 Tucupita Ven
51B1 Tudela Spain
93C3 Tudmur Syria
101H1 Tugela R S Africa
109D2 Tuggerah L Aust
12D3 Tugidak I USA
79B2 Tuguegarao Phil
63F2 Tugur Russian Fed
72D2 Tuhai He R China
4E3 Tuktoyaktuk USA
58C1 Tukums Latvia

99D3 Tukuyu Tanz
84B1 Tukzar Afghan
60E3 Tula Russian Fed
60E3 Tula Division Russian Fed
23B1 Tulancingo Mexico
78A3 Tulangbawang R Indon
32B3 Tulcán Colombia
60C5 Tulcea Rom
100B3 Tuli Zim
94B2 Tulkarm Israel
48C2 Tulle France
19B3 Tullos USA
45C2 Tullow Irish Rep
18A2 Tulsa USA
93C3 Tulūl ash Shāmiyah Desert Region Syria/S Arabia
63C2 Tulun Russian Fed
78C4 Tulungagung Indon
32A4 Tumaco Colombia
108A3 Tumby Bay Aust
74B2 Tumen China
87B2 Tumkur India
77C4 Tumpat Malay
85D4 Tumsar India
97B3 Tumu Ghana
109C3 Tumut Aust
27L1 Tunapuna Trinidad
93C2 Tunceli Turk
100A3 Tunduma Zambia
101C2 Tunduru Tanz
54C2 Tundzha R Bulg
87B1 Tungabhadra R India
68D4 Tung-Chiang Taiwan
38B2 Tungnafellsjökull Mts Iceland
12J2 Tungsten Can
63B1 Tunguska R Russian Fed
87C1 Tuni India
96D1 Tunis Tunisia
88E4 Tunisia Republic, N Africa
32C2 Tunja Colombia
12B2 Tuntutuliak USA
7B2 Tununak USA
34B2 Tunuyán Arg
34B2 Tunuyán R Arg
22C2 Tuolumne Meadows USA
35A2 Tupã Brazil
35B1 Tupaciguara Brazil
30D3 Tupiza Bol
15D2 Tupper Lake USA
34B2 Tupungato Arg
29C2 Tupungato Mt Arg
86C1 Tura India
63C1 Tura Russian Fed
61K2 Tura R Russian Fed
90C2 Turān Iran
63B2 Turan Russian Fed
91A5 Turayf S Arabia
80E3 Turbat Pak
32B2 Turbo Colombia
54B1 Turda Rom
Turin = Torino
61K2 Turinsk Russian Fed
99D2 Turkana,L Kenya/Eth
80E1 Turkestan Region, C Asia
82A1 Turkestan Kazakhstan
92C2 Turkey Republic, W Asia
80D1 Turkmenistan Republic, Asia

90B2 Turkmenskiy Zaliv B Turkmenistan
27C2 Turks Is Caribbean S
39J6 Turku Fin
99D2 Turkwel R Kenya
22B2 Turlock USA
22B2 Turlock L USA
25D3 Turnagain,C Nic
22B2 Turneffe I Belize
16C1 Turners Falls USA
46C1 Turnhout Belg
13F1 Turnor L Can
54B2 Turnu Măgurele Rom
63A3 Turpan China
26B2 Turquino Mt Cuba
80E1 Turtkul' Uzbekistan
18A2 Turtle Creek Res USA
13F2 Turtle L Can
63A1 Turukhansk Russian Fed
68C1 Turuntayevo Russian Fed
35A1 Turvo R Goias, Brazil
35B2 Turvo R São Paulo, Brazil
58C2 Tur'ya R Ukraine
19C3 Tuscaloosa USA
19C3 Tuscola USA
90C3 Tusharik Iran
Tutera = Tudela
87B3 Tuticorin India
54C2 Tutrakan Bulg
57B3 Tuttlingen Germany
68C2 Tuul Gol R Mongolia
105G4 Tuvalu Is Pacific O
63B2 Tuvinskaya Respublika, Russian Fed
23A2 Tuxpan Jalisco, Mexico
24B2 Tuxpan Nayarit, Mexico
23B1 Tuxpan Veracruz, Mexico
23B2 Tuxtepec Mexico
25C3 Tuxtla Gutiérrez Mexico
50A1 Túy Spain
75D3 Tuy Hoa Viet
92B2 Tuz Gölü Salt L Turk
93D3 Tuz Khurmātū Iraq
54A2 Tuzla Bosnia-Herzegovina
60D2 Tver' Russian Fed
60D2 Tver' Division Russian Fed
42C2 Tweed R Eng/Scot
109D1 Tweed Heads Aust
42C2 Tweedsmuir Hills Scot
7E5 Twillingate Can
38B2 Twin Falls USA
111B2 Twins,The Mt NZ
14A2 Two Rivers USA
82E3 Tygda Russian Fed
19A3 Tyler USA
35B3 Tym R Russian Fed
69G1 Tymovskoye Russian Fed
42D2 Tyne R Eng
38G6 Tynset Nor
12D3 Tyonek USA
7E5 Tyne Can
Tyre = Sur
45C1 Tyrone County, N Ire
108B3 Tyrrell,L Aust
53B2 Tyrrhenian S Italy
Tyumen' Russian Fed
44B3 Tywyn Wales
55B3 Tzoumérka Mt Greece

U

99E2 Uarsciek Somalia
31B4 Uauá Brazil
35C1 Ubaí Brazil
98B2 Ubangi R CAR
47B2 Ubaye R France
75A2 Ube Japan
50B2 Ubeda Spain

6E2 Ubekendt Ejland I / Greenland
35B1 Uberaba Brazil
35B1 Uberlândia Brazil
76C2 Ubon Ratchathani Thai
58D2 Ubort R Belarus
98C3 Ubundi Zaire
32C5 Ucayali R Peru
84C3 Uch Pak
63F2 Uchar R Russian Fed
74E2 Uchiura-wan B Japan
63B2 Uda R Russian Fed
85C4 Udaipur India
86B1 Udaipur Garhi Nepal
34D3 Udaquiolla Arg
39G7 Uddevalla Sweden
38H5 Uddjaur L Sweden
87B1 Udgir India
84D2 Udhampur India
61H2 Udmurtia Division, Russian Fed
76C2 Udon Thani Thai
63F2 Udskaya Guba B Russian Fed
87A2 Udupi India
75B1 Ueda Japan
99C2 Uele R Zaire
96C2 Uelzen Germany
98C2 Uere R Zaire
61J3 Ufa R Russian Fed
61J2 Ufa R Russian Fed
100A3 Ugab R Namibia
99D3 Ugalla R Tanz
12D3 Ugak B USA
99D2 Uganda Republic, Africa
12C3 Ugashik B USA
12C3 Ugashik L USA
47B2 Ugine France
69G2 Uglegorsk Russian Fed
60E2 Uglich Russian Fed
60E3 Ugra R Russian Fed
44A3 Uig Scot
98B3 Uíge Angola
61H4 Uil Kazakhstan
8B2 Uinta Mts USA
100B4 Uitenhage S Africa
59C3 Újfehértó Hung
75B2 Uji Japan
99C3 Ujiji Tanz
30C3 Ujina Chile
85D4 Ujjain India
70C4 Ujung Pandang Indon
99D3 Ukerewe I Tanz
86C1 Ukhrul India
21A2 Ukiah California, USA
20C1 Ukiah Oregon, USA
58C1 Ukmerge Lithuania
60C4 Ukraine Republic, Europe
68C2 Ulaanbaatar Mongolia
68B2 Ulaangom Mongolia
72C1 Ulaan Uul Mongolia
82C1 Ulan Gol L China
68C1 Ulan Ude Russian Fed
68B3 Ulan Ul Hu L China
32B2 Ulapes Arg
74B3 Ulchin S Korea
54A2 Ulcinj Montenegro, Yugos
68D2 Uldz Mongolia
68B2 Uliastay Mongolia
58D1 Ulla Lithuania
109D3 Ulladulla Aust
44B3 Ullapool Scot
38H5 Ullsfjorden Inlet Nor
42C2 Ullswater L Eng
74C3 Ullung-do I S Korea
57C3 Ulm Germany
108A1 UlooWaranie,L Aust
74B3 Ulsan S Korea
45C1 Ulster Region, N Ire
66K5 Ulungur He R China
66K5 Ulungur Hu L China
44A3 Ulva I Scot
42C2 Ulverston Eng

109C4 Ulverstone Aust
63G2 Ulya R Russian Fed
61G3 Ul'yanovsk Division, Russian Fed
60D4 Uman Ukraine
6E2 Umanak Greenland
86A2 Umaria India
85B3 Umarkot Pak
108A1 Umaroona,L Aust
20C1 Umatilla USA
38L5 Umba Russian Fed
99D3 Umba R Tanz
38L6 Umba Sweden
38J6 Umea Sweden
101H1 Umfolozi R S Africa
4C3 Umiat USA
91C4 Umm al Qaiwain UAE
92C1 Umm as Samim Salt Marsh Oman
99C1 Umm Bell Sudan
98C1 Umm Keddada Sudan
99D1 Umm Ruwaba Sudan
91B5 Umm Sa'id Qatar
20B2 Umpqua R USA
85B4 Umred India
100B4 Umtata S Africa
35A2 Umuarama Brazil
52C1 Una R Bosnia-Herzegovina/Croatia
35B1 Unaí Brazil
12B2 Unalakleet USA
80C3 Unayzah S Arabia
16C2 Uncasville USA
101G1 Underberg S Africa
60D3 Unecha Russian Fed
94B3 Uneisa Jordan
7D4 Ungava B Can
30F4 União de Vitória Brazil
35B1 Unión Arg
18B2 Union Missouri, USA
17B1 Union S Carolina, USA
14C2 Union City Pennsylvania, USA
17A1 Union Springs USA
15C3 Uniontown USA
91B5 United Arab Emirates Arabian Pen
36C3 United Kingdom Kingdom, W Europe
2H4 United States of America
6B1 United States Range Mts Can
13F2 Unity Can
20C2 Unity USA
46D1 Unna Germany
86A1 Unnao India
44E1 Unst I Scot
92C1 Unye Turk
61F2 Unzha R Russian Fed
33E2 Upata Ven
98B3 Upemba Nat Pk Zaire
6E2 Upernavik Greenland
22D3 Upland USA
100B3 Uplington S Africa
14B2 Upper Arlington USA
13D2 Upper Arrow L Can
111C2 Upper Hutt NZ
20B2 Upper Klamath L USA
20B2 Upper L USA
45C1 Upper Lough Erne L N Ire
27L1 Upper Manzanilla Trinidad
39H7 Uppsala Sweden
72B1 Ural Dianqi China
91A4 Urairah S Arabia
61H3 Ural R Kazakhstan
109D2 Uralla Aust
61H3 Ural'sk Kazakhstan
65G4 Uralskiy Khrebet Mts Russian Fed
5H4 Uranium City Can
75B1 Urawa Japan
18C1 Urbana Illinois, USA
14B2 Urbana Ohio, USA
52B2 Urbino Italy
42C2 Ure R Eng
61G2 Uren' Russian Fed

80E1 Urgench Uzbekistan
84B2 Urgun Afghan
55C3 Urla Turk
54B2 Urosevac Serbia, Yugos
31B4 Uruaçu Brazil
23A2 Uruapan Mexico
35B1 Urucuia R Brazil
30E4 Uruguaiana Brazil
29E2 Uruguay Republic, S America
29E2 Uruguay R Urug
62H2 Urümqi China
69H2 Urup I Russian Fed
84B2 Uruzgan Afghan
61F3 Uryupinsk Russian Fed
61H2 Urzhum Russian Fed
54C2 Urziceni Rom
82C1 Usa Japan
75A2 Usa Japan
64G3 Usa R Russian Fed
92A2 Usak Turk
100A3 Usakos Namibia
99D3 Ushashi Tanz
65J4 Ush Tobe Kazakhstan
29C6 Ushuaia Arg
63E2 Ushumun Russian Fed
43C4 Usk R Wales
92A1 Usküdar Turk
63C2 Usolye Sibirskoye Russian Fed
34B2 Uspallata Arg
69F2 Ussuriysk Russian Fed
47C1 Uster Switz
53B3 Ustica I Italy
57C2 Usti nad Labem Czech Republic
65J4 Ust'Ishim Russian Fed
58B2 Ustka Pol
65K5 Ust'-Kamenogorsk Kazakhstan
63B2 Ust Karabula Russian Fed
61J2 Ust'Katav Russian Fed
63C2 Ust'-Kut Russian Fed
61E4 Ust Labinsk Russian Fed
63F1 Ust'Maya Russian Fed
1C8 Ust'Nera Russian Fed
63E2 Ust'Nyukzha Russian Fed
63C2 Ust'Ordynskiy Russian Fed
64G3 Ust'Tsil'ma Russian Fed
63F2 Ust'Umal'ta Russian Fed
65G5 Ustyurt Plateau Plat Kazakhstan
75A2 Usuki Japan
25C3 Usumacinta R Guatemala/Mexico
101H1 Usutu R Swaziland
38K5 Utsjoki Fin
74D3 Utsunomiya Japan
76C2 Uttaradit Thai
86A1 Uttar Pradesh State, India
65H4 Uval Russian Fed
107F3 Uvéa I Nouvelle Calédonie
99D3 Uvinza Tanz
99C3 Uvira Zaire
6E2 Uvkusigssat Greenland
39J6 Uvsikaupunki Fin
68B1 Uvs Nuur L China

74C4 Uwajima Japan
72B2 Uxin Qi China
63B2 Uyar Russian Fed
30C3 Uyuni Bol
80E1 Uzbekistan Republic, Asia
48C2 Uzerche France
59C3 Uzhgorod Ukraine
54A2 Uzice Serbia, Yugos
60E3 Uzlovaya Russian Fed
92A1 Uzunköprü Turk

V

101F1 Vaal R S Africa
101G1 Vaal Dam Res S Africa
100B3 Vaalwater S Africa
38J6 Vaasa Fin
59B3 Vác Hung
30F4 Vacaria Brazil
35C1 Vacaria R Minas Gerais, Brazil
21A2 Vacaville USA
85C4 Vadodara India
38C3 Vadso Nor
47C1 Vaduz Leichtenstein
38D3 Vägar Faroyar
29E3 Va Gesell Arg
59B3 Váh R Slovakia
87B2 Vaigai R India
65K3 Vakh R Russian Fed
60B4 Valcea Brazil
29C4 Valcheta Arg
47D2 Valdagno Italy
60D2 Valday Russian Fed
60D2 Valdayskaya Vozvyshennost' Upland Russian Fed
32D2 Val de la Pascua Ven
50B2 Valdepeñas Spain
12E2 Valdez USA
29B3 Valdivia Chile
46B2 Val d'Oise Department France
17B1 Valdosta USA
20C2 Vale USA
13D2 Valemount Can
31D4 Valença Bahia, Brazil
35C2 Valença R de Janeiro, Brazil
49C3 Valence France
51B2 Valencia Region, Spain
51B2 Valencia Spain
32D1 Valencia Ven
45A3 Valencia I Irish Rep
50A2 Valencia de Alcantara Spain
46B1 Valenciennes France
47C2 Valenza Italy
43C4 Vale of Glamorgan County Wales
32C2 Valera Ven
39K7 Valga Estonia
54A2 Valjevo Serbia, Yugos

39J6 Valkeakoski Fin
25D2 Valladolid Mexico
50B1 Valladolid Spain
47B2 Valle d'Aosta Region, Italy
27D5 Valle de la Pascua Ven
23A1 Valle de Santiago Mexico
47B2 Valle d'Isére France
32C1 Valledupar Colombia
97C3 Vallée de l'Azaouak R Niger
97C3 Vallée Tilemsi V Mali
30D2 Valle Grande Bol
22A1 Vallejo USA
30B4 Vallenar Chile
53B3 Valletta Malta
8D2 Valley City USA
16B1 Valley Falls USA
15D1 Valleyfield Can
13D1 Valleyview Can
47E2 Valli di Comacchio Lg Italy
51C1 Valls Spain

Virei

100A2 Virei Angola
35C1 Virgem da Lapa Brazil
101G1 Virginia S Africa
10C3 Virginia State, USA
10A2 Virginia USA
21B2 Virginia City USA
27E3 Virgin Is Caribbean S
52C1 Virovitica Croatia
46C2 Virton Belg
87B3 Virudunagar India
52C2 Vis I Croatia
21B2 Visalia USA
70B3 Visayan S Phil
39H7 Visby Sweden
4H2 Viscount Melville Sd Can
54A2 Višegrad Bosnia-Herzegovina
50A1 Viseu Port
83C4 Vishākhapatnam India
47B1 Visp Switz
49C1 Vissingen Neth
21B3 Vista USA
Vistula = Wisła
57C3 Vitava R Czech Republic
87A1 Vite India
60D2 Vitebsk Belarus
52B2 Viterbo Italy
50A1 Vitigudino Spain
63D2 Vitim R Russian Fed
50B1 Vitoria Spain
31C6 Vitória Brazil
31C4 Vitória da Conquista Brazil
48B2 Vitré France
46C2 Vitry-le-Francois France
38J5 Vittangi Sweden
53B3 Vittoria Italy
47E2 Vittorio Veneto Italy
59H2 Vityaz Depth Pacific O
50A1 Vivero Spain
63B1 Vivi R Russian Fed
34D3 Vivorata Arg
63C2 Vizhne-Angarsk Russian Fed
83C4 Vizianagaram India
54B1 Vlădeasa Mt Rom
61F5 Vladikavkaz Russian Fed
65F4 Vladimir Russian Fed
60E2 Vladimir Division, Russian Fed
59C2 Vladimir Volynskiy Ukraine
74C2 Vladivostok Russian Fed
56A2 Vlieland I Neth
46B1 Vlissingen Neth
55A2 Vlorë Alb
57C3 Vöcklabruck Austria
76D3 Voeune Sai Camb
47C2 Voghera Italy
101D2 Vohibinany Madag
101E2 Vohimarina Madag
99D3 Voi Kenya
97B4 Voinjama Lib
49D2 Voiron France
54A1 Vojvodina Aut Republic Serbia, Yugos
26A5 Volcán Baru Mt Panama
23B2 Volcán Citlaltepetl Mt Mexico
30C3 Volcán Lullaillaco Mt Chile
30C3 Volcáno Copahue Mt Chile
34A3 Volcáno Domuyo Mt Arg
Volcano Is = Kazan Retto
29B3 Volcáno Lanin Mt Arg
30C3 Volcán Ollagüe Mt Chile
34A3 Volcáno Llaima Mt Chile

34B2 Volcáno Maipo Mt Arg
34A3 Volcáno Peteroa Mt Chile
34B3 Volcáno Tromen V Arg
23A2 Volcán Paracutin Mt Mexico
32B3 Volcán Puracé Mt Colombia
32A3 Volcán Tinguiririca Mt Arg/Chile
61J2 Volchansk Russian Fed
61G4 Volga R Russian Fed
60E2 Volgoda Division, Russian Fed
61F4 Volgodonsk Russian Fed
61F4 Volgograd Russian Fed
61F4 Volgograd Division, Russian Fed
61G3 Volgogradskoye Vodokhranilishche Res Russian Fed
60D2 Volkhov Russian Fed
60D2 Volkhov R Russian Fed
61G3 Volkovysk Belarus
101G1 Volksrust S Africa
61F2 Vologda Russian Fed
48B2 Vologne France
55B3 Vólos Greece
61G3 Vol'sk Russian Fed
22B2 Volta USA
97B3 Volta Blanche R Burkina
97B4 Volta,L Ghana
97B3 Volta Noire R Burkina
35C2 Volta Redonda Brazil
97B3 Volta Rouge R Burkina
61F4 Volzhskiy Russian Fed
12D2 Von Frank Mt USA
6J3 Vopnafjörður Iceland
47C1 Vorarlberg Province, Austria
47C1 Vorder Rhein R Switz
56C1 Vordingborg Den
64H3 Vorkuta Russian Fed
39G6 Vorma R Nor
60E3 Voronezh Russian Fed
60E3 Voronezh Division, Russian Fed
61F3 Voronezh R Russian Fed
38M5 Voron'ya R Russian Fed
39K7 Võru Estonia
49D2 Vosges Mt France
39F6 Voss Nor
63B2 Vostochnyy Sayan Mts Russian Fed
112B9 Vostok Base Ant
61H2 Votkinsk Russian Fed
46C2 Vouziers France
60D4 Voznesensk Ukraine
54B2 Vozroja Serbia, Yugos
54B2 Vratsa Bulg
54A1 Vrbas Serbia, Yugos
52C2 Vrbas R Serbia, Yugos
52C2 Vrbas R Bosnia-Herzegovina
54B2 Vrbovsko Bosnia-Herzegovina
101G1 Vrede S Africa
33F2 Vreed en Hoop Guyana
54A1 Vršac Serbia, Yugos
52C2 Vrtoče Bosnia-Herzegovina
100B3 Vryburg S Africa
101H1 Vryheid S Africa
54A1 Vukovar Croatia
13E2 Vulcan Can
53B3 Vulcano I Italy
77D3 Vung Tau Viet
38J5 Vuollerim Sweden
38L6 Vyartsilya Russian Fed

61H2 Vyatka R Russian Fed
69F2 Vyazemskiy Russian Fed
60D2 Vyaz'ma Russian Fed
61F2 Vyazniki Russian Fed
60C1 Vyborg Russian Fed
64G3 Vym' R Russian Fed
43C3 Vyrnwy R Wales
60D2 Vyshiy Volochek Russian Fed
59B3 Vyškov Czech Republic
60E1 Vytegra Russian Fed

W

97B3 Wa Ghana
13E1 Wabasca Can
5G4 Wabasca R Can
13E1 Wabasca L Can
14A2 Wabash USA
14A3 Wabash R USA
5J4 Wabowden Can
7D4 Wabush Can
17B2 Waccasassa R USA
16D1 Wachusett Res USA
19A3 Waco USA
85B3 Wad Pak
95A2 Waddān Libya
5F4 Waddington,Mt Can
93E4 Wadi al Bātin Watercourse Iraq
93D3 Wadi al Ghudāf Watercourse Iraq
94C2 Wadi al Harir V Syria
93D3 Wadi al Mirah Watercourse Iraq/ S Arabia
93D3 Wadi al Ubayyid Watercourse Iraq
93D3 Wadi Ar'ar Watercourse S Arabia
91A5 Wadi as Hsabā' Watercourse S Arabia
92C3 Wadi as Sirhān V Jordan/S Arabia
94C2 Wadi az Zaydī V Syria
94C3 Wadi edh Dhab'i V Jordan
94A3 Wadi el 'Arish V Egypt
94C3 Wadi el Ghadaf V Jordan
94C3 Wadi el Hasa V Jordan
94C3 Wadi el Janab V Jordan
94B3 Wadi el Jeib V Israel/Jordan
95B3 Wadi el Milk Watercourse Sudan
92A3 Wadi el Natrun Watercourse Egypt
94B3 Wadi es Sir Jordan
94B3 Wadi Fidan V Jordan
94B3 Wadi Hareidin V Egypt
93D3 Wadi Hawrān R Iraq
95B3 Wadi Howa Watercourse Sudan
98C1 Wadi Ibra Watercourse Sudan
94C2 Wadi Luhfi Watercourse Jordan
94B3 Wadi Mujib V Jordan
94B3 Wadi Qitaiya V Egypt
80B3 Wadi Sha'it Watercourse Egypt
99D1 Wad Medani Sudan
93E4 Wafra Kuwait
6B3 Wager B Can
6A3 Wager Bay Can
109C3 Wagga Wagga Aust
106A4 Wagin Aust
95A2 Wāha Libya
21C4 Wahaiwa Hawaiian Is
18A1 Wahoo USA
8D2 Wahpeton USA

87A1 Wai India
111B2 Waiau NZ
111A3 Waiau R NZ
111B2 Waiau R NZ
71B3 Waigeo I Indon
110C1 Waihi NZ
110C1 Waikaremoana,L NZ
110C1 Waikato R NZ
108A2 Waikerie Aust
111B3 Waikouaiti NZ
21C4 Wailuku Hawaiian Is
111B2 Waimakariri R NZ
111B2 Waimate NZ
21C4 Waimea Hawaiian Is
106B1 Waingapu Indon
13E2 Wainwright Can
4B2 Wainwright USA
111B2 Waipara NZ
110C2 Waipukurau NZ
111C2 Wairarapa,L NZ
111B2 Wairau R NZ
110C1 Wairoa NZ
110C1 Wairoa R NZ
111B2 Waitaki R NZ
110B1 Waitara NZ
110C1 Waitomo NZ
110C1 Waiuku NZ
75B1 Wajima Japan
99E2 Wajir Kenya
75B1 Wakasa-wan B Japan
111A3 Wakatipu,L NZ
74D4 Wakayama Japan
42D3 Wakefield Eng
27H1 Wakefield Jamaica
16D2 Wakefield Rhode Island, USA
76B2 Wakema Myan
69G2 Wakkanai Japan
108B3 Wakool R Aust
59B2 Walbrzych Pol
109D2 Walcha Aust
58B2 Walcz Pol
46D1 Waldbröl Germany
16E2 Walden USA
43C3 Wales Country, UK
12A1 Wales USA
6B3 Wales I Can
109C2 Walgett Aust
112B4 Walgreen Coast Region, Ant
99C3 Walikale Zaire
21B2 Walker L USA
14B2 Walkerton Can
8C2 Wallace USA
108A2 Wallaroo Aust
109C3 Walla Walla Aust
20C1 Walla Walla USA
16C2 Wallingford USA
105H4 Wallis and Futuna Is Pacific O
20C1 Wallowa USA
20C1 Wallowa Mts Mts USA
111B2 Wallumbilla Aust
18B2 Walnut Ridge USA
110C1 Waiouru NZ
43D3 Walsall Eng
9C3 Walsenburg USA
9C3 Walsenburgh USA
17B1 Walterboro USA
17A1 Walter F George Res USA
16D1 Waltham USA
100A3 Walvis Bay Namibia
103J6 Walvis Ridge Atlantic O
97C4 Wamba Nig
98B3 Wamba R Zaïre
18A2 Wamego USA
8B2 Wana Pak
108B1 Wanaaring Aust
111A2 Wanaka NZ
111A2 Wanaka,L NZ
14B1 Wanapitei L Can
109C1 Wandoan Aust
108B3 Wanganella Aust
110C1 Wanganui NZ
110C1 Wanganui R NZ
109C3 Wangaratta Aust
99E2 Wanle Weyne Somalia
76E2 Wanning China
87B1 Wanparti India